RAISING THE BAR

EMPOWERING FEMALE LAWYERS THROUGH COACHING

NIKKI ALDERSON

Disclaimer

All names in the main body of the book have been anonymised to preserve client confidentiality

Copyright © 2019 by Nikki Alderson

ISBN: 9781700332011
ISBN13

CONTENTS

About the Author 5

Preface 9

Reviews and Testimonials 11

Part I
WHO AM I, AND WHY THIS BOOK?

1. Where it all began 17

2. The female retention crisis 30

3. Coaching and mentoring 54

Part II
WHO ARE YOU?

4. Women leaders in the making 63

Exercise 1 94

Exercise 2 96

Exercise 3 98

5. Working parents and career break returners 100

Exercise 4 115

Exercise 5 117

6. Career changers 119

Exercise 6 130

Part III
HOW I HELP : TIPS ON GETTING THE CAREER YOU
WANT, YOUR WAY

7. Mindset and mental toughness 135

Exercise 7 158

8. Digital distraction and how to avoid it 160

Exercise 8 173

9. How to say no but keep the opportunities flowing   175
Exercise 9   186
10. Women's wellness at work   188
Exercise 10   201

Part IV
COACHING EXERCISES TO SUPPORT CAREER
PROGRESSION

11. Making your career work   205
Exercise 11   220

Afterword   222
A Note of Thanks   224
Further Reading   226
Notes   228

ABOUT THE AUTHOR

NIKKI ALDERSON

"If it is to be, it is up to me"

Nikki Alderson has 19 years' experience at the Criminal Bar in Yorkshire, working from Broadway House Chambers, Bradford & Leeds.

She now works as a specialist Corporate and Executive Coach:

- Supporting law firms and Chambers to attract and retain female talent; and

- Empowering female lawyers to achieve career ambitions.

Nikki has learnt a lot from her successful career as a barrister, having gained great insights into the responsibilities, pressures and "expected" career paths of those, particularly women, working in law.

She sees a challenge within the profession of retaining talented female role models, given the dearth of women in senior partnership roles and within the judiciary, and is passionate about addressing these issues through the coaching services she provides.

Nikki specialises in three areas of coaching, whether for law firms, Chambers or for individuals:

- Enhancing support for career break returners and those in career transition;
- Providing a benefit for those recently promoted in the first one hundred days of their new role;
- Increasing awareness around workplace confidence, wellness, resilience and mental toughness.

Although her work is focused predominantly on one to

one coaching within the workplace, she also offers bespoke workshops and speaker events.

Nikki lives by the mantra *"**Live a life true to yourself, not the life others expect.**"*

Follow Nikki on

https://www.linkedin.com/in/nikkialdersoncoaching/

Or refer to www.nikkialdersoncoaching.com

facebook.com/nikkialdersoncoaching

twitter.com/NikkiAlderson2

DEDICATION

To the Death Row prisoner, wrongly convicted, who helped change the course of my life.
CM, in recognition of your strength, courage and faith in me; you continue to inspire me daily.

PREFACE

HOW TO USE THIS BOOK

If you are seeking untold secrets to nailing your career, you've come to the wrong place. This book in many ways states the obvious. And yet, there is something about the obvious that at times in our daily lives we neither see nor tap into, firefighting the next task, project or idea without looking at the bigger picture or goal.

So often we deny ourselves time in the present to become absorbed in quiet reflection which, if embraced, reaps massive reward.

This is your invitation to do so now.

You will find a collection of simple hints and tips which, when put together, provide a powerful blueprint for being the best at work that you can be. You may have forgotten things; you may find them a challenge to implement. They are here for the taking.

Use this book in a way that works for you. Feel free to adopt a selective approach. Dip into the chapters and concepts that resonate; park those that don't. Think about who you are, how you present yourself at work, and in what aspects of your career or business you desire to show up as your best self.

In pretty much every aspect of our working lives there are challenges that, whilst overwhelming at times, are common to at least someone. Acknowledging this empowers us and offers reassurance so that we soon come to realise these ideas are easy to access and implement, if only we permit ourselves time and space to consider them and allow them back into our consciousness.

Use this book as a handy reference guide for getting stuff done, things that you already know about but may have forgotten along the way.

It's a book about taking action. Let's get to it: dive in!

REVIEWS AND TESTIMONIALS

"A great guide for female lawyers (and women more generally in any career), trying to balance the pressures of work and personal lives in a society where "having it all" isn't straightforward. A wonderful mix of personal experience and insights with practical coaching skills".

— **LAURA**

"An important book for lawyers, male and female alike, in finding and understanding your goals and aspirations, what success means to you and overcoming the challenges many of us, particularly working parents, face in the legal profession. Raising the Bar is a refreshingly honest mind recalibrator".

— **KAYLEIGH**

"Nikki's book is an honest account of what is happening for women in the legal profession. By sharing some of her coaching agendas, lawyers and barristers can be reassured that they are not alone in their experiences. There are some excellent tips that can be followed in the moment and highlights the impact that coaching can have in helping individuals move past those barriers that may be holding them back".

— **WENDY**

"Raising the Bar" is a compelling read. It is based on the author's varied international experience as a Barrister. The wealth of factual anecdotes, gleaned from life as a woman with a long career at the Bar, are cleverly woven throughout the book so that the positive suggestions are not only interesting, but also applicable to many situations in which female lawyers (and others) often find themselves. I would highly recommend it"

— MARY

"A gripping read with considerable, well thought out, practical advice based on Nikki's obvious experience. It was particularly useful to find bite-size sections offering day to day coping strategies".

— ANTONIA

"An excellent guide to dealing with those everyday situations that I largely tolerate due to a lack of in-house support - I now have a set of go-to strategies. At least now I can overcome my own frequent bouts of self-doubt. Thank you Nikki!"

— ISLA

"Nikki has gently guided me to a better understanding of how I work most effectively and helped me focus on what it is I want out of my career and how best to go about getting it. She has provided me with some simple tools to break down my goals into bite-sized, achievable objectives and to avoid a sense of overwhelm. I have felt like a new woman – enthused, optimistic, efficient and effective. I have recovered the positive mind-set I lost some time ago and now feel excited about the possibilities open to me".

— LAW FIRM PARTNER

"Nikki helped me to identify my short and long term goals and break down my journey to realistically achieving those goals. Nikki helped me to "dig deep" to find solutions myself and her approach to self-accountability focuses the mind on achieving and not letting things drift. Nikki understands the legal profession and challenges that all lawyers (male and female) face. I think that insight provides an invaluable angle".

— SENIOR ASSOCIATE SOLICITOR

"Nikki has great coaching tools and skills to help you hone in on which goals you truly want to accomplish. Nikki helps set you up for success and is a powerful motivator".

— INTERNATIONAL HUMAN RIGHTS ADVOCATE

PART I
WHO AM I, AND WHY THIS
BOOK?

1

WHERE IT ALL BEGAN

*O*ver-powering heat, still air, the acrid stench of stale sweat mixed with desperate hope. Those are my abiding memories of my thirtieth birthday in March 2004. I'd spent the morning talking to an inmate in a shadowy Jamaican gaol. He was nervously chatty, at times speaking incomprehensible Patois. He appeared in a hurry yet with no place to be. He'd spent longer on death row than I had been alive, his sentence eventually having been commuted to life. He was being rehabilitated ready for release. I felt, with him, the chance of freedom and an end to a lifetime of psychological suffering.

In my diary, I'd simply written "Goblin Hill", the name of the remote tourist spot where I'd spent the rest of the weekend with friends. We'd sipped Appleton Rum and

Coke beside the ice cool Blue Lagoon, surrounded by lush, tropical greenery. No reference to the earlier prison visit, although that's what will remain etched on my brain.

I was a volunteer Barrister working in Downtown Kingston, at that time the murder capital of the world, assisting in the Defence of Capital cases for the Bar Human Rights Committee. I normalised being in that cell at that particular moment because that was what I did. Just part of the job, given all that I'd already seen, experienced and been personally affected by.

It was an extraordinary assignment, a seminal moment in my history, and one of which I remain immensely proud. Barrister colleagues asked whether I was worried about the impact that such a placement might have on my practice back home. I wasn't known for taking the easy or expected path in life so the short answer was no, I wasn't. I'd been right. My profile, and consequently that of Chambers, was raised. More significantly, at least two lives were saved.

And it also revealed an internal conflict in terms of how I felt I "should" behave professionally. The things I witnessed there, and at home, (dealing in the main with child sexual abuse cases), were enough to make me weep, warping my ordinary sense of right and wrong; yet over the years I learnt to adopt the requisite impassive, emotionless veneer.

Pondering how I came to be there, in that prison, I reflect on my childhood. Travel, the outdoors, making human connections - these have always been significant influences in my life. I read law at Balliol College Oxford and quickly discounted the "city slicker" London Solicitor career path, opting instead to become a Criminal Barrister. Fighting hard at the coal face for the underdog felt to me more worthwhile, raw and real. After Bar Finals, I secured pupillage, then tenancy, in Yorkshire.

In and amongst developing a successful career, I now see I'd forgotten what made my heart sing. The perfectionist in me was a hard and unforgiving task mistress: She would dismiss insecurities and anxieties, telling me to suck up the responsibility, the pressure, the desire to do the best job possible for clients, regardless of personal sacrifice or cost.

Escapism was my coping strategy, and set me on course for an unconventional career path. When a rare Scholarship opportunity presented itself, working alongside a Silk (Queen's Counsel) in Wellington, New Zealand, it was an absolute "no-brainer". Many Bar colleagues didn't "get" this approach. They were on the career progression treadmill, hobnobbing with Judges and taking on as many cases as possible on a clear upward trajectory, without deviation or let up. I was happy to lap up the opportunities for the here and now, without too much thought for the next best case. Whilst others raised eyebrows, I remained authentically me.

On my return from New Zealand, it soon became apparent during my annual practice review meetings with clerks, that I wasn't moved by the "expected" career path of a fledgling barrister, not sharing the common career goals of Silk, Recorder (part-time judge) or Judge.

Instead, I avidly pursued my passion for travel, frequently on my own, visiting Australia, Brazil, Thailand, Tanzania, St. Lucia and America to name but a few. Every time my over-packed purple trolley hit the baggage carousel ready for another exciting excursion, I experienced an immediate and all-pervading sense of relief. Job stress and responsibility melted away.

It was only whilst away that I was able to appreciate just how unhappy I was. The intense pressure was hard to handle; the subject matter of the cases I was dealing with weren't just unpleasant, they were downright unpalatable, skewing my own moral compass. The working conditions, with unpredictable and antisocial hours, added to stress levels.

The first time I went to Jamaica was different. Uncomfortable even. Usually, I am talkative, irrepressible. I arrived with my parents at Manchester Airport, about to embark upon the latest in a long line of travel adventures, albeit on this occasion for work, and sat in stunned silence. Mute through fear, I was scared. Scared of the unknown, scared of the negative reports about life out there: guns, gated communities, violence, murder. During my "What the heck am I doing?" airport moment, it took my deepest reserves of determination, perseverance and courage to fight back tears and board the flight.

My Jamaican exploits could fill a book of their own, and maybe one day they will. During the initial placement, thankfully, with caution and a willingness to take sage advice from my local hosts, my fears subsided. In eighteen months, I re-visited that beautiful, troubled and contradictory country many times. I felt compelled to continue working to assist in the defence of those caught up in the most shocking cases of injustice I had ever witnessed.

I became involved with one case, in particular, that was life changing not just for the defendants involved, but also for me personally.

Over two weeks, I observed what felt like a slow motion

car-crash: a miscarriage of justice happening before my
very eyes. Inadmissible evidence being presented to the
jury, third-rate legal representation, judicial bias, media
interference, violent attacks on defendants whilst incar-
cerated, even the murder of a recently released former
death row inmate. As a lawyer, I couldn't fail to be
moved and inspired.

I was in my element. The pressure was intense but the
difference was that the work was voluntary, I was doing
it because I was passionate about the cause, AND I
worked behind the scenes in a supporting role, as
opposed to the buck stopping solely with me.

After a career rollercoaster like that and, over eighteen
months later, ultimately celebrating both men's release,
it is no surprise I had something of a "career crossroads"
moment.

Progressing in my career on returning home certainly
wasn't the problem envisaged by the more senior and
traditional bods in the profession. Nearly two years later,
I was experiencing real success. And the daily diet of
sexual abuse trials, particularly relating to children,
created within me a conflict as to the worth and value of
my UK practice. I was dealing with "heavyweight"
cases, so on the face of it, a great job and income. In reality, I had no time or headspace for anything else. I was

becoming cynical, my thoughts warped by the day to day reality of some of the individuals I was dealing with. I saw the road ahead and wanted to take the nearest u-turn.

In 2008, I first experienced Coaching. As a result, I examined my values and beliefs and came to understand the benefits of going, as Jim Collins put it, "from good to great." My work at the Bar was, as a direct consequence, revitalised. I discovered a new sense of purpose, vigour and personal congruency. Coaching got me back on track in a career that, without it, I could well have left. At that time, it would have been twelve years too early. Instead of resenting the job and feeling trapped by it, I resolved to make it work for me. And so I did.

The positive difference to my career – and whether I stayed or not – was undeniable. It is this experience that I draw on to support my clients. I've already trodden the path where being stuck you become unstuck, where you can't see the next career progression move then take one. And all thanks to coaching.

Such was the profound effect upon me of coaching that between 2010 and 2012, I qualified to become a Corporate and Executive Coach and NLP Practitioner. During that time, with a clear goal and an action plan to achieve it, combined with lots of energy and enthusiasm,

I surprised myself how easy it was to motivate myself to work hard on additional projects over and above an already demanding professional job. It also gave me a glimpse of an alternative course: my own coaching business.

Around the same time though, late 2010, I met my husband. Relatively swiftly we started a family. Any thought of starting a new business was almost immediately shelved. Instead, reluctantly, I returned to full-time barrister work after six months with my first child. This felt too soon, and yet the expected norm is around three months. There's a lack of flexible part-time working options at the Criminal Bar and the continued risk that stepping out of practice for too long makes any return harder.

Before her first birthday, my daughter was twice hospitalised for over a week, directly as a result of the childcare choices we'd made – once at seven months old, (causing my husband and I to postpone our honeymoon), then at ten months old (the ill-fated honeymoon being cancelled altogether).

On this second occasion, I was already pregnant again. I have a vivid recollection of an overwhelming, near suffocating, sense of "mother guilt" engulfing me. I'd placed my baby in full-time childcare purely to service a career that I had worked hard to achieve yet which had, by then, become unfulfilling, draining and downright depressing.

Like a brick to the face, it struck me. I was at court, defending a part-heard jury trial. The judge was mid-way through his summing up. My baby girl was miles away from me in hospital hooked up to various wires, tubes and machines. My notes of proceedings became less ordered and sensible as my sight began to blur. I had a fiery red burning sensation in my ears. Turmoil coursed through me – the intuitive feeling that I was needed elsewhere. What the hell was I still doing in court anyway? Some things were just more important.

In that instant, I understood how the most compelling goals are those kept under constant review. Outlooks alter, and priorities change to flex with prevailing situations. Career decisions made almost twenty years before shouldn't define me or keep me shackled to them forever. I'd worked hard to achieve all that I had in my career to date, yet all that melted into insignificance in the face of my daughter's hospitalisation.

With my middle child then, I made changes. I took longer maternity leave. I went back when I felt ready, having enlisted the services of a nanny. She played mum while I paid her for the privilege of returning to work.

Having been out of the court environment for nearly twelve months, channels of communication between myself and my clerks who managed my diary broke down. A request to "ease me back in" to the job as part of a phased return was interpreted by them as a free-for-all on any case, any time, anywhere.

For me? A baptism of fire. A wounding with intent case where the defendant had broken a glass and twisted it into the face of the complainant who consequently suffered life-changing injuries; a murder trial; a rape trial where the client I represented was just thirteen years old. This was the beginning of the end. The relentless-ness of the criminal bar had me running on empty.

Having a career challenge brought about by significant changes in personal circumstances is of course not unusual. What is more uncommon is the ability to accept, or get comfortable, with them.

When I was seven months pregnant with my third child, a last-minute case was returned to me from another set of Chambers. It was a serious and complex Prosecution sexual abuse re-trial with multiple complainants. Papers more than two feet deep, the pink brief ribbon barely holding them together due to their sheer weight and volume, were couriered to my home address late after the close of business. The brief contained no indictment, no opening note, no case summary and there were several complainant DVD recordings of evidence to view. My other children were 2 years and 17 months old respectively at the time. My husband still worked away. I had to be ready for a clean start the next morning in a non-local court.

I wrestled professional ethics, guilt, anxiety and a deep sense of obligation. And then I said "No". For the first time in sixteen years of practice, I refused to take a brief.

It was the most liberating experience, a coming of age. Like David Bowie said: *"Aging is an extraordinary process where you become the person you always should have been"*.

In that single moment, I embraced a momentous change. I learnt to say no. This became the catalyst for something far greater.

Less than a month later, I was back on maternity leave. I'd worked full time on returning to work with both of my first two children. Now, with three children under the age of four, and a husband working away mid-week, I wasn't in a rush to repeat my most recent return to work experiences. That said, being self-motivated, determined, resilient, resourceful, independent, and formerly the family breadwinner, I certainly wasn't going to sit idle, waiting for the hubby to bring home the bacon.

It was then that I realised I wasn't alone, both in the challenges I had faced battling personal demons within my career around confidence, internal stress and conflict, and with the obstacles re-surfacing around the ease or otherwise with which I could return flexibly. Highly successful and hugely talented women are leaving the legal profession "mid-career" in droves.

In 2017, while on extended maternity leave, I undertook a further course of coaching. Empowered, I re-embraced, with confidence and excitement, the world of work. And so my new business launched; the Bar was no more.

Now, as a specialist coach supporting law firms to retain female talent and empowering female lawyers, I "get" the responsibilities, pressures and "expected" career paths of female professionals. I empathise with clients describing frustrations with their job, such as overwhelm due to over-work and inadequate financial reward when pitted against the burgeoning cost of childcare. I understand when they lament a lack of life balance, a need to more effectively prioritise, time-manage, avoid distraction and increase productivity, and when they share often deep rooted confidence issues around pursuing promotion, returning to work after a career break or starting new roles after promotion.

This journey has taught me to recognise and honour my own value and how to say no. I also know from personal experience how effective coaching is at increasing personal performance in every aspect of life, and have used it successfully to achieve the Bar career I wanted, and beyond, by deciding upon a career change strategy, and successfully navigating transition from professional into business life.

This is the motivation behind the book.

I recall the day I was almost immobilised through fear at the airport en route to Jamaica. I realise now that it led without question to the most influential period of my life and gave me the opportunity to live a life true to myself, not the life others expect.

As my experiences in Jamaica taught me, with authenticity, self-belief and an excellent, supportive team, the most challenging of obstacles can be overcome and goals can be achieved. In this book, the book I wish I'd had, I share the things I have learnt and found useful along the way, hoping to empower and inspire others to achieve success, their way.

2

THE FEMALE RETENTION CRISIS

This Chapter discusses the challenges around being a working parent, judicial bullying, harassment, unconscious bias and gender pay gap, and considers possible solutions in terms of, amongst other things, improved internal working practices and external societal change.

In July 2018 I attended the spectacular Temple Women's Forum Summer Garden Party, in the exquisite Temple grounds, London, reportedly attended by over 700 guests. The Forum was founded by Her Honour Judge Deborah Taylor in 2012 to encourage and support women barristers throughout their careers and so increase retention within the profession:[1]

I was struck by a number of things. Firstly, there was obviously sufficient impetus for founding the Forum around the time of its original inception. Secondly, six years on, for there to be such a massive show of support, not only must female lawyers still be facing ongoing challenges but, more positively, there was clearly a massive groundswell of support for tackling and overcoming these obstacles, enabling women in law to achieve bright futures within the profession.

8th March, International Women's Day, is always a good day to reflect on how far we, as professional women, have come, where we are now, and how far still there is to travel. 2019 was no different, save for being more poignant than most, given it was the year we celebrate one hundred years of women in law.

The week before, I had been at another Temple Women's Forum event, doing precisely that, with the likes of Baroness Helena Kennedy QC, Dana Denis-Smith, Founder of the First 100 Years Project and Maggie Semple, Member of Queen's Counsel Selection Panel. Celebrating a female President of the Supreme Court; more women than ever before entering the profession; and accessibility to groups, such as the

Forum, Women in the Law UK, Women Lawyers and Mothers and Women in Criminal Law, seemingly at an all-time high, to support, upskill and mentor female lawyers.

And yet I couldn't shake the feeling that there was a huge way still to go.

Retention rates for female talent remain low: in 2019, 52% of new entrants to the solicitors profession are women, down to 29% at partner level, and just 19% equity partners. That's not to mention the disparity in numbers of female Silks (15%), Judges (28%) and Court of Appeal Judges (21%).

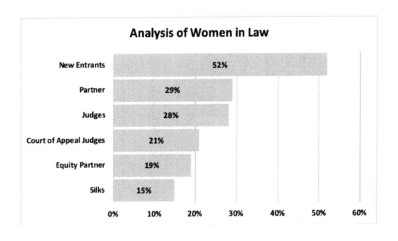

On 12th July 2016, the Bar Standards Board (BSB) published a report entitled "Women at the Bar".[2]

The research behind it was carried out in part to explore issues which may be contributing towards the lack of retention of female barristers. Respondents stated they were more likely to consider leaving the Bar if they had experienced discrimination or harassment, or if they had primary caring responsibilities for children. Family reasons or the difficulties of combining a career at the Bar with caring responsibilities were the most common reasons given for considering leaving the Bar. Doubtless bourgeoning childcare costs and cuts in fees at the publicly funded Bar will also impact upon the high rates of female practitioners leaving.

For too long whilst in the profession, I'd been politely beating around the bush. The challenges for women in law are still acute and, now outside the profession looking in, I feel empowered to say that without a significant cultural shift, the gender narrative will remain the same as it ever was when Baroness Helena Kennedy QC wrote her damning critique of the British Legal System, *Eve was Framed*, over a quarter of a century ago.

Working Parents

The Western Circuit Women's Forum "Back to the Bar" Survey examines "what makes it possible or impossible for parents to return to the bar after parental leave". [3]

Some of the findings were discussed on Radio 4's
Woman's Hour, 15th February 2019. [4]

Ever since its publication, pretty much every report,
tweet and media comment I've read about a female
lawyer's life reveals a daily, and often overwhelming,
struggle for career survival, never mind progression.

Almost two thirds of those who left the Bar on that
Circuit over a six year period were women, most citing
difficulties balancing work and family commitments as a
determining factor in their decision. Those remaining
did so with the assistance of significant shared care with
partners or family members. Flexible working arrangements were also important, the availability of which
depended on the Chambers you were in, the clerking
teams' ability to break from tradition, and whether your
practice was court based or not. The countless personal
stories are as heart-wrenching as they are compelling;
talented, successful women thrown to the long grass due
to the incompatible demands of career and home life. I
related to each and every one.

My own experiences of the baptism of fire on my second
return from maternity leave added grist to the mill, and
exposed the difficulties faced by many Chambers in
understanding how to manage any degree of flexible
working outside the usual "traditional" clerking

approach. Likewise, the "learning to say no" moment, at about eight months pregnant with my third child, revealed an insurmountable combination of lack of thought, understanding and communication on behalf of clerks which left me with no choice. These two experiences in the space of just seven months were, for me, an awakening.

Returning to the BSB Women at the Bar survey, it found flexible working, which clearly enables many female barristers to remain in practice, impacted negatively on them, both in terms of the type of work they received and their career progression. In addition, many cited problems combining flexible working with the unpredictability of courtroom practice, where expectations around last-minute availability or work outside standard "office hours" is the norm in many areas of practice. In addition, many felt taking parental leave had negatively impacted on their practice, for example on work allocation, career progression and income, such that it became known as "the maternity penalty." Difficulties were also highlighted on returning to work, in particular combining courtroom practice, with its lack of flexibility and unpredictable hours, when balanced with caring responsibilities.

·   ·   ·

Judicial Bullying

More insidious obstacles were brought to the public's attention on 11th February 2019. The Chair of the Criminal Bar Association's Monday Message that day was entitled "The Problem with being a woman at the Criminal Bar".[5]

The article would have been more accurately entitled "The problemS." It didn't just concern career break-returners. Chris Henley QC raised, amongst a litany of other challenges, the spectre of abuse of power by Judges, impacting upon all counsel, and women in particular, together with the consequent impact on well-being and morale. "It is little wonder that so many women (and men) are turning away from the criminal bar" he said "the environment is increasingly hostile".

Even new and welcome initiatives, such as The Bar Council's February 2019 Guide: "Advice to the Bar about bullying by judges" [6] reveal a profession only now waking up to reality after a half century sleepwalk.

The judicial abuse of power has been tolerated by the Bar for years, described recently on Twitter by a senior silk as the profession's "dirty little secret," to be joked about at Mess Dinners where offensive nomenclatures are bestowed upon the offending characters, but no formal complaints procedure ever widely or effectively invoked.

And here I see one of the major problems: The old boys' network. The "revels", or after-dinner speeches, the domain of white, middle class men, using alcohol-fuelled humour and bravado to laugh off and excuse otherwise reportable conduct.

My experience in pupillage of one particular judge set the tone for sixteen years' worth of ill behaviour of him towards me: "Your argument is worse than that of a child in a school playground," he hectored. Senior practitioners present at the time offered a supportive ear and remarked specifically about the unfairness of the comment, and agreed it had been designed to humiliate. But neither they nor I "called it out" publicly in court at the time, or raised complaint through formal channels, due to the delicacies of self-employment, reputational damage and the sensitivity of client-counsel relations and client confidence.

I've been complicit in this too; staying silent when the worst offenders turned their vile attention to others, grateful that their poor conduct was pointing elsewhere than in my own direction.

. . .

Harassment

A day after that Monday Message, Criminal barrister Joanna Hardy's tweet about these issues "went viral." What was interesting was that she offered a multitude of sensible and workable solutions to some of the many well documented challenges faced by women at the Criminal Bar: Abolishing 9.30am listings and so called "warned lists" to aid those with caring responsibilities; supporting fellow females through kindness; improving Chambers maternity policies; introducing mentoring schemes to name but a few. And yet the media attention honed in on her complaints around the "stag do behaviour" of men towards female colleagues.[7] She provided a depressing and all too familiar insider view of a male dominated, inherently sexist culture, and one in which women are disadvantaged, their needs overlooked in particular due to traditional court listing practices and hearing times and "old boy" behaviour.

According to the BSB survey, around two in every five respondents said they had suffered harassment or discrimination at the Bar, with only a small proportion (one in five) reporting it. Barristers at an early stage of their career – in particular pupils – were particularly vulnerable to harassment. Discrimination within a Barrister's chambers or organisation was found to be more common than discrimination from external individuals (such as judges or clients) and that the most prevalent form of such internal discrimination was in the behaviour of the clerks and issues around work allocation.

This macho culture isn't hard to recognise or spot. I worked for well over a decade in an environment tolerating bad behaviour by a number of more senior male colleagues towards myself and others simply because that was "just the way it is," preferring not to be singled out as a so-called trouble maker.

During a case as a junior, being led by a senior barrister, in response to an email containing my editing proposals for a police interview, I was sent a sexual fantasy of his involving me. At a case dinner, I was subjected to a lewd proposition by a man well over thirty years my senior. Seeing it now, I accept being a protagonist to the problem. Again, I never spoke out, even when a former partner made it perfectly plain to me that in any other walk of life, conduct such as this would be a disciplinary matter, especially when I had the email evidence to prove it.

Unconscious Bias

Based on my own experiences when in practice, and

now coaching female lawyers still exposed to the negative effects of this toxic, male-dominated environment, I
recognise that it will take some seriously creative, positive and controversial thinking to avoid women feeling
hopeless or helpless about their futures in law. Even
enjoying a drink at the Inns of Court before the Forum
event in 2019, I noted the bar walls draped with twenty-
one paintings of male barristers and judges of yesteryear.
Not one single painting featured a woman.

According to the Law Society's Women in Leadership in
Law Toolkit [8], published July 2018, unconscious bias
was found to be present even from the outset in the
recruitment process, then in how work is allocated, and
continued throughout the various stages of career
progression from performance reviews, to promotions
and selection for partnership. A good example recounted
to me of this recently was a part-time female equity
partner in a law firm being told in a partners' meeting
that she hadn't been put forward for a particular client
role because she was "likely to be at soft play."

*By way of client example, Becky was a committed
Senior Associate in private practice with an eye on
partnership, but was doubtful it was the right firm in
which to achieve that. She had her suspicions confirmed
when announcing a short maternity leave, with the*

Equity Partner's reaction to the news: "This is why we shouldn't hire women as lawyers."

Another client recalls several examples of bias in an international law firm, including both male and female lawyers, suggesting that when considering working mothers' PQE, time should be deducted for the amount of maternity leave they have had.

Gender Pay Gap

Additional challenges highlighted in the toolkit included fewer opportunities for good quality client work, promotion and reward, particularly bearing in mind gender pay gap: Men out-earned women at every level of the legal profession despite, since 1990, women representing over 60% of new entrants into the profession, and as of 2017 women are the majority of practising solicitors.

It comes as no surprise, then, that there are problems attracting talented women to, and retaining them in, senior positions within the legal profession as a whole. Not dissimilar to other professions: finance, dentistry and STEM (Science, Technology, Engineering and Mathematics) to name but a few.

. . .

The Antidote to the Retention Challenge

Internal Culture

Nearly twenty years at the Bar, yet it was only recently that I made a interesting discovery. Thanks to attending the Manchester Roadshow event of the First 100 Years Project,[9] which "celebrates the past to shape the future for women in law", I became aware that the hierarchical, linear business model of traditional law firms is based upon the structure of the army over one hundred years ago. No women allowed then!

It's perhaps no wonder that in the present day, this model looks out-dated and inflexible, particularly for women wanting to progress through the ranks. No surprises that in 2019 we are here now, still losing women left, right and centre, haemorrhaging talent. This exodus will continue until there is profession-wide acknowledgement of its negative impact, rather than adopting the convenient "that's just the way it is" attitude.

It's here that the key to unlocking the elusive, and as yet untried, solution can be found. Massive, ground-breaking, cultural change from within – eradicating the old boys' network in relation to unconscious bias as well as blatant sexism, re-training clerks to challenge traditional concepts around case allocation and working practices, and reducing or removing the inflexible "time-based targets" model within law firms which tend to work against women and in favour of men.

Retaining the "time-based target" model runs the risk of promoting a disconnect between employer and female employee (possibly male too). Whilst ever a hot house mentality is promoted by firms, at the expense of work life boundaries, a lack of shared vision or congruent goals, and between values and beliefs, working practices will keep coming up short for employees. Women (and, with the increasing awareness of Wellness within the workplace, men) will continue to leave.

And speaking out, without fear or favour. Loudly. And repeatedly. In my current role, some within the profession are telling me that they are silently, supportively watching as I gently poke the sacred cow of Bar culture and vocalise the things they wish they could say but feel unable.

Internal Organisational Support and Communication

Organisational support and clear communication between, for example, clerks, Chambers and Barristers are likewise at the heart of the matter. My own experiences of support on return from maternity leave left something to be desired.

You will recall after my second child, having been out of court for twelve months, I requested clerks "ease me back in" to the job. Instead, within the first forty eight hours of my return, I was briefed in those three very serious cases: a wounding with intent, a murder and a rape. For many career break return clients of mine, confidence issues are very real, particularly having spent an extended period out of court and are trying to re-establish themselves as a serious practitioner whilst spinning an ever-increasing number of plates. Knowing to whose agenda you are working is key.

So too is being able to communicate this effectively and with clarity, so that others not only hear but also understand. As a woman at the Criminal Bar generally, whether with children or not, time ownership and task prioritisation frequently present as challenges. I recall the running joke in Chambers being that the clerks would ask when you had time blocked out of your diary, "Yes, but are you 'Away' or 'Away Away'?" in an effort to persuade you to cancel that pre-booked time out of court. Learning to say "No" is an important skill to develop, a challenge which frequently comes up in client coaching and workshop sessions.

Flexible Working Practices

Flexible working within law is thankfully less ground-breaking these days and access to it, and the main-streaming of it, seems critical, in particular, to the successful retention of working parents.

An effective antidote to the traditional business model is witnessing the success of "role model" lawyers and firms embracing these more modern working practices. Gunner Cooke, for example, is already successfully adopting more flexible practices. Flexible working arrangements can be facilitated by reliable remote digital technology, and a more positive, holistic view of productivity, judged on output as opposed to time.

In the Women at the Bar report, the BSB highlighted that "prevailing attitudes" within the legal profession were a key issue to address in order to improve the retention of women. One particular part of this battle can be won by increased awareness of the language we adopt, particularly around flexible working: "flexible" is not the same as "part-time."

Much still needs to be done, however, to convince law firms and Chambers of the benefits: Coinciding with a new CIPD (The Chartered Institute of Personnel and Development) report, the Flexible Working Task Force recently had to launch a campaign (January 2019) to boost flexible working, as uptake has stalled for nearly a decade.

At the Criminal Bar, however, for a serious trial advocate, like me when in practice, flexible working is a fantasy. In this regard, practising in Criminal Law presents its own unique challenge for working mothers. To service the demands of the profession, heavy reliance on childcare, and more often than not a full time nanny, is the norm. Jury trials take place every Monday to Friday during court hours, 9.30am-4.30pm, and that is that. It is important to be realistic. Whilst in practice, where diary commitments would allow, I and many female colleagues would work "two months on, two weeks off", to give a degree of flexibility and time with my family. Clearly though, at the senior level I was working, with a daily diet of child sexual abuse trials, "flexible" hours, during the weeks I was available to work, were impossible. Put simply, a Crown Court jury trial cannot, nor should it, function around childcare drop offs and pick-ups.

That said, more encouragingly in other areas of law, such as clinical negligence and employment law, the situation is not so rigid, as demonstrated in an article for Counsel Magazine.[10]

Support for flexible and affordable childcare options around The Temple in London and at Combined Court Centres around the country would make good alternative options. Some have been mooted yet, as I understand it, still remain untested.

My advice? Start planning early, and be honest about what you are and are NOT prepared to compromise, whether at work or at home. And enter the profession with eyes wide open, and a mind similar.

Women "Doing it for themselves"

There has been a recent rise in women either opening their own firms (I can readily think of three doing so successfully in Yorkshire alone) or working on a consultancy basis e.g. through companies like Obelisk Support. Those who have the courage to be confident and take a leap talk persuasively about reaping the benefits. Such benefits include not only the ability to work more flexibly, but crucially retaining control over their own legal destiny.

The more women doing so, and vocally, the more they become role models for others. Their reasons and motivations for doing so will then be heard, understood and replicated.

. . .

Role Models

Additional support and inspiration for women in law should be available from those who have already climbed the ranks.

Who are the modern day role models? Are they women who have made it because they had to "think and act like a man," to quote a female partner in a leading Yorkshire Law Firm I met recently? Perhaps those who give more junior women a harder time because they've had to "do it the hard way" themselves? Like the senior female barrister (now judge) who berated her former pupil for considering flexible working in family law to fit in with her home commitments, on the grounds that it would "damage" her practice.

Or are they women who have achieved career success whilst working in a more flexible way, a way more appealing to new upcoming millennial and Generation X lawyers? Interestingly on this point, the Law Society Toolkit states "We want to empower all women to lead as women and to enable everyone to have more flexibility." The promotion of authentic leadership and equality within our working practices are both admirable and, more importantly, achievable goals.

The power of role models to influence positive behaviour in others cannot be underestimated. In her career break return sessions, Kath, a Senior Associate and leader in the making, was deciding to decide about when would be the right time to go for partnership. She recognised an area of development in herself that she wanted to lead in the right way, by being motivational rather than hectoring. We used role models to identify what she felt were signs of a good leader allowing her to emulate and develop them where appropriate to support her application for promotion further down the line.

Male Champions

In the Women Leaders in Law Toolkit, The Law Society highlights that those male partners who are "male champions for change" also have a significant part to play. Which senior male figures in your profession do you know who have challenged gender stereotypes, perhaps by taking paternity leave or championing flexible working whilst still achieving silk, a judicial role, partnership or a senior position within the firm? I can think of some, albeit currently they are something of a rarity.

When equality becomes the norm, filtering down from the higher echelons, through senior role models of whatever gender, AND from the grass-roots up, past concerns about outdated "prevailing attitudes" within the legal profession and the potential negative impact upon one's career about reporting harassment or discrimination, will surely be reduced if not entirely eradicated.

Societal Change

For women with childcare responsibilities to be retained in any profession, some creative thought is required to provide confidence in the chosen childcare support plan, such as increased input from a spouse, grandparent or nanny, perhaps even in a nanny-share arrangement with others in a similar position. A simple point to consider in terms of wider, societal change is the division of labour within the home. A former colleague, recently appointed to the Bench as a Circuit Judge, often remarked how she felt she had done a full day's work even before leaving the house to conduct her very senior barrister day-job. She is not alone.

In Britain in 2016, according to the Office for National Statistics, women did almost 60% more of the unpaid work, on average, than men. Are we having the right conversations at home to equally split household chores and childcare responsibilities? Ensuring household tasks and childcare responsibilities are equally divided, or at least shared, will certainly go a long way to supporting the smooth return to work after parental leave and ongoing careers in highly demanding professions.

Just as women struggle shouldering a multitude of domestic burdens and are consequently held back in their careers, men struggle equally, yet differently, frequently with huge financial expectations upon them and little dialogue around the consequent impact on them of stress or missing out on seeing their children grow up. Starting these hard conversations and challenging these outdated attitudes will engender a *united* approach to developing solutions, which currently appears elusive.

Research by Manchester Metropolitan University which produced tools to "Generate Routes for Women's Leadership" [11] in workplaces generally considered other examples to challenge such obstacles. These include:

- thinking how girls and young women can be encouraged into a traditionally male dominated profession to avoid future gender bias
- creating non- linear leadership pathways for women
- challenging bias that a career "gap" relates to a deficit in skills and experience rather than

recognising and valuing continuous learning
and development that occurs outside work
- meaningfully engaging men in the debate

The answer clearly lies in men AND women seeking to eradicate the barriers for women and encourage a level playing field for ALL. Making it a male v female issue has so far been counterproductive. If flexibility is made accessible, and equality made attractive to ALL, then progress will surely be expedited and the legal profession be shaken from its sleep. To do otherwise is to perpetuate a retention crisis which shows little sign of abating.

External Support

The support from women's groups and networking is invaluable. In the same way as I access, even now, incredible inspiration and motivation from groups like the Temple Women's Forum and First 100 Years Project, I would encourage women lawyers to seek out other opportunities to speak to, and support, others; for example, through groups such as Women in Criminal Law, Women Lawyers and Mothers, and Women in The Law UK, for whom I am an Ambassador.

As I see it, it isn't a matter of "fixing women" to (as Sheryl Sandberg put it) "*Lean In*" to a male dominated working culture. Instead, I subscribe to the Mary Portas *"Work Like a Woman"* approach, which everyone, man AND woman, should support and foster, challenging deep rooted inequality and lack of fair opportunity in an antiquated and at times positively hostile environment.

Whilst ever there is client need, I for one am happy to step up to the plate to empower women through coaching, knowing from my own personal experience how much it influenced my decision in 2004 to stay within law and successfully so, for at least another decade.

3

COACHING AND MENTORING

*I*ncreasingly there is an interest in and demand for coaching and mentoring within the legal profession. I have recently delivered coaching workshops to several organisations for female lawyers. Notably, of those, Women in Criminal Law, Midland Circuit Women's Forum and Women in the Law UK all have, as part of their own initiatives, mentoring programmes. Women lawyers are welcoming this independent, impartial support. Some are unclear however as to the distinctions between coaching and mentoring to make an informed choice as to what would empower them the most.

Although there are many similarities between coaching and mentoring, such as the need for good rapport, effective questioning and active listening, they are distinct disciplines, both with their own individual process and differing purpose. Here, some observations about the differences between the two to help inform choice about "Which is right for you?"

Mentoring

Mentors usually work on an informal and voluntary basis with those less experienced than themselves seeking direction, most often on an ad hoc basis. They tend to be more senior with experience and knowledge in the same professional area. The person being mentored (let's call them the "Mentee") is therefore able to learn and benefit from their Mentor's own previous experience, and use them as a role model or guide, to demonstrate what worked for them, what did not, and how to avoid the pitfalls which Mentors themselves have previously experienced and learnt from.

Like coaching, mentoring is a supportive process, but in a more directive fashion, i.e. it is perceived that the Mentor has all the answers in a particular scenario and provides the solutions for their Mentee to assist them in achieving their goals. By this process, the Mentor's past shapes the Mentee's future, regardless of their different personality traits, individual values and beliefs and, in some cases, diverging overall objectives.

One complaint that comes from Mentees is the fact that the mentoring relationship is built upon this hierarchy of experience. Mentors are necessarily more senior, experienced and, more than likely, busy practitioners, mentoring on a voluntary basis. Actually being able to pin them down to speak to on a regular basis, and at a time of the Mentee's choosing, can be something of a challenge, and on occasion impedes useful progress.

Coaching

Coaching on the other hand is usually a formal, paid arrangement which, when done most effectively, is (unlike mentoring) non-directive, encouraging Coachees to identify their goals, and supports them in their desire to move forward and achieve those ambitions. It is usually over a set time-period and with regular, pre-arranged meeting slots. The Coach has coaching experience and should have formal training albeit not always with the same industry experience as Coachee.

Coaching provided a confidential conversation between Coach and Coachee, during which the Coach assists the Coachee move from where they currently are to where they want to be, more quickly and effectively than if they had acted alone. By using insightful questioning, a Coach (unlike a mentor) puts aside their own experiences and allows the Coachee to explore their own possibilities, "next move" or solution, make their own choices and achieve their own outcomes. Personal accountability and responsibility is key to ensure Coaching does not become a crutch. The relationship between Coachee and Coach is an equal one.

Coaching can work powerfully on an individual basis or within the Corporate setting. In the late 90s, an American study for the Public Personnel Management Association examined the impact on managers of a two month, one hour a week, one to one coaching programme in comparison to classroom style training workshops.

The training intervention increased manager productivity by 22%, but adding the eight week coaching programme after the training increased productivity to an impressive 88%.

The distinction with Corporate Coaching is that it acknowledges multiple stakeholders within the process and has at its root the overall objectives of the company as opposed to the individual, perhaps in terms of organisational performance or development.

On an individual basis, client testimonials report the positive impact of coaching: clearer focus, improved productivity and increased levels of achievement.

"The sessions with Nikki have... really made me reflect on existing habits and how I can change these to improve my working day and become more efficient...I liked that the sessions were tailored to me and what I wanted to achieve".

— SENIOR ASSOCIATE SOLICITOR

Coaching or Mentoring: Which is Right for you?

Any decision around coaching or mentoring will doubtless be influenced by the stage reached in our professional lives, and our desired outcomes from the relationship. A significant part of this may be influenced by whether we wish to be advised or guided around certain work challenges and objectives.

Without doubt, for me, coaching is the most powerful tool as a means by which to stay "on purpose" in your career: your journey, your terms. One of my barrister clients, Felicity, on the verge of, as she put it, "jacking it all in" when she came to me felt, at the end of our sessions, "more serene about the current state of play and how it will affect change for the future."

Many coaching tools and tips to empower women to achieve their full potential are dealt with in the later chapters of this book.

PART II
WHO ARE YOU?

Over the years, I have coached hundreds of women whether individually or in workshop settings, both from the legal profession and elsewhere. What is interesting is the commonality of challenge faced by them all, and how evenly this is split between them:

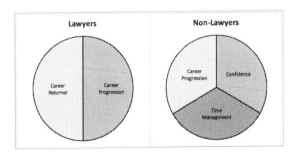

This book applies equally to women in law as women outside the legal profession "deciding to decide" on their next career move, whether up, across or out. By deciding to decide, I mean going all out, with purpose, foot to the floor.

4

WOMEN LEADERS IN THE MAKING

CAREER PROGRESSION AND DECIDING TO DECIDE

Challenges and solutions in this Chapter are around imposter syndrome, starting before you feel ready, deciding what is it you DO want, what success means to you, moving successfully through and beyond your first one hundred days and self-promotion.

The Challenge overcoming imposter syndrome.

Over the time that I have been coaching female professionals, a recurring theme around career challenges is confidence, particularly around a return to work after maternity leave, or applying for promotion or a judicial post.

One topic that seems to be on the increase is so called "Imposter Syndrome", the feeling that we "shouldn't really be there", are somehow "winging it" and at risk at any moment of getting "found out." Time and again amazing, competent, capable women express the view that they simply "aren't good enough" for the next promotional position. A good example of this in practice was given at the Temple Women's Forum "Applying for Silk" Workshop. There, a psychologist encouraged women to be more confident and apply for the prestigious role of Queen's Counsel, not when 90% sure of success as her research showed, but, like men, when 60% sure.

Imposter Syndrome is real. It can keep us "safe", but have you ever heard the saying that when you push beyond your comfort zone, that's where the magic happens? So if you are that woman deciding to decide on your next steps career-wise, get ready to grasp the nettle.

According to whom

Dock leaves at the ready, the good news is, you're not alone. Thinking back to my career at the Bar there were times when, in order to progress my practice, I took on cases outside of my comfort zone. Of course they challenged me. On other occasions they made me feel out of my depth, and in some instances, downright incapable.

Having recently come across the term "imposter syndrome" for the first time, Shabina, partner in a Law Firm, described feeling relief that it was an actual "thing" because she was not on her own in experiencing those limiting beliefs. Likewise, I heard a recently appointed Judge talking at a women's event about similar internal battles.

I have read some negative feminist commentary around the concept recently – the label becomes a self-fulfilling prophesy, somehow, and plays into the "fixing women" narrative. But in my experience on the coal face, empowering women to stay successfully within their professional settings, I have only ever seen it bring about empowerment as they gain some understanding of their inner wranglings and discover ways to overcome them.

How to...deliver the knock out blows to imposter syndrome

So what can we do to harness the feelings which inevitably come in the "Stretch Zone" territory and keep us focused on working hard and doing a good job but which can on occasion have the ability to make us feel debilitating fear and overwhelm?

Here are my suggestions:

1. Create a **Success Board**, a visual representation of your life to date, what you have done well, what you have achieved, what you have succeeded at: Your graduation, your entry date in to the profession, securing your first job, promotion etc. It is a great reference point to go back to on days when motivation is hard to come by and self-doubt is creeping in, to remind you of just how valuable and successful you already are. This works wonders for mindset, and steels you to approach career progression opportunities more positively.

> *Rosemary, Law Firm Partner, used this tool to stop her looking at why she couldn't do things and look instead at how she could. Shifting your focus to your strengths can also be done by preparing a CV or updating your Linkedin profile. By identifying her fabulous skills and achievements to date, thinking about her vast experience, and becoming empowered to talk about them with confidence meant she was able to focus on what she was capable of. By making herself believe it by reaffirming it and visualising the end result, effectively she got out of her own way.*

> *Zoe, locum solicitor, applying for pupillage did similar: by preparing her CV she was challenged to frame each point in a positive as opposed to passive way, think*

about all her cross-transferable skills, and experienced her "first opportunity to shine."

2. Repeat daily **positive affirmations,** positive statements written in the present tense designed to inspire and motivate you and remind you of your own value. Tony Robbins, an American Coach, talks of the brain as a muscle, and just in the same way as a muscle requires consistent exercise to develop and grow stronger, so too your mind needs training to think differently and more positively about you and your situation. *"If it is to be, it is up to me"* is a favourite of mine which I say daily and repeatedly to myself.

Holly was a dually qualified client, having done the Bar exams then, after law school, pursued a solicitor's training contract. She hadn't pursued the Bar because as she put it she had "talked herself out of it" and when we re-visited whether this was still something she wanted to do, she would tell herself, "Don't be silly; you're not good enough." You can imagine our mutual delight when, before the end of our sessions together, she had her first pupillage interview and as preparation beforehand she repeated her motivational motto "Go for it!" Without it, she said she would never had the courage to cross the threshold of the Chambers to be interviewed.

Kerry, one of my barrister clients, used our coaching sessions to devise a new way to approach with conviction meetings with solicitors and win more work. First, she looked at her success board to remind herself of all her strengths and skills. Then, she repeated her positive affirmations to ger her into a winner's mindset. Finally, she thought how her role model would tackle the meeting, modelling similar behaviour to increase confidence and convert business.

3. **Confidence breeds confidence**: As a former criminal barrister I've had nearly twenty years to perfect my "game face." It's so important when representing people anxious about the likely outcome of their case to instil in them confidence that they are in a safe pair of hands. Whilst you might hear your own internal chatter, it is important to manage your own state and give the appearance of external control and confidence. It takes work, and by working on your own thoughts and words you can practise and develop your game face until it becomes second nature.

Externally you may appear like you've got it all together. That's not to say you won't have the occasional wobble brought about by imposter syndrome. Maria, a Senior Associate, had progressed quickly through the ranks, and was readily identified by the partners in the firm as a rising star. And yet, whilst on the one hand she felt a pressure to maintain her "superstar" image, she often worried that people would think: "Who does she think she is?" She was a great example of the fact that you don't have to be under-confident to experience imposter syndrome – in her case, she simply had a long way to fall. By looking in our sessions at things from the viewpoint of others, both those at a senior level, and those causing her most "challenge" i.e. her peers or below her, she was able to re-adjust her mindset.

4. Spend time with and seek feedback from a **trusted circle** of colleagues. Whilst to be meaningful, confidence must come from within, on the down days, it doesn't hurt to remind yourself of the positive stuff that others say about you to win your own battle with your mind to tell it that it is wrong when suggesting you can't do something or your weaknesses will be discovered.

5. Develop a support **network**, both internally and externally. Go to events which will enable you to meet like-minded people and grow your trusted circle to good effect.

6. Work hard to firstly **identify areas of development** so you know the obstacles you are dealing with. Then work equally hard to counter-act them. For example, transitioning from jury advocate to workshop deliverer and key note speaker was a challenge for me at the start of my business. I was heavily dependent on notes, had no experience whatsoever of power point slides nor had I ever had to speak from the heart about personal stories. I knew only the art of persuasion based on the analysis of evidence. So I pushed myself, did the thing I feared, (repeatedly and in a safe environment), and kept doing so until I broke through the barriers of those limiting beliefs.

Lucy, an Associate Solicitor career break returner, had "decided to decide" very quickly in our sessions that she needed to go into business development mode, even though the thought of it made her feel awkward, not very good at it, and at worst invisible. She soon realised that often times, it's just a matter of pushing beyond our comfort zones and doing the one thing that we are most afraid of, and the more she did so, the easier it became. She flipped her thinking from negative to positive, even when she'd made what she described a faux pas at a recent event, got back in the saddle, so to speak, and told herself, "you've got this". Her network extended, her business development activities grew exponentially, and by the time our sessions had come to an end she had not only submitted her application for promotion but had also been awarded it.

7. **Quieten the negative voices** in your head. Acknowledge them and thank them for keeping you safe, but bat them away by saying to them that you want to break free of them this time. Tara Mohr, in her brilliant book, *Playing Big*, develops this theory and practice in greater detail.

Annabelle, a career break returner client, was happy to practise techniques to turn down the volume on the destructive internal chatter particularly as she came to associate the negative stress with those voices telling her "You're not good enough."

8. **Read *Becoming*** by Michelle Obama, a strong, powerful, female leader and ex-lawyer who describes being dogged by the question "Am I good enough?" throughout her life. Her advice to overcome it? To work hard and let your work speak for itself. That said, in my experience, the odd bit of self-promotion never hurt. See how to find the perfect balance in the section on "Using self-promotion for maximum impact" below.

Louisa, a partner in a law firm, was experiencing a struggle similar to that of Obama. She described loving what she did for years, and in the last couple of years being really unhappy at her current firm. She had hit a career cross-roads. What was interesting was that when we talked about some of the things holding her back, a large part of it was her own sense of not being good enough. She actually took great comfort from the fact that she had "discovered" imposter syndrome, from that was able to identify firstly that she wasn't alone in these experiences, and further she was then able to more readily identify techniques to overcome it. A great example of owning it and moving on.

9. **Remember your raison d'etre**, your "what's it all about?" Why are you doing what you are doing? Focus on your career goals and ambitions and work back from there. Put an action plan in place for their achievement. If you have a plan, even if you are knocked temporarily off course by imposter syndrome, you can course correct and get straight back on your clear path to success.

10. **Work with a coach or mentor**. Having identified which is the most appropriate support for you, you can explore further ways to boost your confidence and side step the negative impact of imposter syndrome by

having someone in your corner, shining a light on your strengthens and, more to the point, empowering you to reach your full potential.

> *It's worth pointing out that at the end of a course of coaching I conduct a review session, in which the client is asked to identify her top three strengths and the three things that have changed since we started. Laura, barrister on the cusp of leaving the Bar when we started, found it a great way to demonstrate her capacity for dealing with tasks and evidencing the fact that she could succeed far more than she ever thought possible at the outset.*

The Challenge...starting before you feel ready

So we've got imposter syndrome under control. What next? In the process of "Deciding to decide", we can sometimes feel the need to get organised, become fully competent, and turn uncertainty about promotion into certainty. I'm all for doing the research, being ready and prepared, especially as a career break returner dealing with lots of change, a drop in confidence, possibly even overwhelm. But in truth, isn't some of this simply procrastinating, in a way that lets others, often men, elbow ahead?

According to whom

"The key to success is to start before you are ready". Marie Forleo's great advice not only got my coaching business off the ground but catapulted it beyond expectation, simply because I let go of the feeling that I had to know all the answers.

How to...overcome stagnation through procrastination

You may never feel it's the right time. Success can't always be guaranteed. But how would it feel then to know that in not "going for it" you've ended up standing in your own way?

If you don't step up, who will? How will you feel when others, perhaps more junior or less capable or experienced than you, overtake you? "You've got to be in it to win it", after all. A dear friend of mine in Chambers took this advice some years ago before applying for her Recordership, a part-time judge position. It was enough to jolt her into action. If it's what you want, what's to stop you? She's now a Circuit Judge, so testament to what's out there for you if only you dare.

It might even be something more basic: for Jane, career break returner, a simple task of ringing the Solicitors' Regulatory Authority to enquire whether she was still on the Solicitor's roll initially felt overwhelming. After one coaching session, she felt sufficiently emboldened to make that all important call. Her confidence grew exponentially in the knowledge that she was indeed still "a solicitor" and was safely off the starting blocks.

The Challenge...deciding what it is you DO want

If you are still umming and erring about whether promotion or career progression is truly what you want, what WILL make you sure when the time is now? Over and above setting goals and making an action plan to get you there, how can you get clear about what it is you DO want?

According to whom

Whilst I was happy at the Bar to take on more serious and complicated cases, successfully becoming the most junior Grade 4 Prosecutor in Chambers and Rape and Serious Sexual Offences Prosecution Specialist, when it came to the annual practice review with the Senior Clerk about applying for Recordership, we were completely mis-aligned. It was something he wanted for me (and doubtless Chambers) but it was never something I wanted for myself.

What I did want was to help people in a more positive and less pressurised environment.

How to...know what it is you want, then go for it

Develop an emotional "buy-in" to your end goal to reinforce it and find motivation towards it. Another way of putting it is to "know your why". I think of how proud my kids will be of their Mummy, taking a major leap of faith to implement (not just a change of career but to start my own business) and learning to fly on the way down.

In addition, what better way to increase personal confidence in making that decision than by having a genuine connection with yourself. I know from personal experience how effective coaching is at increasing personal performance and confidence in every aspect of life. Engineering a convincing method by which we step up and make our job or business work more effectively for us is essential – even if this means progressing our career, whether legal or otherwise, in a way that is individual to US rather than in line with what others expect.

This leads me on to one of my favourite quotes which came to light in Research by Bronnie Waring, Australian Palliative Care Nurse, who compiled research on the top five regrets of the dying: *Live a life true to yourself, not the life others expect*

The Challenge...what success means to you

What success means to you will be influenced by your values and beliefs, goals and ambitions. It is entirely individual.

When giving yourself permission to start the conversation with yourself ask: What do you want? What do you really want? These questions are personal to YOU, and shouldn't be influenced by others. Ask yourself "what success means to me?" Explore how you define and visualise it. And be honest about it.

Success can mean many things to many different people. In law it might be being a silk, a judge, a law firm equity partner OR none of the above, in other professions, a CEO, a Director, on the Executive Board or again, something else entirely. In a world where "wellbeing", "life balance" and "flexible working" are all important buzz words, think of the Millennial definition of success, which considers life outside of your profession, as opposed to the "expected" route to success through promotion in a traditional, hierarchical law firm.

We all have very different, and individual, ideas around success and what it means to us: no "one size fits all".

Develop personal confidence around what success truly means as opposed to being held back by it. Give yourself permission to ask those questions of yourself and allow yourself time to reflect and come up with your own answers.

> *Whilst touching here on confidence, it reminds me of career break return sessions with Claire, Senior Associate Solicitor, who had been working a four day week in the office since her return. She had actually been offered a four day week, three days in the office and one day from home, but since she had started the precedent of all days in the office, she felt unable to ask to revert to the original offer. Having focused clearly on the things that were important to her, and worked on her personal confidence in that regard, she was ultimately able to adopt a "if you don't ask, you don't get" approach, and was rewarded when her request was granted. Her terms, her success.*

Only when you have a clear view of what it looks like to

YOU can you make plans to achieve it. Above all else, be authentic. When discussing a recent judicial appointment with a senior male colleague, he told me he would not be applying to the Bench or for Silk because success to him meant defending those who would otherwise not have a voice to do so themselves. This was his own version of success; this for him was more than enough.

For colleagues in Chambers who would moan about hating the job, but "what else could I do?" I always thought, with their many cross-transferable skills, they could perhaps be a bit more precise, truthful even, about their drivers: What they actually meant was "what else could I do that pays X amount of money?" Perhaps they were limiting themselves to a definition of success based purely on financial reward?

According to whom

In her autobiography, *Becoming*, Michelle Obama's searing honesty about this resonated: "I hated being a lawyer. I wasn't suited to the work. I felt empty doing it, even if I was plenty good at it. This was a distressing thing to admit, given how hard I'd worked and how in debt I was. In my blinding drive to excel, in my need to do things perfectly, I'd missed the signs and taken the wrong path."

In my experience, what is essential is to connect with yourself. Now bear with me here. I'm not going "woo-woo." It was Steven Covey in *7 Habits of Highly Effective People* who explained how easy it is to get caught up in life's busy-ness, working hard to climb the ladder of success, only to discover that once you get to the top you discover that all the time the ladder had been leaning against the wrong wall. I can totally relate to this.

Whilst in Jamaica, doing my Death Row work, I was working with passion and authenticity. It was on my return home to the "everyday grind" of child sexual abuse cases that I experienced an internal conflict, my "career crossroads moment." Coaching got me back on track – my focus became more around income and lifestyle. I enjoyed eating and drinking in fancy restaurants, razzing around in my natty little sports car and holidaying in Caribbean resorts. Those that know me know I'm not materialistic, so unsurprisingly, after a further 8-10 years, things still weren't "right". My internal conflict returned because of a lack of authenticity in that path.

This is when we have to get honest about our own values, beliefs and drivers, to ensure we put the ladder against the right wall before starting the climb; otherwise things will always come up short.

. . .

How to...move forward with conviction

Find ways to fall in love with your job again, and if not, make plans alongside it, to improve it – by tweaks, to establish clear boundaries, perhaps by resolving not to work past X time at night; by bigger adjustments like re-training in a different area within the same profession; or by going all out for whole scale career change, as I did pursuing my business as opposed to continuing a career at the Bar.

Don't fall into the trap of thinking "I'm not happy about this, but I'm powerless to do anything about it". Be prepared to do the necessary. I know former Criminal barristers who have successfully strategised and re-trained to specialise in Family Law, for example, to provide a certain degree of flexibility over and above the jury trial v life balance conundrum. Likewise, my Corporate and Executive Coach Training began in 2010, and I completed my thesis in 2012, all whilst working in full time practice at the Bar: I was playing the long game. It wasn't until 2018 that, with mounting family commitments, I finally knew it was the right time to call "time at the Bar".

It's only when we focus on what it is we want, however far ahead that might be, rather than what it is we don't want, that we can put the smaller plans in place and formulate an action plan to make it a reality.

Remain authentic. Being passionate about your role and your career calling will give you longevity and an edge.

So how to settle on a forward trajectory? I am a big believer in Covey's Second Habit of Highly Effective People: Start with the end in mind. Be clear and honest about your goal, visualise the end-point then, working backwards, put plans in place to get there. Everything you do thereafter will be "on purpose" towards that outcome.

> *Whilst mulling over when and if to start that forward trajectory, Sophie, a Senior Associate, was honest to acknowledge whilst liking her job, she didn't love it. She was debating how much to put in and to what end. That said, she was astute enough to realise that even if not yet, networking was a huge part not only of business development, but also of creating opportunities for herself to move role if and when the time became right.*

The Challenge...navigating your first one hundred days and beyond

So you've secured your next promotion. You've asked for and been given the best pay cheque, because you know your own value and how to communicate it. You're suited and booted ready to take on this next important challenge. You've dived right into your stretch zone. What next then to hit the ground running and navigate your steepest learning curve to date?

According to whom

In your first one hundred days, you need to support yourself and find others who support you. Firstly, have confidence in yourself that you are up to the job. You may not be the best YET, but you are in position, and bring to the post all your previous experience and strengths together with all massive future potential. It's good to remind yourself of what you do well and your past successes: you can absolutely do this! Add to, and remind yourself daily of, your success board.

Keep a sense of humour and stay humble, by being self-aware. You've already identified the stuff you do well and by conducting a SWOT (Strengths, Weaknesses, Opportunities, Threats) analysis for example, you will also have the opportunity to acknowledge and, more importantly, work on the areas where you have to dig that little bit deeper.

What challenges do you need to work on to support your own learning, or as a way of upskilling? This might include gaps in knowledge around technology, leading a team and also knowing your own limits. I'm thinking here about your ability to set boundaries and, where necessary, say no.

Moving away from self-reflection then, turn to those around you. What courses or other external support do you need to utilise? Who or what else needs to be involved? How do the logistics at home need to function in support? Put yourself in the best position to make yourself invaluable to your seniors.

Slow down to speed up. Take time to find your feet in the new role before introducing any wide-spread, unsettling or controversial change. That said, don't hang back from the quick and meaningful wins. Take the lead in meetings. Take the opportunities to show the boss they chose well, and your team that you are more than capable; you are on it.

How to…move successfully beyond your first one hundred days

Now that you are conducting yourself effectively as the leader you were meant to be, and you are increasing your qualities and skills daily, how can you maintain this forward momentum over time? This is when there comes a time to embrace self-promotion and use it for maximum impact.

Document, "shout" even, about your success: Use the power of social media and other "platforms" to good effect. It's free marketing for goodness sake, why wouldn't you use it?

In the first instance, update your social media to reflect your new position and skills set. Then consider writing articles or blogs for other publications. By so doing, you build not just a business but a brand, and establish a persuasive platform from it, albeit remaining mindful of the limits imposed by professional bodies about the extent to which it is wise to comment, share or tweet.

Recognise there is a balance to be struck:

> "*She who is humble is confident and wise; She who brags is insecure and lacking.*"

> — ANON

When I was a criminal barrister, I wouldn't shout about it. In some respects, the professional status I was afforded thereby meant I didn't have to. Yet at times, I reflect, this approach held me back professionally. Others, frequently men, happily stepped up to the plate to contribute articles to Chambers monthly newsletter, present quarterly legal update seminars, and entertain instructing solicitors over lunch.

Michelle Obama writes in her brilliant book, *Becoming*, of letting others judge her by her work. But when consummate self-promoters are doing otherwise by creating fast track opportunities for career advancement, aren't the more shy retiring Obama-types at risk of being left behind? If you aren't prepared to shout about your own successes, why on earth should others do so on your behalf? As a coach empowering female lawyers, I'm all for finding a happy medium between wall-flower and braggart.

With analysis and self-reflection, I see two things at play – confidence and authenticity.

Whilst at the Bar, I'd frequently go on holiday abroad alone, then meet up with a group whose only common bond was an interest in that particular desti-nation, trip or adventure. Adrenalin seekers, philan-thropists, culture vultures, interested in the immediate discoveries; the back story of fellow back-packers was less important. And when I told them about the job, the frequent response that greeted me was "you don't seem the type." Whilst pondering what exactly was " the type", that reaction perhaps came as no surprise. For well over ten years, I had felt like a square peg in a round hole. Part of me didn't fit somehow.

What's interesting is that now, as a coach, I shout much more (albeit that it's all relative). The reason for this, I'm sure, is because I'm operating in an area which now feels authentically me.

So how do we use noise to be heard? Some adopt the lion approach, whose roar can be heard over five miles: the loudest shout can be heard the farthest. But how often is it said that "*She who shouts loudest, has the least amount to say...*"? Shouting causes noise. And in this increasingly 24/7 digital age, we are constantly on a knife edge between FOMO (the Fear of Missing Out) and the overwhelming cacophony of email and text notifications and social media updates breeding unhelpful comparisons between us and our colleagues and competitors. It's all about getting an effective balance.

The Challenge...using self-promotion for maximum impact

By whom do you want to be heard? Be clear about your target audience: who are your clients? By doing so, when you have something to say, you can ensure that your content speaks exclusively to them.

Where does your target audience hang out? Consider

the best strategy to adopt to find those clients and speak to them in their preferred arena or on the right platform. Do they use Social Media? If so, what is their platform of choice? Are they more likely to read articles in professional publications? Do they show up at face to face networking events? If so, which ones?

What content are they looking for? Once you have a clear idea of your typical client, and the arena in which they operate, then think about the beneficial content they seek. Think of how you can add value by applying two tests:

- Check the content is useful, not just interesting
- Imagine them reading your content and responding "So what?" Then think how you can overcome that possible reaction by cross-checking your content's value.

According to whom

Certainly Sophie, Senior Associate, had some fears around self-promotion, knowing her own strengths and seeing the importance of telling people about them, but wanting to do so in a way that did not come across as big-headed or arrogant. My suggestion? Be helpful, organically establishing yourself as an expert, and do so without boast or brag. There's a fine line to tread and it simply comes down to practice.

Likewise, whilst coaching Mary, locum solicitor, going for a new position at a different firm, I reflected back to her some of the self-deprecating language she used about herself in our sessions to bring into her awareness how it potentially undermined her attempts to promote herself positively. With awareness and practice, she was able to overcome these self-limiting beliefs to more readily appear confident, positive and, consequently, employable at the new firm.

How to…present content

1. Content Delivery and Tone

Assuming you now have the perfect, useful content, how is it to be presented?

If self-promotion doesn't come naturally, think about one great thing you have done as a team or organisation at work, something on your Success Board perhaps; then think about your individual contribution. Start formulating your individual message from there. The more you do it, the easier it becomes. This was certainly my experience at monthly networking meetings where, each time I delivered my one minute "pitch", I defined with greater clarity what my offering was, to whom I was offering it, and how I could articulate it with as much precision as self-belief.

2. Work on Relationships...

... both in terms of building and developing relationships, and then in terms of maintaining a supportive team. As Zig Ziglar said, "*If people like you, they'll listen to you; If they trust you, they'll do business with you.*" It's certainly been my experience that the more people know and trust you, the more likely you are to hear of the next opportunity. References for future positions are a great example of this.

> *Thinking creatively about how to approach business development activity is a way of acknowledging the importance of self-promotion whilst avoiding the more distasteful "salesy" element. A career break returner, Niamh, found a neat way round this challenge by thinking not in terms of networking but rather "shared interest". She found an exercise class for working mums and also thought about her extended network of friends, those with whom she shared mutual interests, even those she met at the school gates, adopting effective seemingly "rainmaker" techniques which soon converted into business.*

A similar approach was encouraged at a law firm keen to retain female talent who had previously been put off by the onerous business development activities that had traditionally taken place after work at times inconvenient to working parents. Here the approach was once again common interest (in one case, a Senior Associate won business via a phone call with a farmer client through their mutual love of horses). Likewise, online network building was also encouraged. Certain it is to say I don't know where my business would be without Linkedin.

A supportive team having your back cannot be underestimated. Without, communications can break down, (just as they did with my clerks on return to the Bar after my second maternity leave), and consequently, effectiveness and productivity nose-dive.

Choose that circle wisely. I'd always recommend quality over quantity. Given it is said that you become the sum of the parts with whom you mostly spend time, remember the saying: *"Eagles don't fly with pigeons."* I know which one I'd rather be.

3. Establish yourself as an expert: Know your niche

I know from my Bar days that, at the outset of any career

journey, as a pupil barrister or with a solicitors' training contract, there is a need to "try before you buy," keep an open mind and say yes to varied opportunities. This lead to my Pegasus Scholarship with the Inner Temple to work at Capital Chambers, Wellington, New Zealand for three months and then my Bar Human Rights Committee Death Row Work in Jamaica. Baroness Hale said at the Temple (North) Women's Forum event in 2018, there is a huge variety available within law, so consider not just the obvious jobs. From my experience, I agree.

She went on to say, however, that finding your niche is the most important thing. Of that, there can be no doubt. At the point at which absolute clarity on career or business direction is sought, remember *"Generalists seek clients, clients seek specialists."* This is as true with coaching as in law – First I was a Criminal Specialist, then I became an experienced Grade 4 Prosecutor, finally a Rape Specialist. By the time I finished my career at the Bar I had a successful "heavy weight Prosecution sex" practice as a result.

To niche or establish yourself as an expert means you become the go-to person, the specialist, the person who if someone has a particular problem they know you are the one (and often only) person who can solve it for them.

It's the same with coaching: I receive referrals now as the "go-to person" for specialist empowerment coaching for female lawyers. In turn, it's amazing what this can also do for your self-worth: establishing yourself as an expert not only promotes the confidence of others in you, but also allows your personal self-confidence to sky-rocket.

Exercise 1

Jot down your own thoughts here and use as a checklist for action

Have you ever felt like you are winging it or feared you will get found out?

If so, what could you do?

Here is a reminder of some suggestions:

- Success board
- Positive affirmations
- Work on game face
- Develop network
- Identify areas of development
- Quieten negative voices
- Read *Becoming*
- Remember your "raison d'etre"
- Work with a coach or mentor

What WILL you do and WHEN?

Exercise 2

Jot down your own thoughts here and use as a checklist for action

Are you ready to get clear about your next career move?

If so, what could you do?

Here is a reminder of some suggestions:

- Start before you are ready
- Remember your why
- Connect with yourself
- Know your end game

What WILL you do and WHEN?

Exercise 3

Jot down your own thoughts here and use as a checklist
for action

Are you newly promoted?

If so, what could you do?

Here is a reminder of some suggestions:

- Document your successes to date
- Identify and locate your target audience
- Consider what content your audience
  considers is "value add"
- Decide your niche

What WILL you do and WHEN?

5

WORKING PARENTS AND CAREER BREAK RETURNERS

Challenges and solutions in this Chapter are around how to be a career professional and parent and succeed at both, preparing for and overcoming career break return challenges and how to progress your career when you are ready.

The Challenge...how to be a career professional and parent – and succeed at both

Michelle Obama broke the bad news to working mothers whilst promoting her biography, *Becoming*: 'That whole, "So you can have it all." Nope, not at the same time. 'That's a lie." Famously she went on to use colourful language to criticise Sheryl Sandberg's philosophy around women leaning into their careers to succeed. There is a certain irony here, because in Sandberg's *Lean In* book, she actually agrees with Obama, describing 'Having it all' as a myth.

This is not simply the domain of women. The Western Circuit Women's Forum Back to the Bar Survey found that male barristers rarely took parental leave for any significant period. Men at the Bar often experience a sense of obligation to return to work quickly, inextricably linked to the financial pressures of self-employment.

In an example from the survey, a male barrister '*will not be open about his real problems juggling childcare responsibilities... because he feels he needs to "man up".*' Wider, societal issues about gender roles and stereo-typing clearly come into play.

So if 'having it all' is a lie and a myth for both women and men, how are we to be professionals, parents and succeed at both? The preferable question I think is to ask what our own definition of success is, and how that can be achieved as a working parent within our careers.

According to whom

It's important to be realistic about our options and accepting of our choices. Being a parent means making daily compromises and decisions which we may not like, but can live with. How to do so is another matter.

To those outside looking in, a successful barrister is confident, focused and present in whatever case they are instructed upon. They are available to undertake last minute case preparation outside of normal office hours. They go above and beyond to fight their client's case.

They are also human, not robots or superheroes: parents, carers, people who may have been up all night with a demanding baby, or putting small children to bed late, then settling down to prepare a jury speech late in to the small hours.

Yet there is an expectation that we show up next morning at court, ready to go, 'game face' engaged. There is a big difference between image and reality.

How to...ditch the "having it all" myth and learn to live with compromise

To give ourselves the best chance of preserving the image and living with the invidious compromises that we, as parents, inevitably have to make, childcare will have to be in place which is affordable and in which we feel confident. Flexible working arrangements are also important as a means by which to control our own schedule. The downside, however, according to the earlier mentioned BSB Report is that for many, it can negatively impact on the work women received and their career progression.

Again, this applies equally to men. At the Women Lawyers and Mothers launch event in Manchester in 2018, a male panel member working flexibly in a law firm recounted an occasion when he was deliberately discriminated against by a senior partner, who called into question his commitment to his role and the firm due to him working flexibly.

> *Marianne, career break returner and law firm Senior Associate soon learned to live with her changed priorities. She acknowledged the demanding nature of the profession, target driven, with client needs paramount. She was also aware of the expectation that she would be operating at the same level as before her maternity leave with increased demands on her time at home and changed priorities in terms of how important things felt to her at work. Pre-maternity, her career goal was partnership; as a working mother, the emphasis had altered - "I'd love to be partner, but how realistic is that for me, since traditional business development and networking activities are challenging due to time pressure and working hours?"*

As Sandberg says,

> '*the best way to make room for both life and career is to make choices deliberately.*'

The Challenge…Career break return

In the latter five years of my career at The Criminal Bar, I started a family and became all too familiar with the so called "juggle" between work and family life. What struck me reflecting on those experiences was that even within the same family, circumstances change. Deciding on the right childcare options requires a combination of creativity, flex and review.

As mentioned in Chapter 1, with my first child, I returned to full-time work after six months, before I felt ready, with the support of grand-parents and nursery care. This was due to financial considerations and not wanting to step out for too long in case my career progression was hindered and fearing the so called 'maternity penalty'.

With my second, I increased maternity leave to twelve months. I returned when I was in a better position to do so, full time nanny in place.

By child number three, I was ready for an extended

period of maternity leave, which I had no interest in before.

These three, and very different, scenarios serve to illustrate that no 'one size fits all'.

According to whom

I've heard it said on countless occasions that those working part-time can often end up in a situation where there is an expectation that they do their normal full time work simply in less hours. It is imperative then that from the outset, lines of communication are open with the managers and leaders in organisations so that there is a clear understanding of how you and they define and practically implement the term "flexible working". This can differ wildly depending on the sector, company or organisation in which you work. Communication is key – both verbal as well as written.

There is an increasing number of law firms paying more than lip-service to the needs of parents returning from maternity leave to whom I deliver career-break return coaching. These female lawyers commonly experience a lack of confidence resulting from changes in:

- the day to day work, ordinarily second nature,

but which becomes more burdensome after an
extended period away;

- technology and personnel whilst away from the
office;
- priorities concerning their next career move,
how that looks, and in what direction.

I can understand for career break returners, confidence
may be at a low ebb wanting to get back into the swing of
things, at a manageable pace. I'm all for getting your
ducks in a row. However, I frequently hear damaging
internal dialogue around not being good enough (good
old imposter syndrome creeping in again) and feeling the
need to prove something. Additionally, there are practical challenges around time management, productivity,
and the need to establish clear boundaries.

However, my experience of career break returning and
returners, both personally and professionally as a coach,
is that when parents have to leave at 4.30pm to fulfil
nursery collection for example, they simply HAVE TO
leave. The positive consequence of this is our productivity within the hours actually in the office increases
immeasurably. That said, in an age when digital distractions have become both reality and the norm, there are
certain things which can be put in place to better
manage a return to work.

All of these challenges are common place. Clients can be reassured that they are not alone. How to manage and overcome the challenges is another matter.

How to…overcome the common career break return challenges

1. Consider your childcare options. Can childcare be shared equally between parents? Does the cost of external childcare outweigh part-time working opportunities? Is flexible working available? What are your childcare preferences?

> As my career break return client, Jo, said, she had intricate childcare arrangements to put in place to support a return to work, so setting boundaries was important to facilitate a four day week, with a 5pm latest finish, and possibly accommodating a day or two working from home. That brings me on to the tricky matter of communicating it to your organisation.

2. Communicate clearly with leaders and managers in your organisation, both verbally and in writing, so that they not only *hear* what it is you are communicating to them about back to work expectations but more importantly that they *understand* it. Learning to say no can also be an important part of the communication piece.

Career break returner Anya provides a great example as she felt she was being pushed too much by her managing partner immediately on her return. She learned quickly the need to get her priorities in order, time manage, establish boundaries, learn to say no, and communicate this effectively to her boss so that he not just heard but understood.

3. Use Keep in Touch (KIT) days during maternity leave, or a phased return, to upskill on technology and current working practices, network within new teams and gradually ease back in. This way you can break the ice on a career break to avoid the significant pressures to be expected of a "hard" return.

Lucy, career break returner, had to cope with a new area of law on her return, together with new technology, a new environment and personnel since the team had not only expanded but also moved floors to accommodate the growing numbers. It was a lot for her to take in, but she found useful her Success Board to boost her confidence and maintain her focus on the more overwhelming of days.

Similarly, another Career Break returner at the same firm, Kim used as many of her KIT days as were available to her to get ahead of the game, get to know people again and feel more integrated so she could hit the ground running on her return and maintain her visibility within the firm should she wish to quickly pick up her career progression and business development activities again, as opposed to leaving things to the last minute then feeling overwhelmed on her first day back.

4. Align yourself with and listen to the shared experiences of a supportive "team": an empathetic boss, a friendly colleague, inspiring role model, coach or mentor for example. This way you will realise your experiences are completely normal, not unusual and most importantly, not insurmountable.

5. It is absolutely essential that you have the ability to not only plan your day in terms of the priorities you have, and the order in which to tackle tasks, but also to have a clear ability to categorise tasks into important, urgent, not important and not urgent, as Stephen Covey does in his book, 7 *Habits of Highly Effective People*. His best advice is to "Put first things first."

6. Once categorised, tackle each task in a manner that allows you to be fully present in it to maximise focus and time. Likewise, make life easier for yourself where you can by avoiding digital distraction.

7. Examine whether your habits and behaviours help or

hinder your levels of personal confidence. Do you listen to, and are you influenced by, unhelpful negative internal chatter? Whatever the internal chatter, it is important to manage your own state to give the appearance of external control and confidence. Do you adopt a positive mind-set and use correspondingly positive, empowering language?

Progressing: Moving Onward and Upward when the time is right

Some career break returners want to successfully manage the day to day transition from home to working life before ever considering putting their foot to the floor on the career progression path. Often at that time, nothing could be further from their minds, in fact.

Others see the return to work as just the right point in time to go for it, all hands to the pump, with a clean slate, and work towards the next promotion.

In my experience, the vast majority of women fall into the category of those "deciding to decide", a pool of hugely talented women who, having become mothers for the first time, are suddenly plunged into a brave new world of changed priorities – feeling in that particular moment that getting to the next nativity play or sports day is far more important than moving up to the next rung on the partnership or promotional ladder – whilst having no desire to give up on their future career progression. Nor should they have to.

Career break returner clients ruminate on the age old dilemma of how flexible work options may support or potentially hinder them. In coaching sessions, clarification is often sought about career progression, albeit without rushing any decisions to move rapidly up the promotional rungs. One in particular, Bettina, Senior Associate, wanted to be sure that if she went for partnership, she could do so whilst part time with family commitments. She devised a realistic two year plan, to avoid any sense in between times of treading water. Interestingly, over that time she identified her area of development to be the need to project more confidence and gravitas in her role, particularly in meetings. She wanted to speak more forcefully, and to strip out her subconsciously weak language, such as the use of words or phrases "just" and "it will only take a minute." As she saw it, the law firm was still looking for a traditionally "male" skillset (visibility in meetings, confidence, bringing in business). She wanted to develop her leadership skills but was torn with how exactly she should do so – between a Sheryl Sandberg approach requiring her to "Lean in" to and get on with male culture, or bringing her "whole self" to work, as advocated by Mary Portas, in her brilliant book "Work Like a Woman – A Manifesto for Change."

For each of us, how we react and feel is deeply personal; there are no rights or wrongs. Here is the advice that helped me get my own next move right:

1. Take your time

Whilst I'm a big advocate of the Maria Toledo's *"Start before you're ready"* approach in business as a means by which to to overcome limiting beliefs, in the case of career break returners, I caution initially doing anything in a hurry. Take time to adjust, if that is what you need to do. The transition of returning to work after an extended period away cannot be under-estimated.

2. Be honest and authentic

After you have had children, the wall you wish to climb now might or might not be the same one as you were climbing before. There are additional considerations – not least an increased burden on finances if, for example, you are working reduced hours, earning less money, and you have increased outgoings due to exorbitant childcare costs. Look at your goals and ambitions as they are <u>now</u>, not as they were when you were younger and child-free.

What now is your authentic path? Keep your "why" under constant review.

3. Don't forget you

During the two and a half years that I was on extended maternity leave I learned so much about little people, and of course myself. The unconditional ease with which we prioritise, as though our life depends upon it, another human being's needs over and above our own. The compromising of so many of our own personal pleasures to ensure, as best as we are able, the unshakable confidence and all-encompassing happiness of someone else, comes with the territory.

> *Thinking of Ruth, career break returner, I realise these are not uncommon feelings. As she put it, she'd been out of law for so many years raising a family she had "lost something of me over the last thirteen years." This manifested itself in lost confidence and a loss of financial independence too. It's worth remembering though that whilst out of professional life for a while, we each develop a multitude of cross-transferrable skills and whilst we should become savvy about how we package them up on a CV, we should do exactly that – and invite employers or recruiters to consider our skills based on our potential as opposed to current position.*

The brief moments free of responsibility when I used to sneak to my beloved exercise class (as I did religiously twice a week), when childcare, energy levels and mummy guilt allowed, were priceless.

And yet at night, and during nap times, I realised there was a very large part of me that I hadn't compromised or lost: The hard working, determined, financially independent Barrister come Coach. Whilst the period of time I had spent away from Chambers might have been unusually long, I had been working creatively, strategising in an unconventional way whilst still keeping those little people at the core of my very being.

Bronnie Waring's research found that one of the other top five regrets of the dying was "I wish I hadn't worked so hard." People don't look back at life wishing they'd spent less time with their kids now, do they?

Exercise 4

Jot down your own thoughts here and use as a checklist for action

Are you a working parent?

If so, what could you do?

Here is a reminder of some suggestions:

- Consider what are the pros and cons of flexible or part-time work
- Consider how you can redefine success for better outcomes

What WILL you do and WHEN?

Exercise 5

Jot down your own thoughts here and use as a checklist for action

Are you a career break returner?

If so, what could you do?

Here is a reminder of some suggestions:

- Consider how to communicate your career expectations clearly to work
- Consider childcare options
- Consider how to use KIT days or phased return
- Consider who is in your supportive team
- Consider categorising tasks
- Consider how to focus
- Consider how to maintain positive mindset
- Consider how to progress your career when you feel ready

What WILL you do and WHEN?

6

CAREER CHANGERS

Challenges and solutions in this Chapter are around maintaining the status quo with minor tweaks, redefining your career by more significant changes or going all out on your Plan B with full scale career change.

𝒯he Challenge…maintaining the status quo with minor tweaks

Feel like a square peg in a round hole? Fed up with the constant pressure put on yourself to "make it work" because you have strived so hard to do so over however many years yet STILL don't feel fulfilled within your career? You've made some small, then more significant, tweaks to no avail. Now you are intent on career change.

As long as we think creatively about how to make our careers work for us, and are prepared to put in some hard graft re-training if we decide it isn't in fact for us, then either way, we will be keeping up positive momentum towards a defined goal: for me, it was finding a means by which to be authentic. It's worth pointing out too that goals may change, particularly in a long career.

The best way to maintain positive focus is to have a plan, a vision, a goal of where it is we are headed. As the saying goes, *"It's hard to score without a goal."* Peak performers studied by Stephen Covey in his 7 *Habits of Highly Effective People* book were found to be visualisers, had already experienced in their mind's eye standing on a podium as an Olympic medal winner, before doing so for real, or even starting their four or eight year training regime. They *"start with the end in mind"*. Doing so demonstrates the mindset of the mentally tough: to see an end-point clearly, and identify a road by which to achieve it. To do otherwise is to be reactive to or influenced by others.

With any new career challenge, I advocate being pro-active not re-active. *"Life isn't about waiting for the winds to change; it's learning to adjust your sails"*.

According to whom

In my experience, only by allowing myself a safe space with quiet time for example in coaching sessions to plan and strategise can I truly recognise the things that make me tick.

I made the financial incentives work for me for a while, with all the predictable trappings of wealth. But where did that leave me in terms of my personal congruency? Was I being authentic?

My motivations were simply not in sync with my values and beliefs. I had a strong desire to help people, in an authentic and positive environment, which was not being met in law.

What has been interesting about the journey to becoming a successful business woman is that in the background, I always kept a foothold in Chambers, just in case things "didn't work out"; a security blanket or fast track to an income stream if all else failed.

In January 2018, I delivered a workshop specifically for legal professionals. Things were starting to feel more authentic. What was lacking was congruency. I still had that place in Chambers and even then was in discussions about a return to work. It was only really during those conversations that I came to realise that the one thing holding me back in business was the fear of going "all out".

Becoming a specialist coach for female lawyers, pure and simple, was imperative. I could then lose the toe-hold in Chambers which was synonymous to the outside world with my insurance policy for if things didn't work out, a subconscious message that I didn't have 100% faith in the success of my own business: clients could rightly call me out on my own lack of authenticity or personal congruency.

On 10th February 2018, I resigned from Chambers after a career that began in September 1996. The strangest sensation? No histrionics, no drama, just an over-whelming sense of internal calm, and the realisation that without hesitation that was totally the right thing to do. I am back in sync.

How to...change career

My journey from Barrister to career changer is well documented. The missing piece in the puzzle is the "How to..." How does a professional woman with 19 years' experience transition to business woman and specialist coach empowering women?

At the point of my "career crossroads" moment, with the realisation that my inner voice was being silenced and my authenticity compromised due to the dynamics of career and everything else, I set to work to overcome life's immediate challenges by identifying where I wanted to go, the steps I'd need to get there, and made an action plan to start. *"A goal without a plan is just a wish" – Antoine de Saint Exupery.* It was then that I undertook my course with a view to re-training and qualifying as a Corporate and Executive Coach.

I acknowledged that my priorities, and the route to how I would achieve my goals, had altered. These had altered dramatically when comparing the aspirations of a fresh faced twenty-two year old law graduate with those of a forty-something Criminal Barrister, with significantly changed personal circumstances. There is a certain inevitability around the flexing and changing of goals over a period of years. Important then, to keep them under constant review.

I started my coaching business whilst a full time mum working in the nooks and crannies of time. In the beginning, I had just four "day light" hours in which to work the business. I found it critically important when working in such small pockets of time to have a clear vision of what I wanted and a strong motivation for getting there. Also, to be flexible and create time where I thought there was none. Is there something that you could give up, to become more time rich? That was the end of Coronation Street for me. Goodbye, good riddance.

For the "Big Goals" I found two helpful tools:

- Sometimes referred to as Dream boards, I prefer the more tangible and achievable "**Goal Board**" title – a visual representation of "the plan" i.e. what you want, and when, and small steps to progress in between so you can see your achievements as they happen along the way. It's great fun to get out the glossy mags and Pritt stick and spend some time reflecting on what it is you want, and when. Once you have created your masterpiece, find a prominent place to display it. Mine is always displayed straight in front of me at my desk, motivating and driving me forward each day. Included on my 2019 Board was "I am writing a book". Just goes to show they work!

- **Success Boards**, similar to a Goal Board, for the days when you may be lacking that drive to get on with those all important tasks, display visual images of your own achievements to date, so you can be reminded you are a person

of value, feel proud and find motivation to
carry on

Armed with a clear plan, remember, planning is nothing without action: *"Positive intentions without positive action lead to positively nothing."*

A good way to drive action and momentum into your career change or new business, over and above following a good plan, is to know "your why." If you have a powerful enough motivation, you will be driven to act upon it. Ask yourself if you normally start your day at 6am, "what gets you up at 5am?" What are your most important reasons for doing what you do, and desiring that which you want to achieve?

Once you have established a powerful, emotional connection to "your why", implementing your action plan will become more instinctive, more passionate, and you will act with unshakeable conviction: you will put yourself and the plan into forward momentum.

Be authentic, never stop learning or growing as a person, be open to new opportunities, and challenge yourself to think differently and creatively about your current situation and the habits you, for right or wrong, have developed over a lifetime and upon which you have become reliant. *"You can't change your life if you don't change your thinking...Change your thinking; change your actions; change your life..."*

With all this learning and growing during career transition, it seemed fitting to adopt for my Coaching business logo the Maori symbol for an unfurling silver fern frond, "Koru", signifying positive change, personal growth, a new phase in life.

In coaching sessions with Jillian, law firm partner, dealing with her own career cross roads, we explored her options both in and outside of law, identified her career goals with clarity and she became accountable for her next steps. It was only then that she was able to move forward with the next steps in her career with a renewed sense of clarity and confidence.

Likewise, Associate Solicitor Catherine, going through redundancy, was asking herself if she had been unhappy in her role, at her firm or perhaps in law. She had the seeds of a business idea which we explored through a simple pros and cons exercise, and also took time to shine a light on all her achievements to date. On the occasions when she was feeling overwhelmed with the job search and possible options, she had created for herself a firm anchor to feel proud of herself, take control of the situation through research and allowing time to make sense of all her options, and see positives in the leaving process, being the start of new opportunities.

How to...transition from career into business

1. Positive Affirmations

Such was the power and positive impact on me of coaching in 2004, I was inspired to re-train. In 2009, I read a book called *The Guide* by Dr. William Holden after which I penned an affirmation: "I am a successful corporate coach, positively inspiring my clients." Turns out I embedded this by repetition and the simple act of committing it to writing. Ten years on, guess what...? Exactly that.

2. Work the business around the day job

Before taking the entrepreneurial leap, I strongly recommend working the dream around the day job. I already had a number of coaching clients and a strong desire to pursue coaching as a career. I also had a mortgage to pay. It certainly wasn't the right time for me to go all in with Plan B without the right financial backing. In addition, as fate would have it, I met my husband and very shortly thereafter started a family. It was all I could manage to have a period of maternity leave and return to Chambers full time, and again for a second time, whilst keeping alive my business plans with reading and personal development when the rare quieter moments with a baby or two allowed.

3. Adopt the right Mindset

After my third child, and dabbling with another business that coaxed me into the right mindset for a return to work, albeit left me cold on inspiration, I couldn't shake the desire to coach. Even with all the obstacles and doubts, I had a "now or never" moment. I kept coming back to what Marie Forleo said about the key to success: "*start before you are ready.*" And so I did.

4. Use the Power of your Network

I had an incredibly supportive husband, regularly networked with a hugely motivational group of business women, and I had an overwhelming desire to help other women who had hit similar career cross-roads to me after Jamaica.

5. Niche or Specialise

Before Christmas 2017, although I was coaching individual female lawyers in one to one sessions, my workshops were pitched to a generic business audience. It was only really six months into my business journey that a workshop opportunity arose to really hone in on my offering and clearly niche my business. This is what I did – and would recommend similar to new business start-ups. *"The riches are in the niches."*

6. Have What it Takes: Keep Going!

I am reminded of the image of success as an iceberg – the tiny frozen peak of success that people see protruding from the water and what really happens, the massive ice cliff hidden from view below the surface: risk taking; 100% commitment and focus on goals; persistence; hard work; failure; sacrifice like you've never known; daily habits; massive action. When you "decide to decide", go all in.

Despite appearances, journeys like these are neither short nor easy. For me, over the last ten years or more, a tiny idea that has been fed, watered, nurtured, and combined with the most committed action, has finally paid off, to the point that at the time of writing, I'm a finalist for the International Coaching Awards, International Coach of the Year category. Evidence if it be needed that *"if it is to be, it is up to me"*.

My advice to all of you wondering, "Should I?": Keep going. You've got this.

Exercise 6

Jot down your own thoughts here and use as a checklist for action

Are you a career changer?

If so, what could you do?

Here is a reminder of some suggestions:

- Ask whether your "why" or priorities have altered. If so, consider what they are now
- Jot down things to include on your goal board and success board
- Consider what affirmations would serve you
- Think about how you will adopt the requisite mindset
- Consider how you can leverage your network
- Consider whether you have a niche or specialism, and if so, what it is and how it is defined
- Consider what your motivation is for your Plan B

What WILL you do and WHEN?

PART III
HOW I HELP : TIPS ON GETTING THE CAREER YOU WANT, YOUR WAY

7

MINDSET AND MENTAL TOUGHNESS

A CHOICE WE MAKE

Challenges and solutions in this Chapter are around developing mental toughness and resilience, examining perfectionism and knowing when to stop.

$\mathcal{T}$he Challenge...influencing positive outcomes

"It's not what life does to you that is important, but what you do with what life does to you". The words of this Chinese proverb apply equally to work and home life.

According to whom

Having encountered a bump in the road in my business journey around one year in, around a failed collaborative book project, I dug deep, examined my own attitudes to how I react to events and worked hard to challenge negativity. I was able to turn disappointment not only in to a positive learning experience but also a motivator for future behaviour and action.

I am reminded of common themes in coaching sessions, where female lawyers express feelings of overwhelm with competing responsibilities and an inability to time manage or focus. And on a personal level, I reflect on my "glass half full" friend who in the face of two serious cancer diagnoses in the preceding twelve months has the refreshing ability to see the positive in everything and tackle the most arduous treatment regime with admirable strength, resolve, determination and good humour.

An American Business School Case Study undertaken in the Noughties examined perceptions of men and women in the workplace. An identical (and truthful) story about a successful venture capitalist was told to the students with only one detail changed to half the group: her gender. Students, polled about their impressions of the "man" and woman, rated them equally competent, yet the "man" came across as the more appealing colleague, the woman more selfish.

In her book, *Lean in: Women, Work and The Will to*

Lead, Sheryl Sandberg concluded that in light of this unconscious bias women will continue to sacrifice being liked for being successful. More grist to the mill that working women would do well to dig in and develop their mental toughness.

According to *AQR International: Mental Toughness Questionnaire, A Users Guide*, mental toughness is "*a personality trait which determines how individuals respond to challenge, stress and pressure, irrespective of their circumstances.*" It is intrinsically linked to a person's performance, and helps explain why, when looking at two people with similar backgrounds and experience, when placed in the same situation, one may succeed and the other fails.

Resilience on the other hand is "*the ability to recover from an adverse situation or incident – when something goes wrong, the ability to pick ourselves up, dust ourselves off and keep going.*" Resilience therefore has a more passive quality than mental toughness.

Studies demonstrate links between the concept of mental toughness and three significant topics:.

1. Performance

Research in education in the UK and overseas demonstrated mental toughness accounts for up to 25% of the variation of performance in an individual's attainment. When sitting an exam or formal assessment, 25 % of that individual's performance can be explained by their degree of mental toughness. The same was found in the workplace.

2. Positive Behaviours

The mentally tough have a more positive approach to everything they do, a "can do" mindset. They see the world, although challenging, as full of opportunity and have confidence to tackle problems and challenges head on.

3. Wellbeing

The greater the level of mental toughness, the greater the sense of wellbeing.

This translates into outcomes in the workplace such as

- Improved attendance and reduced absenteeism
- The ability to deal more effectively with adversity and difficult days
- Being able to put setbacks into perspective and recover more quickly.

How to...develop mental toughness and resilience

1. Think Positive

Hearing negativity or criticism directed towards us can feel hurtful. It takes an active shift in thinking to master our minds and avoid being mortally wounded by it. As Charles F. Glassman said: *"Sticks and stones can break your bones, but words can never hurt you...unless you believe them...."* Criticism can affect us most deeply when it reflects what we believe about ourselves. Listen out for when your inner critic reinforces any external criticism.

I use NLP techniques with coaching clients to get them to recognise the negative chatter and acknowledge that in some way it is looking out for or protecting them. That way we can accept that there are positive intentions behind the internal dialogue. Then challenge the status quo: when ordinarily we would have listened and more to the point, believed, what that dialogue would have to say, this time, say "Thank you. I'm ok. I don't need you to tell me those negative things to keep me safe."

It was Arianna Huffington, Co-Founder of the Huffington Post, who said that learning to withstand criticism is a necessity for women. Her advice, acknowledging that women don't live in an emotionless vacuum, is to let ourselves react emotionally, feel anger and sadness at being criticised, then quickly move on. She drew an analogy with children, who one minute can express deep, all pervading rage or heartbreak, then in the next, dust themselves off and crack on. I like to think of it as wallowing with purpose and finality.

Tara Mohr, in her wonderful book, *Playing Big: A Practical Guide for Brilliant Women Like You*, advocated "unhooking" from external praise and criticism. She reminds us that feedback doesn't tell us about us; it tells us about the person giving the feedback. Whilst it can be strategically useful to incorporate feedback, letting the rest go is refreshing. In reality, the only people from whom to gather feedback are the audiences and decision makers we need to influence and reach. Unhooking ourselves from praise or criticism or comparisons to our peers and competitors can have a wonderfully liberating and positive effect on focus.

Given that the problem with criticism is usually really a problem with what we believe about ourselves, work hard to address the inner doubt rather than seeking external validation in an attempt to resolve it. Mohr suggests finding an "unhooked-from-criticism" role model to aspire to in support.

As a female leader, doing formative, innovative work, and challenging and changing norms, accept that criticism comes with the territory. Not ruffling the odd feather here or there surely means we aren't making enough progress in the ground-breaking work we are so capable of.

Ask, "What's more important to me than praise?" A significant part of my coaching business is about being authentic, acting with integrity, being true to myself and inspiring others. If you do the same then you can truly enjoy zigging even when others are zagging.

2. Focus: Be present, avoid distractions and learn to say no

With so many electronic devices competing for our attention, and email and mobile notifications pinging left, right and centre, it's no wonder so many of us struggle to silence the noise. Many people find focus a challenge. Planning and prioritisation are both important tools to stay "present" in current tasks.

> *Tracy, career break return senior associate, observed through our sessions that with the right focus she was able to achieve more quality time at work working or playing with her children, if the focus was purely that, work or kids respectively.*

I also understand, and explore with clients, the phenomenon of saying yes "just to prove a point", to tow the "political" office line and fearing that saying no may be interpreted as "not being capable". From experience, better to do a few things well rather than lots of things badly. It may take practice but it pays dividends to do so.

What about your thoughts, and where you put your focus? If I told you, *"you are not your mind; you are what you tell yourself,"* wouldn't you be more cautious about the thoughts you have and the temptation to listen to the negative internal chatter we were just discussing?

Our focus can shape our reality for good or bad, and instantaneously, just as when we focus on a positive as opposed to negative thought which will then influence our experience. Whatever we seek or dwell on, whether consciously or unconsciously, we will bring into sharper focus and it will affect, if not shape, our reality. Being conscious of our words and thoughts is the key to unlocking more positive professional outcomes. Effecting the changes may take a little time; the more awareness and practice we have, the easier it will become

3. Develop Self-awareness

Being aware of our ability to choose our own reactions to

a given situation is hugely liberating. When we regain control of our emotions, how empowering it is to understand and experience how we affect and influence our own outcomes.

Have you ever examined whether the habits and behaviour you have formed over time actually help or hinder in getting to where you want to be? If you consider how you might adopt a different approach, how might that also effect a different outcome?

Whatever you dwell on you bring into sharper focus, for good or bad, positive or negative. Tony Robbins in *Notes from a Friend*, sets a Ten Day Mental Challenge to "train your brain" into having more consistently positive thoughts. In a nutshell, by focusing on solutions not problems, the brain can be trained to search for helpful alternatives rather than allowing old mental habits to hold us back. Just as quickly as we spiral downwards, train thoughts to the positive and see instantly improved results. You only have to think about labelling a frustrating morning on route to work as "one of those days" to think how quickly one negative thought compounds another. So, the end result is an overwhelmingly bad day. In a challenging situation, see the learning opportunities as opposed to the frustrating obstacles.

A simple and effective place to start is by looking at the

thoughts and words we use. Are you a glass half full or empty kind of person? Do you even truly know? Some people can very clearly identify with their own outlook, and for others, whilst they think that they see the world in a positive way, their words and behaviour suggest otherwise. By way of example, those with a great sense of humour albeit that they are always the butt of their own jokes, because in order to get a laugh, they talk of themselves in a self-deprecating way. If you choose regularly to make yourself the butt of the joke, you can't be surprised if colleagues, over time, adopt a similar approach.

Now as a coach, I see countless examples of clients positively influencing their personal performance at work by checking their focus and adopting a more positive mindset. I note with interest how clients' words and tone on occasion betray a lack of confidence not immediately associated with the profession. I encourage them to look at habits and behaviours formed over time and examine whether these help or hinder their own levels of personal confidence, and ask "Would adopting a different approach effect a different, more positive and confident, outcome?"

Similarly, *"Be careful what you tell yourself as you are listening."* From time to time, we're all tempted to listen to negative internal chatter. Be aware, however, that the longer we focus on the negatives, the more likely we are to bring them into sharper focus and negatively affect our own confidence thereby.

A great example of this came for me one autumn day at Centre Parcs with my children after nearly two decades without riding a bike. Although as a teenager a keen mountain-biker, after well over twenty years out of the saddle, the thought of riding a "ladies' shopper" with limited gears and a cumbersome trailer with two children in the back didn't exactly inspire my confidence at the helm.

And there we were, on a beautifully quiet forest track, probably at least eight metres wide, when I saw in the distance a small obstruction which, with each turn of the pedal brought me nearer to it and IT in to sharper focus: a pine cone. A really small pine cone. And yet, all my mind could tell me was "Don't ride over the pine cone, don't ride over the pine cone." With each thought, the pine cone was brought into sharper focus, and with laser precision, I actually ended up riding over it as if it and the bike wheel were an unavoidable magnetic force, with the inevitable negative consequence: a wobble and a fall.

Another example from a previous Christmas, asking my three young children to help hand out pre-dinner nibbles, I learnt by experience better not to have said: "Don't spill it." What's the last thing they heard? "Spill it." As night followed day, they spilt. Instead, when I encouraged them to "Take it through confidently." Guess what? They did.

As Henry Ford said,

"Whether you think you can or you can't, you're right."

Watch your mouth. It pays to take a moment to become aware of the words we use, to see how we might more positively influence ourselves and the view of us that those around us have.

I recall one morning, on one of the last occasions I was enjoying typical robing room banter with Bar colleagues waiting for my case to be called on at Crown court. There, I overheard countless lawyers greeting one another. It caused me to reflect on how frequently it was that when asked "How are you?" barristers and solicitors replied "Busy". Not "Really well, thank you," not "Happy, thanks," but "Busy" – as if their standing as a successful lawyer would in some way be diminished if they didn't take every opportunity to tell their audience that their practice was thriving.

"Good Morning!" "Is it?"; "How are you?" "Busy"... We make jokes at our inability to see the positives in the simple, every day, and wear "busy-ness" like a badge of honour for fear that people might somehow think less of us, or we might collapse without a purpose if we take a moment to reflect and go at a pace slower than a blue-bottle on speed. But how does "busy" really feel? Loaded, pressured, frenetic, even angst-ridden, at times. What happened to the person behind the Practice? Our ability to "simply be" without permanently engaging our "game face"? Think how language does or does not serve. Take a moment to have a go: improve your self-talk and say out loud "I am very well," instead of "I'm busy," and see the difference it makes.

Do you use positive or negative language? If the latter, consider how you can re-frame your language in a more strong and positive way. This, in turn, will have a posi-tive effect on your mindset and levels of confidence.

For example, in a challenging situation at work where others might think "There's nothing I can do," could you be the one to suggest, "Let's look at our alternatives"? If you find yourself saying, "I need to work through lunch," how about, "I choose to..." do so instead? Other exam-ples include, "I must or I've got to... go to the gym," when "I prefer to..." is so much more empowering. Don't get me started on the difference between "I will try to..." and "I will..."! Try is half hearted and weak, and not certain to happen; if you say you <u>will</u> do something, already in your language you are committed to the outcome.

Is what is coming out of your mouth adding to your own sense of overwhelm and consequently impacting on your productivity? Be mindful of inadvertent negative terms and phrases, and their positive or negative power.

It took some time for Jessica, Senior Barrister and business woman, to recognise the destructive nature of her own self talk. She was the first to put herself down, with terms such as "I'm such a failure", "I'm letting myself down" and "I need or expect to apply for Silk or be a judge by now."

It was only when she became aware of how often she did this, and realised the negative impact that it was having upon her state of mind and outcomes, that she was able to challenge herself. Instead she considered what she had already achieved, how things could get better with a plan, and with support, she was finally able to say, "Yes I can, I can do this – I just can't do everything on my own."

The Challenge...recognising the endless pursuit of perfection and knowing when to stop

Have you ever considered, perhaps when preparing for an interview, that in an effort to turn a challenge into a strength, you planned to say your greatest weakness was perfectionism? It is after all, an attribute to which many aspire. Turn a negative to a positive, and all that. When tweaking and re-tweaking a piece of work, do you attribute your high standards to being a perfectionist?

And yet, since perfectionism involves the ceaseless pursuit of unattainable goals, a constant strive for flawlessness, how attractive a trait really is it? Ask yourself honestly whether your own version of "perfect" is ever truly attainable?

According to whom

I recall an example of my own desire to have something perfect from nearly 25 years ago, at Bar School – my advocacy assessment – a plea in mitigation which I practised, re-practised and practised some more. I had it word-perfect, the facial expressions I'd got down to a tee (having even practised those countless times in the mirror). I could recite it without notes, in the dark, with my eyes shut, standing on my head, and quite certain that at the end of it all I'd be getting the all-important T-shirt too.

But, in an effort to get everything just right, I had failed entirely to take into account the possibility of anything unexpected. I certainly hadn't foreseen the video operator opening and then eating very loudly a bag of Walkers Salt 'n' Shake crisps whilst I struggled through my "May it please, Your Honour..." script.

All's well that ends well. After a complaint to the examining board, my performance was re-marked and awarded the highest possible grade. However, it was a good and life-long lesson about how sometimes it is perfectly alright, pardoning the pun, to say "done not perfect".

This was a classic case of how the desire for perfection was unrealistic and became more about control and inflexibility. The initial end result had clearly not served me well.

I've seen it in client sessions too: Aisha, non-lawyer, would set herself unrealistic targets and when she didn't achieve them, she'd feel frustrated and incapable. She soon recognised how helpful it would be to break the cycle of perfectionism, which she did by adopting new techniques: prioritising her work load, delegating some tasks whilst saying no to others, shortening her to do list, time blocking and maintaining strict boundaries around checking emails to avoid distraction.

Other unhelpful consequences of perfectionism include the tendency to self-flagellate when targets aren't met and to view progress or results negatively. Consequently, confidence and mood can be affected adversely too.

Recognising the Signs of Perfectionism

These days, in one to one coaching sessions, I might expect to see in perfectionist clients some of these well-documented tell-tale signs. Do you recognise any of them in yourself?

- Setting demanding and unrealistic standards for yourself and others, for example, by setting unachievable goals
- Displaying high levels of self-criticism and criticism towards others when exacting standards remain unmet: nothing less than perfect will do
- Delegation is a challenge – no one else can do things to the same exacting standards. The desire to control is strong
- Using pressurised language such as "I should do X...", "I need to do Y..." revealing the motivation towards goals is the fear of failure as opposed to the desire to achieve them
- Over-work, and the over-use of lists to measure

progress, which are cross-checked, refined, re-written, ticked off in perpetuity

- Procrastination due to time-wasting on counter-productive activities and, in extreme cases, avoiding situations altogether due to the potential risk of perceived failure
- Not being a "finisher", leaving tasks incomplete because there is a lack of awareness around when to stop, or even when finished, they are never judged truly perfect
- Extreme thinking which is overly results driven, and with a tendency to dwell on the losses, the things that didn't go well, as opposed to the positive learnings and achievements along the way.
- Self-worth and self-confidence being inextricably linked to achievements
- Defensiveness when challenged

Fear not if you recognise some (even all) of these traits in yourself. They certainly aren't uncommon, particularly amongst high achieving professionals.

I can't think of a better example from client sessions than Abigail, a self-confessed perfectionist and highly capable lawyer, who without management help was doing all her own caseload whilst sweeping up all the mistakes of her team too. She struggled with delegation, with the adverse consequence that by covering for others, colleagues were made to look more capable than they were and she herself was suffering overwhelm and burnout. In addition, so consumed was she with the team's needs, she forgot her own career progression and well-being needs along the way having lost sight of the bigger picture. She recognised the need to let her team fail and practise delegation. Whilst she acknowledged giving up control felt unsettling, she saw the benefit of testing it out, and so she did, with far more positive results.

Fionne, partner in a law firm, also had high expectations of herself and others. She set impossible standards for herself from childhood and reported that others had found it hard working with her as she demanded equally high standards of them too. Although she didn't want to drop her standards, she was developing an awareness around the negative consequences for her of perfectionism. Even doing a Goal Board exercise, she had got stuck, was unable to finish, as in her mind it wasn't right, things were missing, there was still more to do, etc. Another example of the destructive effects of perfectionism.

Similarly, Marzena, career break returner and consummate list writer, acknowledged through our sessions that her lists were unachievable and provided her with a constant fear and feeling of failure. That said, she didn't feel confident to function without them. By session three she decided it was time to feel the fear and do it anyway. She went cold turkey on her lists. Instead, she devised a five minute daily review at the conclusion of the working day when she would run though the important tasks and double check she was on track. She performed more productively in the workplace because of it, as she procrastinated less and remained far more positive. By session four she was reporting feeling better, calmer, and could see overwhelmingly the benefits of having ditched her tendency towards perfectionism.

Having some awareness around the tendency towards perfectionism is an essential first step on the road to tackling and overcoming its potentially adverse and damaging consequences.

These include:

- The hindering of progress
- Working under self-induced and unnecessary pressure

- A sense of inner turmoil, constant strife and disappointment
- Exhaustion
- Sleeplessness
- Low self esteem
- In extreme cases, depression and other mental health issues

How to…overcome perfectionism

Some of these have cross-applicability to other areas of challenge which we have touched on already.

1. Mindset

Once it is recognised that "Practice makes improvement" not "Practice makes perfect", it will become easier to recognise and give credit for achievements and progress made along the way, however small, rather than purely focusing on the bigger goals. By celebrating strengths and successes, as opposed to commiserating perceived failures, thinking remains positive and confidence is boosted.

2. Goals

As far as goals are concerned, adjust them. First, check that those bigger goals are realistic and achievable as opposed to burdensome and unattainable. Second, let your motivation to achieve them be pleasure as opposed to "need". Desire the results instead of fearing failure. Then, break down the bigger goals into bite-sized chunks so that they are more manageable to tackle and so that measurability is built in to the plan. That way, progress can be more easily celebrated along the way, and low self-esteem avoided.

3. Habits

Ask whether perfectionist habits picked up along the way serve or hinder objectives. How would outcomes improve with a different response or an adjusted approach? Challenge yourself to overcome those unhelpful habits by testing opinion against reality. For example, delegate a task having asked "What's the worst that could happen?" Go into one day without a list and measure the <u>actual</u>, not perceived, effects on productivity and outcomes.

4. Language

Finally, look at the use of language. Can a kinder, more generous tone be adopted towards yourself and others? Think how outcomes improve with more supportive and encouraging, rather than negative and critical, words. Similarly, learn to handle feedback and criticism of others through practice, and a disassociation from taking it personally.

Suzy's example touches on so many of these different aspects. Having done a Coaching exercise together, she identified that her life balance was exceptionally low down on the list of priorities. She challenged herself to push past her original approach which was to say, "Well that's just the way it is – I haven't tried anything but get on with it." She didn't know how to ask for support, hated doing so in fact, and had become conditioned into thinking that to do otherwise was a sign of weakness in the cut throat corporate world. That said, with some gentle encouragement from me, she felt empowered to ask for help both up the chain from bosses, and down, by delegating certain tasks to more junior members of the team. For the first time in around ten years, she enjoyed not working as late for a whole week, and things improved. Whenever she felt herself slipping back into her old ways, she would reference her bigger goal to stop herself, with much more positive effect.

Exercise 7

Jot down your own thoughts here and use as a checklist for action.

Are you looking to develop your mental toughness?

If so, what could you do?

Here is a reminder of some suggestions:

- Work on positive mindset
- Work on focus
- Work on self-awareness
- Work on reducing unhelpful perfectionist traits

What WILL you do and WHEN?

8

DIGITAL DISTRACTION AND HOW TO AVOID IT

Challenges and solutions in this Chapter are around identifying unnecessary digital distractions, creating boundaries and choices to quieten the digital "noise" and understanding the benefits of "switching off".

The Challenge…avoiding digital distraction

There can be no argument that the digital age has made the world a smaller and more accessible place, and that opportunities, in particular for women, to work flexibly and be retained within the work place have improved immeasurably with the rise in remote working and the so called "laptop lifestyle."

Indeed, technology and innovation have huge potential, harnessed in the right way, for increasing productivity and boosting life balance. Taking the time now to learn something new may reap massive benefits later in terms of time-saving processes, diary management, marketing and the like.

The unexpected cost to our wellbeing, however, is the insidious encroachment into our personal time of work calls and emails as we make ourselves more readily available and contactable 24/7, 365/12. People with the lifestyle that affords them the luxury of taking the laptop with them on holiday can feel a sense of duty or obligation to whip out the mobile or Apple Mac and catch up on work emails or do that "little bit extra" whilst away. The ease with which we can "switch off" in the true sense of the words these days, even when we are supposedly "taking a break", has been seriously compromised.

It is a topic which raises its head repeatedly in coaching sessions, particularly the increased level of distraction and virtual "noise" which contributes to the feeling that we are doing lots of things badly rather than focusing on doing a few things well.

We can all relate to the feeling when we set off in the car, even on a short journey, only to discover we have left our mobile at home. Doesn't it sometimes feel like our right arm might as well have been severed? What will we do if we break down, get a flat tyre, run out of petrol? How will we check those emails, when we eventually reach our destination, to answer those flagged important messages? How will we manage? How will we cope? Gone are the days of snail mail, a 10p coin in the back pocket and, dare I say it, our own grey cells to recall emergency numbers to phone, in the unlikely event we find a functioning phone box nearby.

According to whom

When I first heard on the radio the Arcade Fire song "Everything Now", it stopped me in my tracks. How many of us are wrapped up in this pressure-laden world of clients needing "everything now", where we're on call 24/7 because we're accessible to them, and the world, anytime, anywhere? All the positives we gain from modern day gadgets and gizmos aside, it still reminded me of times during my career as a barrister when I would get calls from the clerks who managed my diary, bookings and work load at the most inopportune moments.

The fifteenth of November 2002 should have been a memorable day for me anyway as I arrived on the beautifully lush Thai Island of Koh Phi Phi for the first time, taking in the impressively steep limestone cliffs, green vegetation peppering the tops, and the turquoise ocean lapping at the almost translucent white sand beaches. Memorable not for the call to my mobile from Chambers telling me, whilst dressed in bikini, sarong and flip flops that there was an urgent advice needing my attention for a Court of Appeal case the following week.

Now more fool me for having had my mobile (a) with me, and (b) on, and (c) having answered it. Yes, of course, I take responsibility for that. But it's the fact that I stewed on the contents of the call for at least 48 hours afterwards, even after giving the clerks short shrift about the unnecessary and pointless interruption to an otherwise idyllic holiday when there was quite literally nothing I could do there to service that particular "crisis".

There are other specific points in my legal career that I remember for similar reasons: the Charles Bridge, Prague on a two night city break; The airport as I was lifting my heavy back pack on to the baggage carousel about to embark on a six week tour of Australia.

And with the challenge to clerks about why the call was even made, the age old retort: "Well your diary was marked Away; Are you Away, Away?!" YES. I AM AWAY!!" Is there no entitlement these days to an uninterrupted break?!

At the end of the day, the world didn't stop turning; the scales of justice never toppled. It's simply that I allowed my mindset to get the better of me and spoil the remainder of my trips. In the case of my lengthy Australian adventures, that was particularly regrettable.

How to...quieten the digital noise

In respect of ongoing tasks, where there is a need to quieten the noise, regain focus and reduce overwhelm, here are my suggestions on how to avoid digital distraction:

1. Firstly, decide what level of interruption you are prepared for, and plan accordingly. If you can't handle the interruption, don't respond, or get a separate personal and work phone. If you do allow the interruption, be accountable for the fact that you personally made that choice and risked the possible consequences.

2. Ensure you communicate clearly with your work or organisation about the boundaries and acceptability or otherwise of calls and other interruptions whilst away as a way of guaranteeing their support.

A great example here is Andrea, struggling with the challenges of open plan offices, digital distraction and the frequent interruptions to her work from a more

junior team member who required a lot of guidance.
Acknowledging the fine line between helping and being
rude, she soon devised a plan (involving a stop and go
system with ear buds in or out) to gently, albeit
effectively, communicate whether or not she was open to
interruption. With ear buds out, she was open to help
out her team, with ear buds in, she was indicating she
was closed at that time to interruption, and people
should come back at a more convenient time for her.

Similarly, get support for your "working from home" boundaries from a spouse or partner to manage everybody's expectations.

3. Whilst at home or work, ask yourself honestly, "Do I have a healthy relationship with my mobile or laptop and life balance?" If the answer is no, consider what improvements, however small, you could make to support your time ownership. For example, start your day with gratitude as opposed to the mobile phone social media "death scroll" – think of, and even journal, a couple of things for which you feel grateful to give you a pro-active sense of your own purpose and owning your day before allowing in the reactive distractions of the digital world around you.

4. Plan your day. As Jim Rohn, American Motivational

Speaker, said *"You run the day or the day runs you."* He emphasised the importance of sticking to your own schedule as opposed to being blown off course by distraction from others. Given the way I worked my business in the early days around significant childcare commitments, I needed laser focus to make most efficient use of small pockets of time, and spent Sunday evenings planning each week day before they happened so when I got a rare and unexpected extra ten minutes during the day, I could get straight to work and know precisely what needed doing, on what particular day, AND in what order of importance.

Have a plan and stick to it. Go back to basics. Prioritise tasks in to most important first. "Put first things first" as Steven Covey puts it. For example, you may wish to categorise them as "urgent", "important" and "to do". Covey's Time Management matrix in which he categorises all tasks into four (urgent and important, urgent not important, important not urgent and not important nor urgent) is equally valid here. I've recently heard a similar summary described as the four Ds : "Do, Diarise, Delegate and Delete".

Tick tasks off a realistic to-do list if it helps, and most of all, tackle the trickiest stuff first to avoid procrastination: *Eat That Frog* by Brian Tracy is a great book to read on this topic. Feel good about your achievements as you meet them, watch the jobs get done. If you are prone to perfectionism, however, also know that with the unpredictability and demanding hours in professional working life, it may be you don't meet all these plans, and that is ok too. Be prepared to carry over some of the "to do" list to another day if it means the critically important tasks are attended to first.

5. For the sake of your own wellbeing, be bold! Consider allocating two or three specific times in the day e.g. 8.30am, 12.30 & 4.30pm to check emails and in between times, remove notification sounds, alerts, banners from all your devices.

Angela, career break returner, initially struggled with setting out her stall to clients to manage their expectations because she was all too aware of the expectation that their lawyer be there any time, any place. She was able to set her own limits around her email sign off and out of office notifications however, and soon came to realise that by setting her own limits, others became respectful of them. That said, as an aside, due to the pressure she felt to respond to emails, the boundaries she set for herself would not necessarily be right for everyone – to check her emails every two hours maximum from 8am to bedtime. I left her to consider

*the reasonableness or otherwise of such late evening
work expectations, particularly given the observations
about wellness with which we are all becoming
familiar.*

An extreme yet effective tool for specific times during the day which require a fully immersive level of concentration is to engage the "Airplane mode" facility. Remove social media apps from your mobile devices and set strict times for access. Similarly, consider using the automatic "out of office" function at set times during the working day, not exclusively for holidays. An effective one I saw recently read: *"This is an auto reply. It may be unconventional, but I usually only check and deal with emails at 12:00 and after 16:00. This means I can provide a better service as I'm not sat in my inbox all day"*. Organisations can support employee engagement here by creating a culture which is respectful of boundaries and leads by example in terms of the expectations of the workforce, such as introducing a moratorium on emails after 7pm.

*By her own admission, Jo, barrister at a career
crossroads, did not utilise her time as she should, and
saw the need for structure and efficiency to allow her to
work more productively. Her preferred strategy to*

overcome this challenge was to create clear demarcations between work and non-work to readily identify the start and end of the working day. In only a matter of a few days, she was already reporting huge benefits to her productivity and wellbeing too. "I feel more relaxed, balanced, calm. I feel lightness and things are easier and more enjoyable."

6. In and amongst, take regular breaks and keep "proper" hours. That way, overwhelm can be avoided and productivity maintained.

7. Be savvy about time ownership: we all have the same 24 hours in a day; how will you best utilise yours, to be at your most efficient and productive? For example, time block. By allocating specific bursts of time to each of your allocated daily tasks you can ensure that every task you put your mind to is in short, manageable bursts which you commit your full attention to: then when you are doing your work or you are with your family for example, you can give 100% attention as opposed to feeling constantly conflicted and distracted. It's a form of workplace mindfulness.

Career break returner, Emma, found this an effective method of time management. She found self-imposed "pressure" to work in time blocks ensured she got tasks done quicker and gained a high level of satisfaction from completing them. The knock-on consequence was that she experienced an increased sense of calm, felt happy and contented at work, and proud of her achievements. Her return to work confidence also improved.

When it comes to organizing activities of your teams, be the organisation that supports and facilitates employee focus – are the open plan office spaces working? How conducive to productivity is the working environment or culture? Have you surveyed staff on this lately?

8. In whatever you do, be present – don't be constantly on the phone dealing with work problems when you are with your children, or when working from home, sit yourself in an area where you can become easily drawn into domestic dramas. Work whilst at work; have family time whilst with your family. When in the office working, consider making it clear to colleagues the times during which you do not encourage interruptions. When you are free to chat, go to the communal areas to make yourself available for a proper chat and a break. By doing so, you provide focus and clarity to you and those around you. It helps you manage your (and their) expectations, plus it allows you to be more productive in the pockets of time dedicated to which ever specified activity you are

undertaking in that particular moment. In turn, this will reduce, if not eradicate, working parent guilt. To focus on what you are not doing at the point you are in 'the other' mode, will serve only to pile on the guilt in the bucket load.

9. If you are a parent working from home around child care, accept that there may be isolated times that distraction is unavoidable, and but for it, you would otherwise be enjoying a full day with your children. The alternative might be having to opt for a full day in the office, no time with the kids at all, and staring aimlessly at their photos all day whilst engaging in a whole heap of mummy or daddy guilt. Acceptance is a very freeing mind-set to adopt. Likewise, keeping reasonable working hours.

10. Unplug. Literally. Switch off. Lock your digital tech in a box for allocated periods in the day. If you don't already, start with the rule "no tech at the (dinner) table". It might be tricky at first, but how many short days of pain for some significant long term gains? Dr. Rangan Chattergee's *4 Pillar Plan* to creating a longer healthier life includes a suggested Seven Day Digital Detox which provides a helpful starting point.

Then the biggie. Switch off: for a full 24 hours – the cold turkey solution to the digital revolution and one which I bet a whole heap of us secretly yearn for. Try it. One day you might thank yourself.

Putting all of this in to the coaching context, would you welcome a calm, safe "space" to assist you move in your career from where you currently are, to where you want to be, more quickly and effectively than if you act alone? Ask yourself, "When did you last, or ever, have the opportunity to switch off the gadgets and devices, and get focused on you – just you – your career or business in an impartial yet challenging support setting, to think, visualise and gain clarity about what you want as an individual or at work, how you will achieve it, and take positive action steps to do so?"

If you are a female professional who would welcome the opportunity to celebrate strengths, anticipate and over-come obstacles, increase confidence and motivation to get the desired results, and welcome increased produc-tivity and a diminution of stress, then "switching off to switch on" through coaching may be just the thing for you.

Exercise 8

Jot down your own thoughts here and use as a checklist for action.

Do you want to strip out digital distraction?

If so, what could you do?

Here is a reminder of some suggested questions to ask:

- What level of distraction will you allow?
- How will you communicate your boundaries to others?
- Do you have a healthy relationship with technology? If not, what tweaks can you make to improve this?
- How will you plan your day?
- What bold steps will you take to do things differently?
- How will you maintain proper hours?
- What tweaks will you make to improve time ownership?
- How can you become more "present"?
- How will you switch off?

What WILL you do and WHEN?

9

HOW TO SAY NO BUT KEEP THE OPPORTUNITIES FLOWING

Challenges and solutions in this Chapter are around how to avoid saying yes to everything, how to say no and still keep future opportunities flowing.

The Challenge...learning to say "No"

Recently, an ex-chambers colleague remarked that he enjoyed going to court for a break. I asked what he meant. He explained the only way to silence what he felt were the incessant demands of clerks and instructing solicitors trying to get hold of him to prepare cases, file skeletons, complete written submissions and the like, was to be in court doing a jury trial where he was completely immersed in the task in hand. There he found respite from the endless noise and digital distraction elsewhere.

How many of us can relate to that? The dread as another email pops onto our phone before we know exactly what it is we are being asked to deal with. The overwhelm as the little red notification circle fills with ever increasing numbers of tasks pinging into our inboxes.

There are a number of solutions to assist with the challenge of digital distraction. But challenge, as I see it, comes at the preventative rather than curative stage. How do we say no in the first place to reduce the build-up of tasks, and yet convey a message, perhaps to those who instruct us, both in solicitors' firms and the clerks' room, that we are very much 'open for business' and receptive to new work and opportunities?

Traditional culture at the Bar has been 'that's just the way it is.' It's ingrained in us. The expectation that we go above and beyond, in terms of out of hours preparation, covering cases at short notice when preparation time is disproportionate to fees received, even covering cases without legal aid for no fee at all. Many argue the criminal justice system would collapse without this degree of goodwill.

Additionally, there is self-imposed pressure. The feeling that to say no is to let others down, to reveal we are not a team player, or is a matter upon which we will be judged as weak or incapable. That's not to mention the phenomenon of saying "yes" to things "just to prove a point."

We've all done it. As a pupil looking for that all important tenancy, we become the Chambers "Yes Woman". The trainee solicitor working towards promotion accepting without question more and more tasks the senior partner is pushing on to us. The associate solicitor taking calls from the CEO out of hours, originally as a means by which to facilitate global conference calling, now becoming a matter of expected out of hours working practice. The career break returner who has an eagerness to please which, if left unchecked, has her left running on empty. The volunteer note-taker in meetings, who ends up lumbered with typing the notes up, spending hours creating an email list to circulate them, consequently tasked with writing the agenda for the next meeting and so on and so forth, simply due to being so obliging. As a member of chambers, asked to cover the 'bag of rats' return that no one else wants to touch, we take it on for fear that to do otherwise, we will be overlooked by clerks in future, preferring to reward with further briefs those who are more amenable to helping out.

Experience from client coaching sessions suggests many more female lawyers feel the need to be congenial and giving of their time compared to their male counterparts. "People pleasing" becomes a sure fire way of pleasing everybody else but themselves, their needs and priorities forgotten about, or at least shoved to the bottom of the pile.

Before mastering the art of saying no, examine to what you are (and are not) prepared to say "yes". At the Criminal Bar, return cases are an unfortunate and unavoidable part of the job, and there is an inevitable amount of flex and spontaneity required, which often results in anti-social working hours. Similarly, as a pupil or associate solicitor, there is a certain degree of "putting yourself out" to achieve a certain position or promotion. You may feel it is politic to "get on" with some things for a short time. If over time, however, it causes you to suppress your true values and beliefs, you will necessarily come to a point where that approach is unsustainable.

Whilst it may be perfectly natural to adopt a professional "game face," rather like the image of a swan gliding gracefully above the water surface whilst its legs are paddling inelegantly below, if by so doing you risk your own standing, or come into conflict with your own values and beliefs, I caution that you should question your own integrity, particularly if you ever do feel tempted to say yes "to prove a point". To whom are you proving a point? And to what end is this ever necessary?

I'm not suggesting don't be a team player. I'm advocating a move away from the misconception that saying "no" means we're not capable. My experiences demonstrate otherwise. For example, I always remember a senior colleague fuming at having been asked by the clerks to take a case far beneath her level of experience and call, which ultimately she refused to do, having the foresight to appreciate that had she done otherwise, her credibility would have been adversely affected.

If you look back at the times in your professional life when you may have said yes to something to prove a point, being honest with yourself, was this not rather as result of a lack of personal confidence, and an inability to effectively prioritise your own values and objectives over and above your perception of the expectations of the organisation within which you worked? Doesn't "learning to say no" really come down to improving our own ability to assert yourself through clear and effective communication?

In my experience, only when I became clear about my own values and beliefs and examined what was most important, did I first recognise the power to say "no" was within me. The confidence to use this power when severely tested, and the liberation felt as a result, was as refreshing as it was unexpected, example being the late return Prosecution Sex Case which ultimately I refused to do.

Looking at values and beliefs is an integral part of coaching:

- Only when you have examined your values and beliefs, and have some clarity around them can you truly understand what it is to be confident in them, and assert them.
- Ask with authenticity - (a) *"What's in it for me?"* to identify your values and beliefs, and (b) does [the task] fit with what I am doing or where I am heading?
- From that authentic position, having gained a clear understanding of the expectations of the organisation and yourself, ask yourself "To whose plan am I working?"

Thereafter, you can more readily learn and apply the art of saying no: and master it by practice, practice, practice!

According to whom

Keeping opportunities open is an important skill, but the obvious consequence of saying yes to everything, without filter or discernment, is that we end up doing everything badly, rather than a few things well. With increasing awareness around wellness, particularly after the Bar Council Wellbeing at the Bar[1] initiative, the ability to give a firm but polite no is becoming an increasingly essential skill, to learn and deploy, for a happy, sustainable life in law without stress or overwhelm.

In the 'Handling Stress' section of that Initiative, Mr Justice Henry Carr suggests: *'Give yourself sufficient time to prepare each case, even if that means turning work down. It will make your performance much better and the working day shorter.'* The advantages of doing so are obvious: improved work performance and an increased sense of life balance. When work performance improves, so does reputation. This in term will have the consequent effect of enhancing work allocation or briefing quality and frequency.

A barrister client, Julia, experienced similar: when she learned to say no, she observed a massive improvement in her wellness as she prioritised her own needs over others and established boundaries within her working day. After one session of embedding her changed habits, she reported feeling better and more relaxed already.

One Senior Associate career returner, Michaela, observed that this challenge seemed to increase with changes in priorities and working arrangements oftentimes "forced" upon her due to nursery closing times etc, where she needing to re-set the firm's expectations of her working hours on her return, and re-establish boundaries to accommodate the need to leave at a certain time. I recall a non-negotiable mantra of another, Helen, being "it's not in my pay grade" as a means by which she categorised things into priorities and learned to say no.

That said, some struggle with using the actual word 'no'. It is worth considering whether couching it, and using alternative words, reduces the power and sense of what we are trying to communicate. If we recognise and accept that there may be occasions when saying no is not just important but imperative, in practical terms how can we say no and still keep future opportunities flowing?

. . .

How to...say no and still keep future opportunities flowing

A great book recommendation on this challenging workplace topic is Geoff McKeown's *Essentialism*. He gives eight simple and effective examples of saying "no" without using the actual word, summarised below:

The direct no

On occasion, only the actual word 'no' will do. In this instance, it goes without saying that to be firm but polite will be most effective. A defensive or rude 'no' does little to curry favour and preserve ongoing relations.

The indirect no

There are also countless other ways to say no which need not offend nor cut off opportunity:

Delivery

If we pause before delivering a no, the person making the request will realise that it is a considered no, and not necessarily a decision that we have come to easily. More so, if we ask for some time to consider our response, we communicate that we are deliberating and not coming to a snap refusal.

Consider using humour to say no. By laughing off a

request, any sense of awkwardness on our behalf or the other person can be dissipated. Having this conversation face to face, where we can use facial expressions to enhance the message, will be more effective than email where any sense of deliberation, disappointment or humour can be difficult to convey or detect.

Language

We can say words to the effect 'it's a no for now'. This allows all parties keep the requests coming, if not now, at a future, and not far distant, point.

Alternatively, deliver a helpful no, and assist the other person find an alternative solution. Perhaps refer the request on to clerks to find someone else to deal with it, or suggest when you are next available, whether for that or another piece of work.

Boundaries

By setting automatic out-of-office email notifications during the day, not just whilst on holiday, we set our own boundaries. We communicate a 'not right now' message, and still allow for the conversation to continue at a point more convenient to ourselves.

If an unreasonable request is made, let's say by clerks, answering with 'Yes, but that will mean I don't prepare

X or Y' will have the same effect as communicating an outright no, without sounding quite as unhelpful or difficult. An added bonus is it bringing into their consciousness the reasonableness (or otherwise) of their initial request.

Exercise 9

Jot down your own thoughts here and use as a checklist for action.

Do you want to learn to say no?

If so, what could you do?

Here is a reminder of some suggested questions to ask:

- What are my values and beliefs?
- Whose plan am I working to?
- To what am I prepared to say yes?
- How will I practice the next no?
- Which is my preferred "no" approach?

What WILL you do and WHEN?

WOMEN'S WELLNESS AT WORK

Challenges and solutions in this Chapter are around how workplace wellbeing is under threat and how to improve wellness at work for more positive mental health and productivity outcomes.

The Challenge...common threats to wellness

Depression and anxiety cost the global economy an estimated US$ 1 trillion per year in lost productivity, according to World Health Organisation figures published May 2019. Whilst such labels aren't common parlance in the legal profession, The Guardian newspaper reported May 6, 2018 that Barristers in England and Wales were "in the grip of a mental health crisis."

A survey for The Bar Council revealed that nearly half of participating counsel said they worked over sixty hours a week and only 50% said they felt able to balance their home and work lives. Statistics for The Bar Council's "Wellbeing at the Bar" initiative suggest that one in three barristers find it difficult to control or stop worrying, and two out of three feel that showing signs of stress equals weakness. The consequent negative impact on wellbeing is obvious.

According to whom

Taking effective actions to promote wellness in the workplace clearly benefits productivity, given that for every US$ 1 put in to scaled up treatment for common mental disorders, the WHO statistics assert there is a US$4 return in improved health and productivity. So what effective actions can YOU take, whether as an organisation or individual to improve work place wellness and productivity?

How to...improve wellness at work

1. Positive Mindset

Firstly, adopt a positive mindset. Whether individually

or collectively, look at thoughts, words AND behaviour and consider whether there are positive adjustments to be made which would more positively influence your wellbeing. Law firms, Chambers and other corporate organisations can work together on inclusive, supportive cultures through positive values and shared mission statements from administrative staff right up to the CEOs and Equity partners to achieve similar, collective outcomes.

2. Wellness Routine

Adopt a non-negotiable wellness routine, whatever works for you, whether that be meditation, exercise, yoga, keeping active, the list is endless. Whilst some things may slip due to unexpected deadlines and work-load, the sooner regular patterns are established, the quicker they become second nature: the benefits become obvious, and a powerful motivator. Regular breaks and keeping "proper" hours promote this too.

3. Keep Well hydrated

Even when it is so easy to skip lunch with deadlines and meetings and countless other things on our "to do" list getting in the way, keeping water levels topped up throughout the day is vital to improve, amongst other things, muscle function, digestion and even our state of mind.

That's to say nothing about avoiding liquid lunches. Thankfully, gone are the days of my mini-pupillages (work experience) thirty years ago, when afternoons turned into evenings whilst the local Bar socialised at the pub, just up from the law courts, some of whom would think nothing of returning to court for the 2 o'clock "session" tanked up on red wine and ready for an afternoon nap. That said, alcoholism within the profession is not uncommon even now, and the regular focus of bar dinners remains heavy or over-consumption of alcohol. The knock on effects to wellness are well rehearsed, including the blurring of acceptable boundaries between work and professional behaviour, low mood and an inability to cope.

4. Practise daily gratitude and journaling

First thing in the morning, think of, and even journal, three things you are grateful for, as opposed to the mobile phone social media "death scroll." This will give you a pro-active sense of your own purpose and owning your own day before you allow in the reactive distractions of the digital world: your family, a sunrise, the peace of an early morning for example.

On the days you come across a difficult judge, managing partner or client, firstly, remember to remain calm under pressure. Then, even in the moments of extreme pressure and stress at work, on the commute home for example, be grateful for a beautiful sunset, your favourite song playing on the radio, your friends and family. Be amazed at how quickly focusing on the positives can put into perspective, and most importantly reduce the extent of, the negatives.

As an organisation, incorporate gratitude into the culture: employee recognition and rewards could assist here, along with a transparent appraisal system. I spoke to an associate solicitor in a law firm recently voted "lawyer of the month." Not only was she incentivised by the nomination but equally grateful: a winning combination for increased productivity.

5. Confidence

From time to time, career break returners and those experiencing Imposter Syndrome can experience dips in confidence which negatively impact on their wellbeing at work. By recognising that self-limiting beliefs hinder wellness, work on strategies to increase confidence and happiness. Become aware of, and make strides to silence, negative internal chatter by changing your self-talk. Focus on, and remind yourself daily of, your strengths.

Keep the company of a supportive, encouraging network.

6. Priorities and Planning

Prioritise workloads and plan the working week with care. It is so easy in this 24/7 digital world to become needlessly distracted. A clear plan of your day and week, with tasks put in order of importance, the less likely it is to have to course correct, even when the inevitable interruptions occur.

Isabelle, international barrister, was a classic example of this: her poor working conditions became exacerbated by an inability properly to identify what her working day should look like and how she could communicate this effectively to her clerks. She was too busy, taking on more work than she could manage and was fast becoming drained, exhausted and overwhelmed. A clear plan of her day and week, with well-established and non-negotiable boundaries around working hours enabled her to regain control and composure, having an obvious knock on beneficial effect to her wellbeing, both physically and emotionally.

Whether we stay within the profession or decide to leave, a structured plan is essential to preserve our own wellbeing. Harriet, partner in a law firm, came to me when she had "had enough". She was unhappy, unfulfilled, overworked, burnt out, stressed, fed up, under appreciated. She hadn't had a holiday for well over a year, was working every weekend and felt trapped on a treadmill of "living someone else's dream", not wanting to continue, but feeling pressured to do so for fear of letting herself or her family down. Even reading Michelle Obama's book will give comfort here that these are certainly not isolated experiences. Harriet was giving serious consideration to a change within her existing role or even an all-out career change. Either way, she recognised that in order to do so, she would need a structured plan to preserve her mental health in the short term, and indeed went about making one – setting boundaries around working hours and the volume of work brought home to work on evenings and weekends.

Finally, shift your focus: focus on performance, not the case result. Harking back to the advice of Mr. Justice Carr: *"Maintaining a healthy life balance helps keep work triumphs and disasters in perspective."*

7. Mindfulness and Getting back to Basics

Strip things back to the bare essentials to avoid overwhelm. Firstly, identify and stick to clear boundaries, particularly important in preserving a healthy work life balance. Then learn to say no and, through practice, work out effective methods of doing so without cutting off future opportunities.

Consider how employee mindfulness could be supported and encouraged. What is your culture and how more can it increase and promote a more mindful approach? Are your employees showing up mindful or with minds full?

8. Change your "state" and environment

Smile. Over and above the thoughts you have, how about improving mood by behaviour? It may seem like the simplest of things, but how often when you are busy, stressed or overwhelmed do you take a moment to consciously smile? Try it. The endorphins released around the body when you do have such an instantaneous effect, you can't fail to feel, even temporarily, a changed and more positive mood.

Breathe: deeply, with your eyes shut, from your core, and with a long exhale to finish. Just allowing yourself that single moment to pump air through your body and take a reflective pause can be all it takes to feel re-centred and back on point.

Change your state. How many of us have experienced

that afternoon eye flicker? I vividly remember the 3 o'clock graveyard slot in crown court trials where interviews were simply being read into the record for the jury, which I already knew like the back of my hand. Paper pushing at my desk when I know I SHOULD be working and when motivation to do so is low.

When you have an opportunity for "a natural break," change state. For the individual, get away from your immediate environment, move away from your desk, even go to the toilet and do some star jumps if you are able! Honestly, try it. Equally, playing your favourite song (with ear buds if you are in open plan offices) can do wonders to boost and improve mood. This change in state works wonders for your energy levels, and can significantly alter how alert you feel.

For the organisation, lead by example. Encourage genuine chances for employees to leave their desks, better still, the office, when and if they want, for a proper lunch break, for example.

9. Where possible, focus on nature.

Even if it's a picture of a country road on the office wall, or a thriving plant in the corner of your room, allow yourself a moment to shift your focus, then return with more energy and vigour. Better still, look, or even get, out of the office. Incorporating voluntary opportunities to exercise and access the outdoors in a working day are frequently credited for an increase in performance, productivity and wellbeing.

"If you always keep your nose to the grindstone, you'll never see the sky".

Promote wellbeing and social events such as yoga and team sporting get-togethers as being an integral and important part of the organisational ethos. Better to shift the social focus here than suggesting the traditional "pint after work".

10. Network and Connect

Fifteen years ago, after working on Jamaican Capital Murder cases then returning to a UK child sexual abuse case practice, I've already said I hit a career crossroads. Did I want to continue in a career with such grave responsibility and depraved subject matters? What could I do to make my everyday working life more palatable and edifying? I sought assistance from a coach. Another tip, then, is to connect by recognising the need, and not be afraid to ask, for support. Far from a sign of weakness, it demonstrates a significant degree of emotional intelligence and is a matter of good sense to preserve a healthy state of mind.

This support can come from any number of valuable sources. If not a coach, perhaps you are a member of a women's networking group or have access to a mentorship programme? Either way, talking is a helpful outlet to keep perspective and avoid overwhelm. As a result of my early coaching experiences, I continued in my career for at least another ten successful years.

Network to build your practice; likewise, network to create a supportive team around you. Your pupil supervisor or managing partner may be the first and obvious port of call; but as your practice develops, think of other important relationships: with instructing solicitors, court staff, senior colleagues who may invite you to be their junior or the next promoted partner, even the judiciary when it comes to writing a reference for when you apply for silk or the judiciary.

Special interest groups also offer important Peer to Peer support e.g. The Criminal Bar Association, Family Law Bar Association, Women In Criminal Law, Women In The Law UK. These organisations can be credited with helping to combat the negative effects of lengthy commutes, long working hours, reducing time with family and friends, the challenges of committing to social engagements, even loneliness.

Contributing to The Bar Council Wellness initiative,

Mr Justice Henry Carr said *"It is vital to recognise that sharing your anxieties isn't a sign of weakness."* Keep channels of communication open to share any bumps in the road with trusted confidantes. Tap into available resources such as Lawcare, promoting and supporting good mental health and wellbeing in the legal community.

11. Preserve Authenticity

Finally, and most importantly, be authentic. As I've touched on before, it's so easy to get caught up in life's busy-ness, working hard to climb the ladder of success, only to discover that all that time, as Covey puts it, the ladder has been leaning against the wrong wall. Put your ladder against the right wall before start climbing: At all times "live a life true to yourself, not the life others expect".

Without authenticity, the risk of internal conflict is high, and likely to cause unnecessary frustration or stress.

This particular issue reminds me of Susan, who had recently changed role from solicitor to senior barrister, but who was without clerking support and needed to source all her own work. It took some time to work out a clear idea of her own brand and offering, and indeed it was tweaked and altered a number of times as sessions

*progressed. She moved from stuck to unstuck, however,
when we spent a session considering her values and
beliefs and seeing how they aligned to how she was
conducting herself at work. Once there was congruency
between her at work and outside of work, she was more
readily able to identify her message and assert it
confidently and win business from it.*

12. You are not alone

For the tricky stuff, always keep in mind one of my
favourite quotes and use like a mantra: *"This too shall
pass"*. It will.

Practice makes improvement. The tips that resonate may
take time to incorporate on a daily basis. Over time, the
positive benefits will undoubtedly outweigh the effort.

Let these suggestions support you in your quest to stay
well. If in doubt, talk: Someone will be better placed to
help if you feel able to communicate and share
with them

Exercise 10

Jot down your own thoughts here and use as a checklist for action.

Do you want to improve your workplace wellness?

If so, what could you do?

Here is a reminder of some suggestions. Consider which method to adopt and how:

- Mindset
- Routine
- Hydration
- Gratitude and journaling
- Confidence
- Priorities and planning
- Mindfulness and getting back to basics
- Changing state or environment
- Focusing on nature
- Networking and connecting
- Staying authentic

What WILL you do and WHEN?

PART IV
COACHING EXERCISES TO SUPPORT CAREER PROGRESSION

Challenges and solutions in this Chapter are around goal setting, prioritising, action planning and doing!

The Challenge...career progression planning and doing

When did you last look at where you want to be in ten years' time or make a serious, detailed plan for your career progression over the coming months and years?

If you are a lawyer wanting to move from associate to solicitor, partner to equity partner, junior counsel to Queen's Counsel, recorder to judge, do YOU have a plan? If your chosen path is outside of law, what is your next promotional opportunity? Do you have a supportive network of people championing you and helping you to get there? And how about if you wish to move from being a maternity career break returner to working successfully with more flexible working?

According to Whom

For me, whilst still at The Bar, and prior to setting up a business, I must have considered the "plan" a maximum of twice a year, and only in passing, without follow up accountability, when reluctantly talking about my pension with my Independent Financial Advisor and, briefly, with my senior clerk at the annual practice review meeting. I understand how easy it is to plough on with the daily firefighting without a clear vision of what you want or a plan of how to achieve it.

Likewise, when we entered the grip of Day Three of The 2018 Beast from the East, a ferocious Siberian snowstorm which caused untold misery for working parents unable to get to work or do business whilst child-care faculties and schools were closed, I totally understood the competing emotions of enforced time to reflect, spending time sledging with my nearest and dearest, and the nagging thoughts of what other business priorities I "should" be attending to. I drew a parallel to an ordinary working day, when competing distractions vie for our attention and steer us off course from tackling our most important priorities.

How to...set goals, prioritise, action plan and do!

Coaching Exercise 1

Firstly, have a goal and make an action plan to achieve it. By this I mean have a clear career strategy. It's often said "*It's hard to score without a goal*". I couldn't agree more. If you don't know what you want, how can you formulate a clear plan to get there? *"Fail to plan, plan to fail"*

Identify the things that are important to you. Consider the consequences of not achieving them. Then stretch yourself to think of your career plan, initially, for the next three, six and twelve months; then for the next three, five, ten+ years.

Then, write down the overall plan. By committing it to writing, you are well on your way to making the first, and most crucial, step: a commitment to taking action. Not only is it helpful to see where you are headed, but also to motivate you to take action to achieve it. Brian Tracy, American Motivational Speaker, suggests that of goals committed to writing, even with no further conscious action on behalf of the writer, 80% of them will actually be achieved, simply because that individual has clarified the vision of what they want.

> *Emma was working in a toxic law firm environment. After being promised court work that never materialised, she was then given a case worthy of someone fifteen years her junior. The firm demanded regular and often pointless business development activity which was anti-flexible working which she had to maintain due to family commitments. She was going to work feeling sick and wanted coaching before she was, to quote, "binned". Ultimately she was unfairly dismissed. No surprise then that she was fragile due to a lack of confidence. Her Plan B was going to take a whole new mindset. And yet a simple shift in focus out of the quagmire of the current state of play, to her twelve month goal, created a visible shift in her, both physically and emotionally. Stated simply, "In a year I want to wake up confident and happy going to work." She set to work that day and over the next few sessions to do exactly that.*

What would you like to achieve in the next three, six and twelve months?

What are your longer term goals? Jot your ideas down here:

3 month goals

6 month goals

12 month goals

Long term goals (3,5,10 year)

Coaching Exercise 2

Identify your priorities around any work-related challenges which, once addressed, will make achieving the plan more manageable.

Order these priorities. Refer back to Stephen Covey's invaluable Time Management Matrix to identify those urgent or important (or neither!) tasks.

With coaching clients, I encourage, as a helpful starting point, the identification of their top 6-8 priorities, after which they can order into levels of importance their will to tackle them. Having spoken recently to a number of solicitors interested in coaching as a means by which to support their employees work more productively and purposefully, I have identified a number of recurring examples of priorities which may resonate.

1. What's in it for me? Why am I doing this?

Life Balance or Boundaries, for example, how much you are willing to put in without compromising other things like home life. Taking calls from your CEO at 10pm at night might be acceptable if you work in a global operation taking conference calls over different time zones, but be aware of unreasonable requests becoming a matter of habit, weekly on a Friday night.

2. Time management and Efficiency

Be ready to plan your week or day to the letter, as far as you are able, to get best use out of them. If you work in two offices in geographically separate locations ensure you are planning all meetings on one site in one day, and vice versa. Do you struggle with the "first in, last out" mentally, with poor productivity in between times? Perhaps consider bringing your finish time forward by an hour and plan in between times to make the fewer, remaining hours count more.

3. Financial considerations

Are you prioritising you own professional worth with your corresponding value? Have you given thought to how your fee accurately reflects the work you do and the hours you put in. I've heard lawyers talk of the "Toilet Thinking Time" conundrum. If you are clear on your worth, you can properly charge the appropriate fee, wherever you do that thinking!

4. Mental toughness, resilience and our ability to deal with overwhelm

See Chapter 7 for further discussion and ideas on this topic.

5. Distraction Avoidance

See Chapter 8 for further discussion and ideas around this topic.

6. Up-skilling

What are your strengths? What are your areas of development?

How do you rate your communication skills? What about leadership or management skills?

Once you have identified around six work-related priorities, consider where you are now, compared to where you want to be. Then break each priority down individually to identify specific plans addressing each one: "*A goal without a plan is just a dream.*"

I then use a really effective coaching tool with clients to examine each priority individually and support them make an action plan for achieving their desired outcomes.

In summary, take yourself through the simple six step process:

1. What is your **final goal**, perhaps for in about a year's time?
2. What is your **first journey goal**, say for in

the next few days or weeks? Much like climbing a mountain, every journey starts with a single step. By breaking it down into manageable chunks you can start the forward momentum and see the path to the end goal more clearly.

3. Examine and write down **your strengths** to support you to achieve your objective, and to encourage you on your less motivated days.

4. Identify the **obstacles** you might face en route to anticipate, and more easily overcome, them.

5. Then commit to what **action** to take

6. Then decide, most importantly, **when**?

Final Goal

Journey Goal

Strengths

Obstacles

Action

When

Committing to a particular action within a specific time frame is an extremely effective method by which to ensure the journey is started.

You will recall the earlier quote, *positive intentions without positive actions lead to positively nothing*, so have the courage to commit, not just to writing down the plan, but getting on with facilitating those actions. **Now**. Then you are on your way!

Coaching Exercise 3

The GROW Coaching Model, an acronym for the 4 step coaching process "Goals; Reality; Options; Will or Way Forward"

Whilst in the park crunching through the reddy-brown autumn leaves of 2017, my youngest delightedly scooting through muddy puddles, we came across a freshly dug mole hill. To him it was huge, and an opportunity to scramble up the loose soil to the top and use as a springboard from which to jump back to terra firma. As an adult looking down, I noticed, with perspective, how the earthy mound appeared flat, or at least much smaller and more conquerable than my then two year old believed.

It reminded me of a life balance workshop I delivered

the week before to Health Care professionals branching out from NHS employment into the private sector and starting or developing their own businesses. Amongst many things, we looked at "the big vision", the reality of their circumstances, expanded our thoughts to consider limitless possibilities around what <u>could</u> be done to achieve the end goal, then put in place the first action steps – what <u>would</u> be done, and when – to move, with positive momentum, towards their overall objective. This in a nutshell is the coaching GROW model.

> *Liz, law student and budding international advocate, did precisely that during our sessions: Instead of asking "am I good enough" and telling herself that she "should" or "would try" to do X, Y or Z to break the cycle of feeling stuck in a rut, she made a plan using the GROW model and then gave herself sufficient thinking time to consider and review her options a number of times.*

I was struck with how, in a similar way to the molehill, the coaching model applied had made her career goal look so much more manageable with perspective – and having considered the bigger picture (child's view of the whole mole hill), then going on to break it down into bite-sized, achievable chunks, it was possible to start the process of first steps towards the overall objective because it made it look easy, possible, simple even.

The positive feedback from such an exercise speaks volumes: *"The workshop was fantastic. Nikki covered so much in a short time and gave us direction. On a personal level, it helped me get some thoughts on paper to develop my business plan. I am planning on making a goal board; was very inspired by Nikki's."*

I understand with renewed insight how, especially in business and our careers, we shouldn't make a mountain out of a mole hill.

Get a vision, get a plan, move.

Exercise 11

Jot down your own thoughts here and use as a checklist for action.

Are you serious about making your career work?

If so, what could you do?

Here is a reminder of some suggestions:

- Consider when you will do Coaching Exercises 1, 2 and 3
- Consider your overall goal
- Consider your short term goal
- Ask what is your next action step?
- Decide when you will take your next action step

What WILL you do and WHEN?

AFTERWORD

Congratulations on getting to the end of the book, whether by working through its natural order, or by curiously opening the back page first.

If the former, further congratulations on being open minded enough to consider, and perhaps even test out for yourself, some of the hints and tips contained herein. How did you get on? Have you felt any lightbulb moments or significant moments of shift?

If you skipped directly here, let me encourage you to go back to the beginning. As a coach, I love the end game, (as must you to find yourself here first), but I'd encourage you to think that working backwards and getting a plan in place from the start cannot be underestimated.

- What is your big picture?
- What are your shorter term goals to get there?

Whatever your circumstance or situation, however inspiring, powerful, motivational or overwhelming, let me leave you with these thoughts:

- What was it that brought you here in the first place?
- What tools and techniques have you been reminded of or learnt to support you in that first objective for reading the book?
- What will you now do?

Even if small, actions, changes, movement of any kind, will propel you forward from here.

To what end, you decide.

Here's to your success.

Nikki

A NOTE OF THANKS

It's a funny thing, looking back on a project like a book – where the idea first started and how I was encouraged, supported and spurred on to get the job done.

In no particular order then, thanks to CM, the Jamaican Death Row prisoner, whose first comment "you should write a book about it" fifteen years ago planted the seed for something back then I could never truly imagine.

To Jaime Harrison, Sharon Bott and Melanie Pledger, without whom I would never have transitioned from barrister to coach and been on this thrilling, exhilarating and rewarding journey.

To the most fabulous women I have met along the way, in addition to my incredible and awe-inspiring clients, altruistically willing to share their network, experience and time to see this happen: Claire Norman, Laura Pacey, Kayleigh Fantoni, Lisa Unwin and Jennifer Holloway to name a few. Specifically, to Sally Penni and Claire Watts, who always said there was a book in me somewhere, and encouraged me against the odds, to get it out there.

To those who gave my blogs a platform in legal circles at The Law Society, Counsel Magazine, Criminal Bar Quarterly and Oxford Women's Law Society.

To the champions of my business, without whom I wouldn't have found the confidence to find my pen and write: Marie Walsh, HHJ Sophie McKone, Helen Saunders at Clarion Solicitors, Richard McCann, Wendy Ramshaw, Steve Kennedy, Dally Purewal and the Leeds Law Society team.

To my husband, Neil, for his unshakeable support and encouragement, and his motto, that I repeat daily like a mantra: "Keep going".

And to my parents, for their unerring encouragement, support and dedication, even when I was living my life true to myself, and certainly not in the way they necessarily expected. Thank you for staying the course, and more.

Nikki, 22.9.19

FURTHER READING

- *7 Habits of Highly Effective People* - Steven Covey
- *Eve was Framed* - Baroness Helena Kennedy QC
- *The Guide* - Dr. William Holden
- *Essentialism* - Geoff McKeown
- *Playing Big: A Practical Guide for Brilliant Women Like you* - Tara Mohr
- *Becoming* - Michelle Obama
- *Work Like a Woman: Manifesto for Change* - Mary Portas
- *Notes from a Friend* - Anthony Robbins
- *Lean in: Women: Work and The Will to Lead* - Sheryl Sandberg
- *Eat that Frog* - Brian Tracy

- *The 4 Pillar Plan* - Dr Rangan Chattergee

2. THE FEMALE RETENTION CRISIS

1. https://www.innertemple.org.uk/your-professional-community/temple-womens-forum/
2. https://www.barstandardsboard.org.uk/media/1773934/women_at_the_bar_-_full_report_-_final_12_07_16.pdf
3. https://westerncircuit.co.uk/wp-content/uploads/2018/11/WCWF-Back-to-the-Bar-Final-version.pdf
4. https://www.bbc.co.uk/sounds/play/m0002hxw
5. https://www.criminalbar.com/resources/news/cba-monday-message-11-02-19/
6. https://www.barcouncil.org.uk/media/723821/bar_council_guides_judicial_bullying_february_2019_final.pdf
7. https://www.dailymail.co.uk/news/article-6699901/London-female-barrister-Joanna-Hardy-Twitter-thread-male-colleagues-joke-breasts.html
8. http://www.bristollawsociety.com/wp-content/uploads/2018/07/Women-in-leadership-in-Law-toolkit.pdf
9. https://first100years.org.uk
10. https://www.counselmagazine.co.uk/articles/flexible-working-flipsides
11. www.mmu.ac.uk/growl

9. HOW TO SAY NO BUT KEEP THE OPPORTUNITIES FLOWING

1. www.wellbeingatthebar.org.uk

Printed in Poland
by Amazon Fulfillment
Poland Sp. z o.o., Wrocław

The Prostitutes of
Serruya's Lane
and other hidden
Gibraltarian histories

About the Author

M. G. Sanchez was born in the British colony of Gibraltar. He is the author of the book of short stories *Rock Black,* and is also the editor of *Writing the Rock of Gibraltar: An Anthology of Literary Texts, 1720-1890.* For more information, please email: rockscorpionbooks@hotmail.co.uk.

The Prostitutes of Serruya's Lane and other hidden Gibraltarian histories

M. G. Sanchez

Rock Scorpion Books
Dewsbury, West Yorks
2007

ISBN–10: 0-9552465-2-0
ISBN–13: 978-0-9552465-2-4

For Jane

Contents

Acknowledgements   8

The Prostitutes of Serruya's Lane   9

'The Mongrel Race called Rock Scorpions'   33

'The Great Depot for Smuggling'   69

'That Dreadful Scourge of Humanity'   125

Appendix A:
The Smugglers Rock, 3, September, 1877   151

Appendix B:
Scene during the plague at Gibraltar (1839)   167

Author Acknowledgements

I would like to thank Mrs. Tanaz Buhariwalla, Mr. Christopher Wall, and Mr. Stephen Wall for all their help.

Special thanks must also be extended to my good Gibraltarian friends Mr. Mark Cooper, Mr. Gerald Mañasco and Mr. Gino Sanguinetti.

Finally, I would like to thank Grant Thornton (Gibraltar) and Barclays Wealth (Gibraltar) for assisting with the publication of this book.

The Prostitutes of Serruya's Lane
An essay on Gibraltar's forgotten red-light district

(i) The Legend of Miss X

It must have been 1974 or 1975. I was about six or seven years old. We were living in Chicardos Passage, a narrow sequence of weather-beaten, clay-coloured steps that skirts the northern side of the civilian hospital. Our flat was one of those typical uppertown abodes that Gibraltarians used to occupy for decades, the kind of cockroach-infested, windowless dwelling that Richard Ford, in his bestselling *A Handbook for Travellers in Spain and readers at home* (1845), describes as 'fit only for salamanders and scorpions, as those born in the Rock are called.'[1] Nowadays I can't remember much about the flat - except that it stank of damp and that to get to the bathroom you had to walk through the living room and the two bedrooms. One Saturday night, while the whole family was asleep in the two adjoining bedrooms separated by a retractable formica screen, there was a knock on our front door. Wearily, my father got out of bed and walked to the living room. He unlocked the front door and pulled it back an inch or two. Through the small gap before him, he saw two drunken sailors, not much more than eighteen or nineteen years old, loitering sheepishly across the broken flagstones leading into our flat. 'Sorry to disturb you, matey,' one of the sailors began with a nervous gulp. 'But we're looking for Miss. X's place? Me and me mate Taffy here got told it was just round back of hospital.

---

[1] Richard Ford, *A Handbook for Travellers in Spain and Readers at Home*, vol. 2 (1845; reprinted 1966), p. 513.

Got any idea where it could be, matey?'[2] 'Miss. X?' my father anxiously replied. 'Yes, yes,' the other sailor now began. 'Miss. X... Scodger down from the *Argyll* told us that he used to know this fellah from the *Anglians* who said that she was a proper Gibraltun goer. You know what I mean, don't you, mate?' Suddenly it dawned upon my father what the sailors were after, a smile simultaneously materialising across his somnolent features. 'Miss. X died about three years ago,' he then truthfully told the young sailors. 'She was about eighty-five. I think you've come about forty or fifty years too late.'

* * *

My father related this story to me around 1986 or 1987. He told me that Miss. X. was an old lady who used to live one or two streets away from us. She had been alive when we had first moved into our flat towards the end of 1969, but had died of an embolism or some other geriatric malady a couple of years later. She had carried with her a reputation for moral looseness, although neither my parents nor any of our other neighbours in Chicardos were old enough to remember to what this uncommon privilege was due. From what I gathered, Miss. X. was a slightly dotty old woman who rarely opened the crumbling persian shutters of her first-floor dwelling except to let down a wicker basket attached to a piece of string. Into this basket the boy from *Juan's* greengrocers in Castle Street would regularly deposit a pint of milk and a loaf of bread, giving the line a little tug just after he had taken the money and the note for tomorrow's order lying in the basket's interior. When she died in 1969 or thereabouts, her flat was taken over by a Moroccan

---

[2] Her real name, of course, was not X.

family and that was that: Miss. X. was well-nigh forgotten. Or maybe not, judging from what happened that night in 1975. Somehow or the other, the legend of Miss. X. had lived on, morphing its way down the fluorescent-lit corridors of Royal Navy frigates and destroyers just like one would have expected from a story involving alcohol and a voracious young Latina...

(ii) Introducing New Passage / Serruya's Lane: Gibraltar's forgotten Red Light Area

What my father did not tell me was that Miss. X. was part of a long-forgotten prostitutional tradition which stretched back to the 1800s and that Chicardos Passage itself lay no more than a stone's throw away from what used to be the epicentre of Gibraltar's infamous red light district. To reach this quarter from Chicardos, all you have to do is walk down the steps, cross a little stretch of badly-tarmacked road and then climb down the steeply-inclined side street known as Pezzi's steps. You will then find yourself in an area known as New Passage, a narrow, ill-paved alleyway that connects Hospital Steps on the South to the broad, limestone-hewn *escalones* of Castle Street on the North. Even now – when almost no-one in Gibraltar remembers what scandalous practices once used to occur in this area – New Passage looks very much like a colonial red light district *should look*: dark, eerie and, if we are to be honest, a little dilapidated. On both sides of the passage we come across tottering nineteenth-century houses, with thickly-plastered facades and crooked little archways through which one can sometimes catch the damp-infested recesses of some half-hidden interior patio. Though no more than five minutes' walk from Main Street, you could be forgiven for thinking that you had been teleported back to the 1870s.

The demographic history of New Passage makes no less interesting reading. Nowadays, the area is populated mainly by Moroccan workers and one or two remaining Gibraltarian families; it is, in effect, one of the last localities left in Gibraltar where you can find affordable housing. Back in the 1970s, when our two sex-starved friends came looking for the long-interred Miss. X, the demographic lay-out would have been reversed: with one or two Moroccans hemmed-in among the cluster of working-class Gibraltarian families. If you were to go back even further in time – say, for example, to the decade straddling the nineteenth and twentieth centuries - the situation would have been even more different. For a start New Passage would not have been known as New Passage at all, but by the rather less impersonal name of Serruya's Lane. Even more so than nowadays, it would have drawn individuals with low disposable incomes - mainly prostitutes from the ten or twelve brothels stretching across the Lane's length and the scruffy, ill-fed ragamuffins from the orphanage near Castle Street. We are able to catch a glimpse of what life must have been like in the lane from a hand-tinted postcard, printed by the local publisher V. B. Cumbo some time around the 1920s. In what is clearly a prearranged tableau, about thirty or forty women and children spill out from a doorway, a teeming mass of humanity peering amusedly at the newfangled contraption that a camera must have seemed.[3] An anonymous English reporter, writing in 1888, has also left us this singular impression of the place:

> [T]here is a whole lane, containing several houses… every
> house being a house of ill-fame…. This lane is a perfect

---

[3] See this book's front cover.

trap for strangers, say sailors and soldiers entering the garrison. I have seen dozens of lads from HM training ships enter this lane on a Sunday afternoon... who would probably have gone back to their ships pure, so far as that day was concerned, had it not been for this same trap door.[4]

Who were the women working in Serruya's Lane and its surroundings and how many were they in number? Records suggest that most of them were Spanish aliens who were allowed to ply their trade by means of rescindable permits issued by the governor. Censuses carried out between 1868 and 1921 reveal that there was an average of 115 registered prostitutes at any one given moment, their numbers fluctuating between the all-time high of 138 recorded in 1913 and the corresponding low of 83 just after the war in 1921. From these censuses, too, we learn that between 1871 and 1921 there were around fourteen to sixteen brothels in operation throughout Gibraltar, each of them containing between four and fifteen prostitutes. Officially their ages ranged between twenty and forty, although an article by the Methodist writer James B. Wookey in 1887 suggests that some of the prostitutes could have been as young as eleven or twelve.[5] Very little is known about the women in question apart from what appears in juridical documents and court summonses, the life of a prostitute, it seems, never being of

---

[4] Anonymous, 'On Guard at Gibraltar,' *The Sentinel*, 10: 10, 1888, p. 125.

[5] Wookey relates the story of three orphaned girls of Anglo-Gibraltarian parentage, Lizzie, Sophie and Lucy Cox, two of whom were raped by their male protectors and one of whom was employed as a child harlot. Wookey subsequently argued for 'a law for the protection of young girls both from the procuresses and vicious men.' See James B. Wookey, 'A visit to Gibraltar,' *The Sentinel*, 9: 11, 1887, pp. 139-140.

any interest to anyone outside the courtroom. In 1919, for example, in a move that anticipated the new gubernatorial Puritanism that was just around the corner, the military authorities decided to close down a brothel on the road to Devil's Gap reserved exclusively for the use of the garrison's officers. The brothel's mistress, a lady by the Gibraltarian-sounding name of Enriquetta Thomas, immediately challenged the decision, arguing that officers and soldiers would henceforth have to suffer the indignity of mixing together in Serruya's Lane, as well as maintaining that it was wrong to close down an institution which 'exceed[ed] the memory of any living inhabitant of Gibraltar.' Apart from anecdotes like this, there is not very much else. Occasionally, we come across a few addresses where the prostitutes actually plied their trade - 35 Arengo's Lane, for example, or 20 Serruya's Lane – but even these are impersonally tabulated details which shed no light on the social and emotional plights of their inhabitants. On their lives and the trials they had to go through, history is conspicuously silent. [6]

(iii) 'A necessary evil': Garrison attitudes towards prostitution in eighteenth and nineteenth-century Britain

For most of the eighteenth and nineteenth centuries, there was an assumption among the British military elite that prostitution was something of a 'necessary evil' that the Army had to put up with. Fighting men, being highly sexualised, needed to release pent-up energies. If they didn't, morale would suffer and the army wouldn't operate to its usual high standards.

---

[6] Most of the statistics in this paragraph has been taken from Philip Howell's impeccably researched article 'Sexuality, sovereignty and space: law, government and the geography of prostitution in colonial Gibraltar,' *Social History*, 29, 2004, pp. 444-464.

'Using prostitutes,' accordingly writes the modern scholar Janet Padiak, 'was considered a natural sequela of bachelor life, and all garrison towns, including Gibraltar, had a large contingent ready to service the men.'[7] Behind this attitude was a Freudian belief that male sexuality was a reckless and an uncontrollable force that had to be given free rein if it wasn't to turn inwards and destroy the repressor. '[L]ust for women is a much more universal and more intense appetite than the craving for alcohol,' for example wrote the military theorist George J. Anderson in 1918[8] - the implication being that it was practically impossible to stamp out the 'necessary evil.' Closely interrelated with this was a belief that the British military in particular, more than perhaps any other fighting unit in the world, was an uncommonly sexualised apparatus that needed prostitution to release its pent-up energies. Peter Baldwin, author of *Contagion and the State in Europe, 1830-1930*, rehearses precisely this conviction when he states that the 'British military was notorious for having by far the worst VD rates of any European force.'[9] A similar point was made by the Victorian journalist James Connolly, who believed not only that British garrisons were 'generator[s] of prostitution, but the British Army is in the last particular the most odious on the face of the earth.' To illustrate this point, Connolly looked at the rate of hospital admissions for venereal disease among different fighting units throughout Europe in the 1860s. Out of every 1000 soldiers,

---

[7] Janet Padiak, 'The serious evil of marching regiments: The families of the British garrison of Gibraltar,' *History of the Family*, 10, 2005, p. 142.

[8] George J. Anderson, 'Making the Camps Safe for the Army,' *Annals of the American Academy of Political and Social Science*, 79, 1918, p. 148.

[9] Peter Baldwin, *Contagion and the State in Europe, 1830-1930* (1999), p. 510.

the Prussians had 26.7 men, the French 43.8, the Austrians 65.4 and the British in India 458.3. '[N]early every second man,' as Connolly ruefully writes about his own countrymen, '[or] ten times as many as in the French Army.'[10]

How did the army react to such high rates of venereal disease? Since the prevailing opinion was that prostitution could never be extirpated, the authorities decided to implement a Foucaultian strategy of control - in other words, they tried to regulate the practice of prostitution with the aim of limiting its impact upon its 'innocent' young soldiers. Within the British mainland this reached its apogee with the euphemistically-named Contagious Diseases Acts of 1864, 1866, 1869, much-maligned pieces of legislation which sought to regulate and demarcate the practice of prostitution within the vicinity of nineteen British garrison towns. Judith R. Walkowitz, a noted feminist historian, puts these Acts in their historical context:

> Concern over the spread of venereal disease among the military led to the passage of the Contagious Disease Acts, pieces of legislation that registered prostitutes in nineteen garrison towns and subjected these women to periodic medical examination. The Contagious Diseases Acts were a blatant manifestation of the double standard; only women, not family men whose innocent wives and children were supposedly being protected by the acts, nor the promiscuous soldiers and sailors, were subject to examination and arrest. A poor woman could be arrested by a special morals officer 'who had due cause to believe' she was a common prostitute. The definition of a common

---

[10] James Connolly, 'Soldiers of the Queen,' *Workers' Republic*, 15 July, 1899.

prostitute was entirely vague and consequently these plainclothes policemen had large discretionary powers. No warrant was needed, and women were effectively deprived of due process of law. When confronted by the morals officer, a woman was forced to sign a voluntary submission that authorized her examination, and, if found diseased, her incarceration in a hospital for a maximum of nine months. If a woman refused, she would be brought before a magistrate, where the burden of proof was on her to prove she was virtuous, that she did not go with men, whether for money or not. Even if she were not imprisoned, she had been publicly degraded and stigmatized for life.[11]

More than any other piece of legislation, the CD Acts show to what extent the British military authorities had institutionalised the practice of prostitution. They also reveal to what degree governmental bodies were prepared to side with the military and discriminate against the prostitute in their attempt to police the sex trade.[12] Men could visit prostitutes with relative impunity, confident that the objects of their desire had been medically inspected *a priori*; prostitutes, by contrast, were being subjected to the most barbarous methods of control. When in 1870 Parliament tried to amend the CD acts so that

[11] Judith R. Walkowitz, 'Notes on the History of Victorian Prostitution,' *Feminist Studies*, 1, 1972, p. 112.

[12] This discrimination extended to all sorts of other areas. Jennifer Ballantine-Perera relates the example of three women, Berkeley, Leslie and Lima, who were accused in 1887 of seriously assaulting a civilian. The Attorney General at the time argued that clemency should be shown to Berkeley and Leslie (who were English), but not to Lima (who was a local prostitute). See 'The Language of Exclusion in F. Solly Flood's 'History of the Permit System in Gibraltar,' *Journal of Historical Sociology*, 20, 2007, p. 231.

they would cover the rest of the civilian population, there was, not surprisingly, something of an outcry. Spearheading the anti-CD movement was Josephine Butler, a feminist from Northumberland with distant family ties to the reformist Prime Minister Charles Grey. Through a combination of public speaking and political lobbying she highlighted the intrinsic unfairness of the CD acts and shortly afterwards forced the authorities to repeal the laws in 1886. This, in the words of a feminist commentator, effectively 'broke the conspiracy of silence on the sexual exploitation of lower class women.'[13]

(iv) Prostitution within a Gibraltar context: police and military strategies of control

But did this conspiracy of silence really come to an end? Had Josephine Butler's valiant efforts really succeeded in dismantling the hypocritical mixture of indifference and misogynistic dogmatism with which the British military establishment viewed the sex trade? Nowadays historians are not so sure. In her book *Prostitution, Race and Politics: Policing Venereal Disease in the British Empire*, for example, Philippa Levine has shown that, while the anti-regulationist brigade won an important victory in 1886, strong regulationist policies were still being followed in the colonies, where similar methods of control had been in place both before the onset of the CD laws in the 1860s and after their abolition.[14] Gibraltar was a case in point. Although it had never been technically bound by the 1860 CD laws, the alien prostitutes of Serruya's Lane were arguably subject to a much tighter form of

---

[13] 'Notes on the History of Victorian Prostitution,' p. 112.

[14] Philippa Levine, *Prostitution, Race and Politics: Policing Venereal Disease in the British Empire* (2003).

control than anything witnessed in the British mainland. For one thing, names and addresses of all prostitutes were recorded, along with their backgrounds, medical histories and other significant details. Then there was the matter of socio-geographical control. In a pioneering essay to which I am much indebted, Philip Howell has shown that from 1866 onwards the geographical spread of Gibraltarian brothels (which in 1866 included not just Serruya's Lane, but also other streets in the vicinity such as modern-day Castle Street, Hospital Ramp and Castle Steps) was being slowly whittled down so that by 1922 all the brothels were situated directly on Serruya's Lane itself. This would have aided the military authorities in policing and controlling the area, just as much as it would have helped them usher the prostitutes to the nearby civil hospital for examination. Those responsible for enforcing these authoritarian measures emphasised that Gibraltar was a place apart, that it needed legislation and policing methods different to those employed in the British mainland. Take the case of William Seed, the colony's English chief of police. In the year immediately after the parliamentary repeal of the CD laws, he maintained that

> ....Gibraltar is a place apart and special rules are necessary. The bulk of prostitutes are Spaniards, who very well know that to be allowed to live in Gibraltar it is necessary that they should submit to examination. They come to ply their calling here with the knowledge that they are to submit to the examination and as they do so voluntarily I cannot see any hardship in it. It is simply a contract they enter into. If they do not wish to enter into the contract they need not come.[15]

---

[15] 'Sexuality, sovereignty and space: law, government and the geography of prostitution in colonial Gibraltar', p. 450.

Seed is here referring to the British military's most important strategy of control: the law which allowed non-British subjects to reside and/or work in Gibraltar on permits rescindable by the governor. An amendment to this law, introduced several decades earlier, stated that alien women who refused or neglected to submit to regular medical examination for signs of venereal disease could be summarily extradited from the garrison. This, in effect, ensured that Gibraltar *did* become something of a place apart, since the treatment of its prostitutes was dependent on social forces and legal variables not present within the British mainland. To quote Howell once again, the residents of Serruya's Lane 'were controllable not because they were prostitutes *per se*, but because they were aliens.'[16] This uncommon situation – which saw regulationism being perpetuated under the guise of immigrational policy – was, not surprisingly, much criticised by the anti-CD activists back in England. In a letter to the Misses Priestman, for example, the indefatigable Josephine Butler complained about the latent hypocrisy of the system employed in Gibraltar:

> As has already been said, there is no special Act applying to Gibraltar, but nonetheless the system is carried out there with a brutality of logic which could hardly be exceeded. It rests entirely on the authority of the military commander of the Rock…. An alien prostitute's permit of residence… is not granted unless she is certified to be physically fit for her calling, and is not renewed unless she undergoes her weekly visit at the civil hospital.[17]

---

[16] Ibid.

[17] Letter from Josephine E. Butler to the Misses Priestman, 19 October 1886. Quoted in Jane Jordan's and Ingrid Sharp's *Josephine Butler and the Prostitution Campaigns: Diseases of the Body Politic* (2003), p. 27.

But Butler was wrong: it was not only alien prostitutes who were coming under such duress. Gibraltar-born prostitutes were also being targeted. There were a number of reasons why this was happening too. Along with naturalised aliens (i.e. Spanish prostitutes who had gained residency status by virtue of marriage) Gibraltar-born prostitutes were exempt from immigrational restrictions and could therefore not be controlled as easily as their Spanish counterparts. This made them virtually untouchable from the point of the law - and also threatened to destabilise the garrison's strategies of civilian control. A resident military surgeon recognised as much in 1867, arguing that while the law provided for 'the removal of aliens known to be diseased[,] those enjoying the rights of British subjects cannot be dealt with in the same manner.'[18] The authorities tried to remedy this anomalous situation through a number of extemporised measures. First, they invested the governor with the right to annul and break up marriages between British citizens and aliens of disreputable character. This is precisely what happened to Carmen Hernandez, a Spanish prostitute and 'woman of infamous character and conduct,' who was expelled from the Rock in 1867 despite being married to a Gibraltarian.[19] In addition, they got the local police to 'lean' on native prostitutes - either by forcing them to work alongside their Spanish counterparts in the Serruya's Lane area where they would be subject to greater control or, what was even better, by discouraging them from prostituting themselves

[18] 'Sexuality, sovereignty and space: law, government and the geography of prostitution in colonial Gibraltar', p. 459.

[19] Stacie D. A. Burke and Lawrence A. Sawchuck, 'Alien encounters: the jus soli and reproductive politics in the 19th century fortress and colony of Gibraltar,' *The History of the Family*, 6, 2001, p. 540.

outright. That they were largely successful in doing this, moreover, can be seen not just from the slow implosion in prostitutional space alluded to earlier, but from the falling number of native prostitutes, which went down from 36 in 1871, to 17 in 1891, to an inconsequential 2 in 1921. Finally, in 1901, an amendment to the Sanitary Orders Ordinance conferred upon the governor the power to terminate the residence in Gibraltar of any prostitute, Gibraltar-born or alien, who had not been granted a certificate of heath following a medical inspection.[20] Josephine Butler, who was seventy-three at the time, must have been wondering what the hell was going on.

(v) Verifying VD: the weekly medical examination

All during this time the main strategy of control remained the weekly medical examination. Lasting anything between ten minutes and a few hours, this was carried out in the civil hospital's VD unit, just yards away from Chicardos Passage. Its proponents argued that it was a safe and fairly painless procedure, and insisted that the prostitutes should be grateful for free medical inspections. They also pointed out that the soldiery was being regularly examined for sexual diseases too - although, in truth, they could not have chosen a more redundant comparison. In general the authorities tended to underplay and even ignore male genital inspections – known by the soldiers as 'dangle' or 'short arm' parades – as they were thought to dent morale and develop 'coarseness and injured modesty.'[21] This was in complete contrast to the total lack of tact and

---

[20] 'Sexuality, sovereignty and space: law, government and the geography of prostitution in colonial Gibraltar,' p. 459.

[21] *Prostitution, Race and Politics: Policing Venereal Disease in the British Empire* (2003), p. 77.

discretion with which registered prostitutes were treated. Consider the following description of the methods employed in a VD clinic within the British mainland:

> The exams were often brutal. Typically, the woman's legs were clamped open and her ankles tied down. Surgical instruments – sometimes not cleaned from prior inspections – were inserted so inexpertly that some women miscarried. Others passed out from the pain and the embarrassment. Some women with harmless conditions were misdiagnosed and locked in hospitals without recourse.[22]

Within the colonies things were arguably even worse. In one of the few surviving accounts left behind at a Commonwealth VD inspection unit, we learn that registered prostitutes were 'made to stand or sit in a tub of water and then freely drenched by means of a syringe... solutions... [which were] subsequently squirted into the vaginal canal.' No less brutal were the 'medicinal' treatments on offer. 'It was common practice,' writes Professor Philippa Levine, 'to dust sores with iodoform powder, in part because many held to the distinction between the 'true' indurated syphilitic sore and the chancroid. Labial abcesses were often opened and drained before being dusted dry. Genital warts, not understood as viral, were painted with acetic or pyrogallic acid or dusted with sulphate of iron.'[23] As if this wasn't demeaning and painful enough, all the examinations had to be conducted

---

[22] Wendy McElroy, 'The Contagious Disease Acts,' *Freedom Daily*, March 2000 (http://www.fff.org/freedom/0300e.asp - 14-10-2007).

[23] *Prostitution, Race and Politics: Policing Venereal Disease in the British Empire*, p. 77.

by men. This was one of those grotesque examples of false propriety that the Victorians, with their extreme sexual hypocrisies and their latent culture of denial, were famous for. It also raises some inevitable questions about the socio-sexual mechanics within the colonial and domestic inspecting units. Although, writing in 1922, Surgeon Rear Admiral Daniel McNabb piously believed that the examinations were not 'relished by the officers concerned,' it is clear that some men must have taken a perverse delight in subjecting young women to such humiliating treatment.[24] Why else would the authorities have been so implacable in their refusal to allow women to carry out such investigations? When the possibility of using lady doctors was mooted before Lord Curzon and his advisers in India, for example, they were quick to 'strongly deprecate' the use of women in VD wards. The Lady Dufferin fund, an organisation which recruited and trained women doctors for India, showed similar resistance to the idea: 'The committee decided that in no circumstances should any lady doctor attached to a hospital connected with the association be employed on any such duty.'[25] Outwardly, of course, the intention was to protect the sensibilities of the middle-class female population – lady doctors being considered too effete and delicate to be dealing with anything vaguely gynaecological. However, taking into account what Lieutenant George J. Anderson and other military men believed about 'lust for women' being 'a much more universal and more intense appetite than the craving for alcohol,' such high-minded principles are very much open to question.

---

[24] Daniel McNabb, 'Notes on Venereal Disease in the Navy,' *Journal of Hygiene*, 21, 1922, p. 1.

[25] Both these examples can be found in *Prostitution, Race and Politics: Policing Venereal Disease in the British Empire*, p. 137.

Despite this false propriety, the methods employed by the British medical authorities in Gibraltar appear to have been reasonably successful. In 1889, two army medics examined over one hundred prostitutes in the Serryua's Lane area and came to the conclusion that 'most of these women are well nourished, cleanly in habits and enjoy good health.' Likewise, Howell notes how at the turn of the century 'police magistrates and medical officers tended to be increasingly skeptical of servicemen's claims to have been infected by residents of Serruya's Lane.'[26] From a twenty-first century perspective, of course, there is something quite repugnant about such a state of affairs. Sailors, alighting from ships, could satisfy their lust in the knowledge that the objects of their desire had been thoroughly examined beforehand; prostitutes, meanwhile, were being treated no better than cattle. Yet it would be a mistake to think that all this was being submerged under a torrent of Victorian self-righteousness. Many saw what was happening – and some, like the Methodist writer and evangelist Mr. R. C. Morgan, chose to express their indignation in the most emphatic terms:

> In visiting some of their houses with a constable for purposes of inquiry, I saw their official certificates for the current week authenticating them as 'healthy.' The majority of soldiers in the garrison are youths in their teens, many away from home for the first time. The hideous hypocrisy of marching these boys to church on Sunday to pray, 'From fornication and all other deadly sins, good Lord deliver us,' while they know that on the previous day provision had been made for them to commit

---

[26] 'Sexuality, sovereignty and space: law, government and the geography of prostitution in colonial Gibraltar', p. 461.

this 'deadly sin' with impunity, places England, 'the heir
of all the ages,' in the foremost files of cant.[27]

Morgan's denunciations were also echoed in an anonymous
article appearing in 1883 under the title 'The Corruption of
Gibraltar.' Published in the reformist periodical *The Sentinel*,
it attacked the military establishment for condoning prostitution
and also rallied against the idea that all soldiers needed to
release pent-up sexual energies:

> Our British authorities have been fostering immorality
> and debauching the population by licensing vice... The
> place swarms with Spanish women and female children,
> whose lives are devoted to immorality.... Houses of ill-
> fame abound. Near the Governor's residence is a lane
> entirely given up to this vice, and there are three or four
> bad houses within twelve yards of the Presbyterian church,
> while there are other such houses in the main thoroughfare
> leading to the civil hospital. Of course the partizans of
> regulated debauchery will endeavour to excuse such a
> state of affairs by pointing out that the population of
> Gibraltar is largely composed of soldiers. These persons
> reason and act as though enlistment changes a man's
> nature, and he thereafter loses all power of self-control.
> Henceforward, it is the duty of the state to expect him to
> be immoral, and, in fact, to tempt him to be so, by
> elaborate, costly, brutalising arrangements designed... to
> enable him to sin without the physical penalty of sin.
> Why, the daily atmosphere they breathe is enough to
> contaminate any man. The men themselves would tell

---

[27] Quoted in *Josephine Butler and the Prostitution Campaigns: Diseases of the Body Politic*, p. 62.

you, as they have told me, that vice is not a necessity, but that the provision made for them, or allowed, is so great, that to resist is almost impossible.[28]

(vi) A New Puritanism: Smith-Dorrien and the end of Prostitution in Serruya's Lane

The salubrity of Gibraltar's red-light district, however, was something of a fin-de-siècle illusion. Within only a few years, prostitute admissions to the civil hospital increased once again and VD rates among the troops also rose. In 1911, 123 out of every 1000 men in the garrison were infected; in 1912, the figure rose to 128.[29] While these numbers, it is true, compare favourably with the incidence of VD in the 1850s and 1860s, they did once and for all destroy the illusion that Serruya's Lane was a place free from the ravages of venereal disease. Sir Archibald Hunter, Gibraltar's governor at the time, was said to be aghast. A dour, cheerless man who according to his contemporaries was 'obsessed about cleanliness,'[30] Hunter complained that Gibraltar was 'like the Augean stables' and maintained that he was 'determined to exact order and decency… from everybody who comes into the fortress.'[31] Meanwhile, speculation was rife. What could be causing the new infection rates? And, more importantly, why was the old system not

---

[28] Anonymous, 'The Corruption of Gibraltar,' *The Sentinel*, 56, 1883, pp. 263-264.

[29] 'Sexuality, sovereignty and space: law, government and the geography of prostitution in colonial Gibraltar', p. 461.

[30] See Roger T. Stearn, 'Hunter, Sir Archibald (1856–1936)', *Oxford Dictionary of National Biography* [http://www.oxforddnb.com/view/article/34059 - 14-9-2007]

[31] Anonymous, 'Compares Gibraltar to Augean Stables,' *The New York Times*, 23 February, 1913.

working any more? Many within the military establishment, including Hunter himself, laid the blame upon an alarming new development: the rise of the unregulated amateur. How else could one account for what was happening? Within no time, lurid tales began to circulate around the garrison about nocturnal encounters in secluded areas like the beaches or Alameda gardens - and it is surely no coincidence that Molly Bloom, James Joyce's famous literary creation, remembers the Alameda repeatedly during her pre-fornicatory monologue in *Ulysses*. The new climate of sexual tension is best captured in a British Lieutenant's memorandum, quoted by Howell, on the recent upsurge of infected cases within his regiment:

> Thanks for letting me see enclosed report from Chief of Police. Really don't know what we can do!!! There must be some free lancers abroad who indulge in al fresco performances in the Alameda or elsewhere. I cannot believe that all this increased venereal [disease] is the result of picnics, fairs, & La Linea. There is some woman or women who are poisoning the unsuspecting soldier. One can take some steps with the professional lady, but it is very difficult to deal with the amateur. [32]

Sentiments like these were common at the time and appear to have induced something of a backlash against the Gibraltarian sex trade. British soldiers were discouraged from visiting the 'Ramps' (as the area around Serruya's lane was popularly called). Police were instructed to 'lean' a little bit more forcibly on prostitutes and their procuresses. The advent of the Great War,

---

[32] 'Sexuality, sovereignty and space: law, government and the geography of prostitution in colonial Gibraltar', p. 461.

if anything, made the situation even tenser. Troop numbers were dwindling; reinforcements were needed; consequently, the men's health had to be protected at all costs. Riding the new anti-regulationist bandwagon, the Deputy Surgeon General of Gibraltar dismissed the existing inspectional procedures as all but worthless and argued that 'the presence of these women under present conditions constitutes a danger to general health and an increasing loss to the Navy.'[33] Thus, we come to a complete and thoroughly remarkable *volte face* on the subject. If in the 1860s and 1870s controlled access to prostitutes had been seen as a prerequisite for British military stability; now, less than fifty years later, regulationism came to be equated with the most noxious forms of physical and moral abandonment.

The final drive for de-regulationism came with the visit of the National Council for Combating Venereal Disease a few months after the end of the war. The NCCVD (later to become the British Social Hygiene Council) was a volunteer association formed in 1914. It organised lecture programmes among the army and the civilian population, and also sent voluntary commissioners to inspect centres of profligacy both at home and abroad. When its experts arrived at Gibraltar in 1919, they were made very welcome by Governor Horace Smith-Dorrien, another strait-laced figure with a Baden Powell-esque obsession with outdoor pursuits and sexual hygiene. Their eventual recommendations, published in 1921, suggested that legalised prostitution was bad for both the health of the garrisoned troops and civilian morale in general. They also advocated that regulationism should come to an immediate

---

[33] Ibid.

end. Faced with what must have been music to his ears, Smith-Dorrien, an uncompromising man who had incurred the wrath of his military superiors during the First World War by repeatedly questioning orders, took matters firmly into his own hands: in January 1922, just months before Joyce's *Ulysses* was published, he gave orders for the immediate closure of all brothels in Serruya's Lane. Regulated prostitution, for so long a feature of the Gibraltarian landscape, had come to an end.

(vii) Decampment to the *Calle Gibraltar*: the end of an era, or a two and a half kilometre shift northwards?

One final question remains: what happened to the prostitutes of Serruya's Lane? The answer is simple: they left their bordellos and decamped to the *Calle Gibraltar* across the border in La Linea, an area synonymous with street-walkers and brothels to this very day.[34] There they continued servicing British military personnel for many decades, unhindered by the demands and

---

[34] There were, of course, one or two exceptions. John David Stewart, author of the largely anti-Gibraltarian history *Gibraltar: the Keystone*, for example, relates the 'tale of Gibraltar's solitary surviving whore.' This was a Gibraltar-born prostitute who had left for Spain in 1922, but who decided to return back to her hometown several decades later. 'Well over fifty,' Stewart rather relishingly writes, 'all passion spent, this poor woman showed her British passport, claimed residence and returned to the Rock, leaving her disappointments behind in La Linea.' Unfortunately (or fortunately, from the old lady's perspective) her arrival back on the Rock coincided with the days when large NATO warships used to regularly visit Gibraltar, bringing with them large contingents of sex-starved sailors looking for women. 'Since [prostitutes]… were not to be found [in Gibraltar],' Stewart takes up the story for us once again, 'and the frontier was closed, this single superannuated whore… put herself back in circulation. Without proper premises, she used to take her occasional suitors up the mountain… and entertain them in the roadside thickets.' This situation continued for a while until the lady in question was finally caught *in flagrante* by the local police and charged with indecent exposure. 'That,' Stewart archly concludes, 'was the end of her public career, and, so far as I know, the belated end of prostitution in Gibraltar.' See John David Stewart, *Gibraltar: the Keystone* (1967), pp. 214-216.

impositions of state regulationism. This, doubtless, was one of
the ironies of Smith-Dorrien's high-minded decision: by pushing
prostitution across the border, he had effectively condemned it
to an unlicensed and thoroughly squalid future, one thoroughly
divorced from the world of doctors and enforced medical
treatment. It was also ironical that it was here in Spain,
pushed beyond the pale as it were, that the prostitutes of
Serruya's Lane finally acquired the representative voice that
had been denied to them for so long. For this we must thank
Jean Genet, the legendary French dramatist whose theatrical
works revolutionised the face of twentieth-century drama and
who as a young man prostituted himself with English soldiers
in the area in and around the *Calle Gibraltar*. Although foreign
and homosexual – and although he only lived in La Linea for
a short while – Genet manages to memorialise the experience
of the Hispano-Gibraltarian prostitute in a way that no archival
records can:

> My path was that of all beggars and, like them, I was to
> know Gibraltar. At night the erotic mass of the Rock,
> filled, thronged, with soldiers and sleeping cannons, drove
> me wild. I lived in the village of Linea, which is simply
> one big brothel, and there I began the period of tin cans.
> All the beggars in the world – I've seen the like in Central
> Europe and in France – have one or more white tin cans
> (which contain peas or stew) to which they add a wire
> handle. They go along the roads and railroad tracks with
> these cans hanging from the shoulder. I got my first one
> in Linea. It was new. I had picked it out of a garbage can
> where someone had thrown it the night before. Its metal
> was gleaming. I pressed down the sheared edges with a

stone so that they wouldn't cut, and I went to the barbed
wire of Gibraltar to pick up the leftovers of the English
soldiers. In that way I abased myself further. I no longer
begged for money but for scraps of food. To which was
added the shame of begging them from soldiers. I would
feel unworthy if some soldier's good looks or the potency
of his uniform excited me. At night, I tried to sell myself
to them, and I succeeded, thanks to the darkness of the
narrow streets.[35]

---

[35] Jean Genet, *The Thief's Journal*, translated by Bernard Frechtman (1949;
reprinted 1987), p. 79.

'The Mongrel Race called Rock Scorpions'

(i) Introduction

It was 1984, and I was having a drink with two friends at a local bar. We had just taken part in the *Gibraltar international half-marathon*, that most inaptly named of athletic competitions, and we were celebrating the achievement by having a shandy at a small, thickly-carpeted wine bar down on Cornwall's Parade. Like most Gibraltarian watering-holes on a Sunday evening, the place was relatively empty – with only ourselves, an old Moroccan and a bored English barmaid sat near the counter. While we discussed mid-race tactics and pollution fumes in Dudley Ward tunnel, a group of about fifteen British squaddies walked in, staggering from side to side and stinking of booze. Being the most pragmatic among the three of us, I suggested we get up and go somewhere else, but M. and E., being slightly older and therefore, in the language of Gibraltarian street slang, *mas pasota*, said that they had no intention of going anywhere just because of a few drunk 'giris.'[1] Some moments then passed. From the other side of the bar, the sound of drunken laughter mingled with talk about 'cocks' and 'cunts' and 'fannies', all but killing off the rhythm of our previous conversation. Then, quite suddenly: 'Ere. Anif yer lot want ter buy us ah lager n' lime, then?' Looking up, we saw a corpulent man wearing a Leeds United shirt, about six foot two and with a suspiciously flushed face, his tattooed knuckles protruding around a pint glass containing some fluorescent green liquid. 'Excuse me?' I just about managed to whisper

---

[1] Colloquial Spanish word for 'Englishmen.'

after looking at my eighteen-year old friends and seeing that
they were as puzzled as I was. 'Do you mind repeating that?'
'Ah says yer wanna bui'off meh ah lager n' lime?' the drunken
six-footer once again said, a hint of irritation already thickening
his voice. Again, the same blank looks of incomprehension on
our part. Again, the same shrugs and nervous glances into our
half-pint glasses. At this point the Englishman shakes his
head and lets a little air escape his lips - like he doesn't know
why he is bothering, like he doesn't know what possessed him
to approach us little colonials in the first place. Then, turning
around to his friends, with an expression of the utmost contempt
stamped across his freckled face, he says two words which I
had never heard in conjunction before, but which, judging
from the sneering tone he employed and the laughter that
greeted them from the other side of the bar, I am destined
never to forget as long as I live: *'Fucking spicks.'*

* * *

Allow me to indulge in a little time travelling now and take
you forward to the year 1999. By one of those perverse
machinations of Fate, I find myself doing a PhD degree at
the University of Leeds. My subject is English Literature and
my area of speciality is anti-Spanish sentiment in early modern
writing. It is a relatively unexplored area and I am spending
a lot of time looking at microfilms in the basement floor of
the Brotherton University Library. To uncover the sort of
texts that will uphold my arguments, I have to consult the
two standard books of bibliographic reference for the early
modern specialist, the *English Short Title Catalogue* and the
Donald Wing manual. Because these two reference works list

titles alphabetically – rather than chronologically or by subject matter – I am having to go through a lot of material that is not related to my subject of research. As I do this, I discover that there are quite a number of eighteenth and nineteenth-century texts dealing with Gibraltar. This surprises me greatly. Like many other Gibraltarians, I had known that Byron and Thackeray had once written about Gibraltar, but I had never imagined that our Rock had also gripped the imagination of other lesser writers. My excitement is great; I feel that I am uncovering a part of our history that has lain dormant for many years. With the help of a government grant first and some corporate sponsorship later, I eventually publish my findings in the form of two anthologies - *Rock Of Empire: Literary Visions of Gibraltar, 1700-1900* in 2001, and *Writing the Rock Of Gibraltar: An Anthology of Texts, 1720-1890* in 2006. In these two anthologies, we learn, among other things, that Byron described the Rock as 'the dirtiest and most detestable spot in existence'; that Coleridge complained that the onset of the Levanter Cloud made him ill with 'a sense of suffocation' that caused his tongue 'to go furry white and his pulse quick and low'; and that George Whitefield believed that 'drunkenness was a sin that easily beset the men of Gibraltar.'… But there is something in all these writings that is conspicuous by its absence: the Gibraltarians themselves. I mention this in the introduction to *Writing the Rock of Gibraltar* itself, while discussing Thackeray's description of his sojourn at Gibraltar:

All this, of course, leaves us with one pressing question: where is the figure of the Gibraltarian among all this? To this there can only be one answer: not exactly at the forefront of things. Thackeray himself, to go no further, rhapsodises about the Sir Robert Wilsons and the Mr. Bulwers of this world and takes great delight in relating the picaresque fortunes of your Captain Smiths and Captain Browns, but never for one minute does he seem to take an iota of interest in your poor little Manuel Cardosos or your bare-headed Giovanni Schembris. The same is true of almost every other writer anthologised in this book. In their quest to ornamentalise the Gibraltarian travel experience, authors like John Galt or Samuel Taylor Coleridge repeatedly marginalise the indigenous Gibraltarians, reducing them almost to background extras in one of those gaudy Covent Garden celebrations of Empire such as James Fennell's *Lindor and Clara; or a Trip to Gibraltar* or *John Dennis's Gibraltar, or The Spanish Adventure.*[2]

In this essay I will argue that this marginalisation has been one of the most important features in our colonial history. Furthermore, I will demonstrate how our relationship with Britain has traditionally been clouded by a strong sense of anti-Gibraltarianism and how, in some ways, we are still suffering from this legacy of prejudice today. In doing so I am conscious that I will be resurrecting a largely forgotten part of 'our history. Although one or two commentators have touched upon the British disregard for the indigenous Gibraltarian population - Philip F. Herring, for example, has stated that 'British commentators of the last century ignored Gibraltar's people, who were generally seen as undeserving alien colonials, slightly more evolved, but less interesting, than the Barbary

---

[2] M. G. Sanchez, *Writing the Rock of Gibraltar: Anthology of Literary and Popular Texts, 1720-1890* (2006), p. 14.

apes'[3] - very little has been written about the British negation of Gibraltarian identity. The reasons for this, I think, have been twofold. First, there are few British historians out there who would be comfortable maintaining that their ancestors were prejudiced not just against Africans and Arabs, but also against other fellow Caucasians. Secondly, perhaps even more importantly, one must not forget that, set aside the more well-known atrocities committed under the banner of Empire, the denigration of a European Caucasian people may not seem like the most fashionable of topics. Yet anti-Gibraltarianism did exist (and what is more, exists even now) and I feel it is my duty as a Gibraltarian to bring to light the bigotry and blind prejudice that our ancestors had to endure. How else is it possible to put into context the rights and liberties that we enjoy today? If it is true, as the cultural philosopher Claire Kramsch asserted in the late 1990s, that national identity is built upon a complex interplay between cultural memory and remembered past, then it is essential that we uncover each and every last fragment of our hidden history.[4] Anything less than that would not only be an insult to our ancestors' memory; it would be a disservice to those generations of Gibraltarians still to come.

(ii) 'The Gibraltar Question' in the eighteenth and
nineteenth centuries: early imperial disagreements
and the marginalisation of the local population

Let us start off by looking at what can be termed 'the Gibraltar question' in the eighteenth and nineteenth centuries. By this I mean the long-running dispute which, almost from the signing

---

[3] Philip F. Herring, 'Toward an Historical Molly Bloom,' *English Literary History*, 45: 3, p. 502.

[4] Claire Kramsch, *Language and Culture* (1998), p. 7.

of the Treaty of Utrecht onwards, saw Britons debate Gibraltar's territorial status. Then, just like now, Englishmen were divided into two opposing camps: those who wanted to retain Gibraltar and those who wanted to cede it back to Spain. While this debate frequently wound its way into parliamentary circles – in 1782, for example, Lord Shelbourne argued that Gibraltar should be handed back to the Spanish and was told by William Pitt the Younger to 'stop dreaming' – it is in its pamphleteering applications that we are most interested here. Between the Treaty of Utrecht and the beginning of the twentieth century an extraordinarily large number of these were published, the topic of Gibraltar, it appears, never being far from Englishmen's thoughts. On the one hand there were reactionary, unashamedly imperialistic texts such as *Considerations offered upon the approaching peace,* and *upon the importance of Gibraltar to the British Empire* (1720), *Gibraltar, a bulwark of Great Britain* (1725), *National prejudice, opposed to national interest, candidly considered in the detention or yielding up of Gibraltar* (1748), *The propriety of retaining Gibraltar impartially considered* (1783), *The Past and the Future of Gibraltar* (1895). On the other we find moralistic, anti-imperialistic tracts such as *A humble proposal that may be a better defence to Gibraltar* (1731), *Reasons for giving up Gibraltar* (1749), *The Uselessness of Gibraltar* (1893) and *An Exchange for Gibraltar* (1893). The irony, as far as the Gibraltarian reader is concerned, is that none of these texts, whether for or against the idea of retaining Gibraltar, appear to show much of an interest in the local population. Again and again, we find that the Rock is focused upon from a purely strategic or economic angle, with the Gibraltarians conspicuous by their absence. Writing in

1720, for example, the vehemently anti-Catholic and anti-clerical Thomas Gordon argued that holding on to the Rock 'gives us the means of carrying a private and advantagious commerce with Spain... [and] obliges all Nations who Trade in the Mediterranean, or have Empire there, to court our Friendship, and keep Measures with us.'[5] Almost two hundred years later, in an article entitled *The Past and the Future of Gibraltar,* John Adye made pretty much the same point when he maintained that retaining Gibraltar 'would be an advantage to our trade and an annoyance to the Spaniard; and [would] enable us, without keeping so great a fleet upon that coast, with six nimble frigates lodged there to do the Spaniards more harm than by a fleet.'[6] The counter to this can be seen in tracts such as *Reasons for giving up Gibraltar* or *The Uselessness of Gibraltar,* the former claiming that Gibraltar 'is a great expense to the nation'[7] and the latter arguing that its 'possession costs us much both in money and anxiety.'[8] What is interesting to note, from our perspective, is that there is hardly any Gibraltarian presence within this spectrum of competing discourses. In fact, the only time that the Gibraltarians appear is when they are treated as an economic liability, as Arthur Griffiths did when he complained that 'the presence of some

[5] Thomas Gordon, *Considerations offered upon the approaching peace, and upon the importance of Gibraltar to the British Empire* (1720), sig. B3v.

[6] John Adye, 'The Past and the Future of Gibraltar,' *Nineteenth Century: A Monthly Review,* 38: 225, 1895, p. 818.

[7] Quoted in Robert Chambers, *The Book of Days: A Miscellany of Popular Antiquities* (1832), p. 116.

[8] William Laird Clowes, 'The Uselessness of Gibraltar,' *Fortnightly Review,* 53: 314, 1893, p. 247.

17, 000 souls over and above the militant population must obviously produce inconvenience in food supply, especially as regards *munitions de bouche.*'[9] Crucially, too, this was a view that was shared *both* by the imperialists and those who wanted to let go of the Rock. Thus, even a stalwart imperialist like Harold A. Perry could round off his arguments by conceding that 'the question of population is, however, much more serious.' For Perry, in fact, there could only be one answer to the problem: ethnic cleansing. To this end, he argues that 'the military unity of the place... [can] only be restored by some very drastic measures, such as enforced migration to some new British acquisition on either shore of the Straits.'[10]

There are some distinct parallels between then and now. Even after ODA (Overseas Development Administration) funding was stopped some years ago and Gibraltar became for all intents and purposes self-sufficient, its detractors have always taken a fiendish delight in misrepresenting it as a major economic burden to the British crown, there being nothing more damning, in the eyes of most modern Englishmen, than the cardinal sin of wasting taxpayers' money. I myself recall listening to a Radio Five phone-in several years ago, in which the Gibraltarian Chief Minister, Mr. Peter Caruana, was being berated by an angry caller who had evidently fallen for all this baseless propaganda. 'Why should Britain be maintaining you lot?' I remember the caller, a gentleman with a very pronounced northern accent, huffing and puffing his way down the line.

---

[9] Arthur Griffiths, 'The Question of Gibraltar,' *Fortnightly Review,* 71: 425, 1902, p. 840. I have already looked at Griffith's other Gibraltar-related writings in my essay 'The Great Depot for Smuggling.'

[10] Harold A. Perry, 'Gibraltar,' *MacMillan Magazine,* 58, 1888, p. 267.

'It's not like we can afford all millions of pounds that we give you, is it? The quicker we give you back to Spain, the better is all I can say.' When the combative Mr. Carauna told him, in no uncertain terms, that Gibraltar had not received a penny of UK money since the 90s, his antagonist quickly put the phone down, presumably, I would have thought, out of embarrassment at not having got his facts right.

(iii) 'English of English': Misrepresentation and the Gibraltarian non-presence

Interestingly, the issue of Gibraltarian dependency is not the only modern anti-Gibraltarian prejudice rooted in the past. Another accusation, much favoured by the Spanish and other modern-day detractors of the Rock, is that there is no indigenous population of Gibraltar as such, but that those who live on the territory are all either ex-pats or British military personnel. This, again, can be traced back to the negation of Gibraltarian identity seen in the eighteenth and nineteenth centuries. Witness, if not, the words of one James Lowry Whittle, an English journalist writing for the *Fortnightly Review* who, in an article designed to attract more Victorian tourists to the Rock, carefully explains that, while some of the inhabitants of Gibraltar may look tanned, they are in fact 'English of English, and will not admit any mixture of foreign blood.'[11] The implication is clear enough: it is not the indigenous Gibraltarian that is of any importance, but his sun-tanned English imperialistic overlord. Even a writer as ecumenically-minded and accommodating in his tastes as George Henry Borrow – whose proselytizing efforts across Europe, it will be remembered, saw

[11] James Lowry Whittle, 'Gibraltar as winter resort,' *Fortnightly Review,* 62: 636, 1897, p. 386.

him fraternise with ethnic groups as diverse as Russian peasants and Spanish gypsies – exhibits a similar negating tendency, going as far as granting citizen status only to those persons 'born at Gibraltar of English parents.'[12] Moreover, Borrow's position is closely echoed in an article in *Household Words*, the magazine which Charles Dickens almost singlehandedly wrote and edited himself. Although Dickens, in this instance, does not appear to have written the article in question, its sentiments are still very revealing for our purposes:

> The men we meet here [in Gibraltar] are not dry, brown-faced, undersized Andalusians, but plethoric, red-faced majors: no dancing-footed and Arab-blooded majos, but puff-faced privates, in white blouses, talking at the corners of streets...[13]

We are, invariably, reminded here of that strain in modern anti-Gibraltarian propaganda which seeks to discredit the Gibraltarians' right to self-determination by suggesting (somewhat idiotically, if you ask me) that there is no indigenous populate to begin with. This is the position that General Franco, a master at propagandistic manipulation within his own domains, always used to employ when speaking about Gibraltar – either by inferring that the Rock was populated mainly by military personnel or by suggesting, as the Spaniards did before the UN in 1963, that the original population of Gibraltar had migrated to San Roque in Spain shortly after the British take-over of 1704. It is also – somewhat ironically - the stance adopted by Labour's spindoctors in 2001/2 when

---

[12] See *Writing the Rock of Gibraltar*, p. 84.

[13] Anonymous, 'Gib,' *Household Words Conducted by Charles Dickens,* 19: 455, 1858, p. 43

Tony Blair was trying to form an Anglo-Italo-Hispanic bulwark that would counter the all-powerful Franco-German alliance in Europe. In those days the Blair administration had somehow convinced itself that the only way to bring the Spaniards on board was by ceding Gibraltar back to them. Hand in hand with this went an anti-Gibraltarian smear campaign designed to persuade the British public that the UK would be better off without the Rock. Among the more unashamed pieces of Blairite spindoctoring that appeared back then was the article 'Go Ape on the Rock,' by *The Daily Mirror* journalist Brian Reade. A rambling, highly inflammatory piece of vitriol, it attempted to convey the impression that Gibraltar was 'a sort of EastEnders-on-Med,' full of 'expatriates[,]… woeful, wizened-up prunes… and tax-dodgers who moved to the offshore-haven to pay less dues on investments, pick up their UK state pensions, vote Tory every four years, and brag about how special the place is because they use Sterling, have red phone boxes, and 'don't have to speak Dago.' '[14] Needless to say, Reade did not mention anything about the native Gibraltarians in his article.

(iv) 'A superfluous adjunct': the negation of Gibraltarian identity set in its imperial context

What has caused this deliberate negation of the Gibraltarian identity? In the eighteenth, nineteenth and first half of the twentieth centuries at least, the answer was very simple: Gibraltarians didn't matter. They were seen by the British as a superfluous adjunct, one of those rather troublesome burdens that necessarily came with Empire. 'The civilian in Gib,' accordingly wrote Walter Thornbury in 1860, 'seems a mere tolerated accident, and the young military blood delights to

---

[14] Brian Reade, 'Go Ape on the Rock,' *Daily Mirror,* 7 February, 2002.

tell you that, in case of war or revolt, the government, to whom nearly all the houses and shops belong, would sweep them away at one swoop, and plant fresh batteries upon their sites.'[15] David Lambert, one of the few modern British scholars to have recognised this culture of negation, sums up what was happening in his article 'As solid as the Rock? Place, belonging and the local appropriation of imperial discourse in Gibraltar':

> Another consequence [of Empire] has been that the non-military population has been marginalized consistently, hidden by the looming shadow of the Rock. Gibraltar, after all, has never just been a 'natural fortress, it has also been a landscape of home and settlement, a contact zone as much as a *lieu de memoire.* The effacement of the indigenous populations is a common feature of imperial discourse, tied to ideas of *terra nullius* and projects of clearance and settlement. Similarly, the reduction of Gibraltar to 'the Rock' effaces its human geographies and histories, aside from the endeavours of transient soldiers. It becomes a place through which British troops pass and perform heroic deeds, rather than a place of continuing residence.[16]

This is nowhere more evident than in guidebooks and other forms of travel writing. Time and again, we find that Gibraltarians are absent from their pages, as if they didn't

---

[15] Walter Thornbury, *Life in Spain* (1860), pp. 310-311.

[16] 'David Lambert, 'As solid as the Rock? Place, belonging and the local appropriation of imperial discourse in Gibraltar,' *Transactions of the Institute of British Geographers,* 30: 2, 2005, p. 212.

exist or were of no interest to anybody. In Richard Ford's bestselling *A Handbook for Travellers in Spain and readers at home* (1845), for example, nothing is mentioned about the local population in the course of close to twenty pages devoted to Gibraltar – other than that they live in airless, vermin-infested houses 'fit only for salamanders and scorpions, as those born in the Rock are called.'[17] A similarly pejorative angle can be encountered in Major George James Gilbard's *A popular history of Gibraltar, its institutions and its neighbourhood on both sides of the straits,* a locally-published guidebook whose only word on the civilian population is to declare that the British have no interest in 'nationalising the aborigines [of Gibraltar], whether men or monkeys.'[18] Likewise, Captain Frederick Sayer, who worked as a civil magistrate in the colony during the 1860s, dismisses the entire population by claiming that '[t]he natives are for the most part idle, dissolute, and phlegmatic.'[19] Even more anti-Gibraltarianism, it has to be said, can be seen in *The Land of the Castanet: Spanish Sketches* (1896), an American travelogue that appeared just before the Spanish-American war of 1898.

> One forgets what a thoroughly detestable fellow the *rock scorpion* is… The Spaniard despises the natives of 'Gib', the Englishman scorns them, the stranger distrusts them, yet there are some twenty thousand of them, living there

---

[17] Richard Ford, *A Handbook for Travellers in Spain and Readers at Home,* vol. 2 (1845; reprinted 1966), p. 513.

[18] Quoted in Andrew Gibson's *Joyces Revenge: History, politics and aesthetics in Ulysses* (2002), p. 259.

[19] Frederick Sayer, *The History of Gibraltar and of its Political Relation to Events in Europe* (1862), p. 460.

under martial rule, their actions regulated, their laws
made and executed by a foreign power. A very good thing
for them, too, as they are made to behave themselves,
and keep themselves - or at least their streets - clean...[20]

Philip F. Herring has highlighted the racist undertones behind
these sort of writings. In analysing the language of *The Travellers
Hand book for Gibraltar by an old Inhabitant* (1844), he suggests
that it 'describes... views and other places of interest in Gibraltar,
but... typical of such guides... leaves us ignorant of peoples'
lives.'[21] The same can be said about the artists of the period.
George Carter, John Singleton Copley, Richard Paton, John Keyse
Sherwin, Clarkson Stanfield, John Trumbull, Thomas Whitcombe,
Joseph Wright of Derby:[22] all of these artists have painted scenes
from Gibraltar's past, but not a single one of them saw fit to
represent the native Gibraltarian.[23] Does this mean, then, that
there are absolutely no references to Gibraltarians in the literature
and art of the eighteenth and nineteenth centuries? That
Gibraltarians have been marginalised to the point of non-existence?
Charles Caruana, one of the few native commentators to have

---

[20] Hobart Chatfield-Taylor, *The Land of the Castanet: Spanish Sketches* (1896),
p. 238.

[21] 'Toward an Historical Molly Bloom,' p. 505.

[22] For a more complete list of artists that have painted Gibraltar, see *Writing
the Rock of Gibraltar,* pp. 257-259.

[23] There is a further irony to be noted here, one which modern-day Gibraltarians,
with their deep-seated anti-Spanish biases, may not necessarily appreciate.
And that is that, for all our professed detestation of all things Iberian, it is
only Spanish writers like Benito Perez Galdos or Vicente Blasco Ibáñez who
have written extensively about the local Gibraltarian population. See *Writing
the Rock of Gibraltar,* pp. 234-345.

grappled with these issues, suggests in his insightful study of local Catholicism *Rock Under a Cloud* that Gibraltarians were not represented until a much later period in time:

> Many authors have written about the Rock from the viewpoint of its flora and fauna, its fortifications and sieges, its military role. Some have made an occasional reference to its civilian population, though for at least one author Gibraltar consisted solely of British army officers and their families. Writers in more recent times have indeed recognised the existence of civilians upon the Rock, some being inclined to look upon them as hybrids, bastards, smugglers, *panzistas,* people with no identity or culture of their own, people without a history.[24]

Bishop Caruana is, of course, right in recognising that Gibraltarians have been vilified by different generations of British writers – but it is not strictly true to claim that the Rock's inhabitants were a non-presence in all early imperial writing. Although attitudes to the local populace have historically been very dismissive, there has also existed a parallel tendency - symptomatic, perhaps, of the Victorian delight in voyeuring subjugated nations - to present Gibraltar and its population as something of an anthropological curiosity. For this to happen effectively, the inhabitants of Gibraltar had to be denied any individuality and turned into an amusing array of national stereotypes:

> It is a curious sight at evening this thronged street, with the people, in a hundred different costumes, bustling to and fro under the coarse flare of the lamps; swarthy

---

[24] Charles Caruana, *Rock Under A Cloud* (1989), p. v.

Moors, in white or crimson robes; dark Spanish smugglers
in tufted hats, with gay silk handkerchiefs round their
heads; fuddled seamen from men-of-war, or merchantmen;
porters, Galician or Genoese...[25]

Not only Thackeray in this passage, but Twain, Disraeli,
Borrow and a whole host of other lesser known writers also
exoticise the Gibraltarian populace. In doing so they are
reducing the civilian inhabitants almost to the status of
objects on display, transforming them into a human freak
show for the amusement and delight of the reader back
home. We are reminded here of the cultural philosopher
Edward Said and the dehumanising exoticism which in his
view underpins European representations of the Orient.
According to Said, the exotic provides a 'vision of reality
whose structure promote[s] the difference between the familiar
and the strange'[26] – usually with the aim of establishing
primacy over the culturally unknown 'other.' This deliberate
exoticisation of locale and population, I believe, repeatedly
surfaces in British nineteenth-century descriptions of
Gibraltar – sometimes to the point of ridiculousness.
'Everything seemed so novel,' for example wrote James Bell
Forsyth about his first day on the Rock in 1861, 'that
you at once felt you had, in reality, entered the portals of
the East.'[27] A similarly exaggerated perspective can be
encountered in the anonymous article 'Gibraltar, its town
and fortifications':

[25] *Writing the Rock of Gibraltar*, p. 113.

[26] Edward Said, *Orientalism* (1978), p. 234.

[27] James Bell Forsyth, *A Few Months in the East* (1861), p. 13.

While passing through the market-place... I was much interested in observing the different color, and character, and costume of the crowds congregated together... Here you meet the grave, stately Moor from Barbary, and his old enemy the Spaniard, each with his distinctive countenance, bearing and attire. The Jew and the Greek jostle each other, and busily ply their different avocations in peace and amity... Here you see the dark-eyed Spanish senorita with her mantilla and her fan; there the *contrabandistas,* ready for any deed of darkness and daring. Genoese and Africans, English soldiers in their red coats, and jolly tars in their blue jackets, meet you at every turn... Indeed, the whole population seemed a medley of the most motley description, the town being peopled... by stragglers and strangers from Patagonia to Poland.[28]

No less dramatic is the view of Gibraltar presented in *The Mediterranean, its Storied Cities and Venerable Ruins* (1902). According to its authors, Gibraltar was 'a conflux of nations, a mart of races, an Exchange for all the multitudinous varieties of the human product':

Tall, stately, slow-pacing Moors from the north-west coast; white-turbaned Turks from the eastern gate of the Mediterranean; thick-lipped and woolly-headed negroids from the African interior; quick-eyed, gesticulating Levantine Greeks; gabardined Jews and black-wimpled Jewesses; Spanish smugglers, and Spanish sailors, 'rock-scorpions,' and red-coated English soldiers – all these

---

[28] Anonymous, 'Gibraltar, its town and fortifications,' *The National Magazine,* 12, 1858, p. 404.

compose, without completing, the motley moving crowd that throngs the main street of Gibraltar in the forenoon, and gathers densest of all in the market near Commercial Square.[29]

This is pure theatre, the conscious and sensationalised rendering of the local citizenry into a compendium of national stereotypes. Somehow we are reminded of one of those early monochrome newsreels, in which reed-skirted dancing women or javelin-throwing warriors are paraded for the benefit of the British viewer. In fact, it is no coincidence that these Gibraltarian ethnological snapshots are frequently presented as a form of entertainment. For Nathaniel Armstrong Wells 'the most *amusing* sight in Gibraltar is the principal street, filled, as it is with an infinitely varied population.'[30] Coleridge, similarly, recounts how he had walked through Gibraltar's streets in a state of great hilarity, 'my poor nose paying for the *amusement* of my eyes.'[31] Likewise, Alexander Slidell Mackenzie, author of the travelogue *A Year in Spain*, admits that '[t]hough this mixed society [of Gibraltar's] must be detestable to the permanent inhabitant, it offers a singular and *amusing* study to the stranger.'[32]

Rather surprisingly, too, there are one or two texts in which we find an individualised Gibraltarian presence. What is not

---

[29] T. G. Bonney, E. A. R. Ball et al, *The Mediterranean, its Storied Cities and Venerable Ruins* (1902; reprinted 2005), p. 10.

[30] Nathaniel Armstrong Wells, *The Picturesque Antiquities of Spain* (1846), p. 306.

[31] *Writing the Rock of Gibraltar*, p. 227.

[32] Alexander Slidell Mackenzie, *A Year in Spain* (1831), p. 258.

so surprising, perhaps, is that these individual Gibraltarians are portrayed in a manner which reinforces Andrew Gibson's assertion that in 'the late nineteenth century, discourses on Gibraltar were … likely to be explicitly racist.'[33] Typical of such attitudes is the anonymous short story 'The Rock Scorpions,' which appeared in the anthological *Omnibus of Adventure* (1930). In its pages we encounter the good Captain Hindhaugh, an Englishman in charge of a steamer lying alongside Gibraltar. Finding himself importuned by 'one of the natives,' Hindhaugh looks 'about for something to throw at the visitor' and then 'addresse[s] the man as one would an ill-conditioned dog.'[34] A similar deprecatory angle can be found in R. D. Clephane's *Rough and Smooth: A Tale of our Times* (1863). Although a likeable chap in most of his dealings, Colonel Tom Clinton, one of the novel's main protagonists, cannot stop himself railing at one point against 'a slovenly waiter… who belonged to the mongrel race ycleped[35] *Rock Scorpions,* and spoke the two languages, to which he possessed a sort of equal right, with similar imperfectness.'[36] Even more damning colonialism, if anything, can be seen in *The Sweet South: Impressions of Spain,* a rambling autobiographical travelogue published in 1856 by the infelicitously named

---

[33] *Joyces Revenge: History, politics and aesthetics in Ulysses*, p. 259. It is no coincidence that both Gibson and Herring, two of the small group of modern scholars to have written about the colonial negation of the Gibraltarian identity, have done so while investigating Joyce's use of Gibraltarian locale in Ulysses. From this we can safely assume that if Molly Bloom had not resided in Gibraltar, their articles would almost certainly have never been written.

[34] *The Omnibus of Adventure,* vol. 2, edited by John Grove (1930), p. 796.

[35] 'Called' (Archaic).

[36] R. D. Clephane, *Rough and Smooth: A Tale of our Times* (1863), p. 387

Emmeline Charlotte E. Stuart Wortley. Her account of meeting
a Gibraltarian in Lyon is so extraordinarily dismissive that I
have not been able to resist quoting from it at length:

> Speaking of Rock Scorpions, I will relate a little adventure
> thereupon that once happened to us at Lyon... I had ordered
> some fine Lyon silks to be brought to the hotel where I was
> staying, and they accordingly arrived; and who began immediately
> talking a kind of severely-fractured English, of which
> accomplishment he seemed very proud. Of what country could
> he be? He looked as unlike a Frenchman as an Englishman?
>
> 'Are you an Italian?'
>
> 'No, no.'
>
> 'A Spaniard?'
>
> 'No, madam: British. I British, and British spikes.
> Yes, I spikes quite clear.'
>
> 'But your English is rather broken, allow me to say.
> Surely you are not an Englishman?' we cried, in wonder
> at the contused language he spoke in: where could he
> have lived in all his British born days?
>
> 'Yes, yes,' he hastily replied, 'and not broken moshe my
> Englands is at all.' (This was, indeed, a mistake; for it
> suffered from severe compound fractures at the very least).
> 'I complete Britisherman self, though I had not been
> parleying Englishes moshe late: far away from my contree:
> but I real right down Britisherman.'
>
> 'Really?'

'Yes; is real Rock Scorpion, now you knows quite well.'

I had never heard of such a thing in my life, and looked, of course, much puzzled. 'Rock Scorpion?'

'Yes, madame. All true dat. Born on de Rock – on de great Rock itself, be sure.'

A passing thought probably crossed the minds of his hearers that the youth was distraught.

'Rock! In the name of Patience, what rock on earth do you mean, man?'

'Why de Rock, de great Rock. I native ov Gib, madame: certain: Gib....'

Gibraltar came then, like a bursting shell, to enlighten us or to confound us. How could we be so stupid, as not to know that Gib was Gibraltar, as well as that that was the Rock, and that Rock Scorpions are Gibraltese, or Gibese, or Gibbers, or Happy Rockers, and all the rest of it. This, and much more, that bursting shell very loudly and fiercely came to express; and how came we not to recognize our countryman instanter, by his beautiful Englishees, and air, and features?[37]

(v) 'Spanish in habits, connections, family predilections, language and religion:' the imposition of 'Spanishness' and the negation of Gibraltarian identity

It is no coincidence that both Wortley and Clephane highlight the Gibraltarian inability to speak fluent English. Since

---

[37] Emmeline Charlotte E. Stuart Wortley, *The Sweet South: Impressions of Spain* (1856), p. 123.

time immemorial, notions of national identity have come inextricably woven with language, its subtly graded variations acting as a kind of differentiating device which separates those who belong to a national collective from those who do not. As Martin Reisigl succinctly writes, 'linguistic devices are employed to construct national sameness... on the one hand, and differences from other national collectives on the other.'[38] To speak 'proper' English, therefore, is to be English; just as not to speak the language 'properly' is a sure indicator of foreignness. What is interesting in this case is that both Wortley and Clephane are *amused* at seeing Gibraltarians attempting to speak English. Not only are the Gibraltarians 'a mongrel race' with no claim to British nationality, they are also to be ridiculed for speaking the language so badly. John Esaias Warren, author of the travelogue *Vagamundo; or, the Attache in Spain* (1851), indulges in such jingoistic jesting when describing a Gibraltarian by the name of Pascual in his narrative of Spanish travels:

> Being a 'rock-scorpion,' his knowledge of the English language was extremely imperfect... [and]... he mangled the innocent words of the noble Anglo-Saxon tongue.... There was something about the clown that pleased us.[39]

There are countless examples of such jingoism in the literature of the period. When, in 1811, a travelling Englishman attended a performance at Gibraltar's only theatre, he could not help hiding his amusement when 'one of the performers,

---

[38] Martin Reisigl, *Discourse and Discrimination: Rhetorics of Racism and Antisemitism* (2000), p. 43.

[39] John Esaias Warren, *Vagamundo; or, the Attache in Spain* (1851), pp. 137-139.

on his benefit night, concluded his address with a wish to have the attendance of *Ladis* and *Gentilmin*.'[40] Nearly a hundred years later, Thomas Lister, a visiting English journalist commissioned to write an article on the Calpe Hunt, thought that it was 'amusing' to see 'a native of the Rock... [who]... wishes to be thought English.'[41]

So, if the Gibraltarians are not British, what exactly are they then? To the imperialist mind the answer was obvious: they were Spanish down to the very depths of their being. This line of thinking has become yet another of those commonplaces of anti-Gibraltarian discourse and deserves to be looked at for a few moments. Robert Gardiner, one of the most notoriously anti-Gibraltarian governors employed by Whitehall, took great pleasure in maintaining that the civilians were 'Spanish in habits, connections, family predilections, language and religion, as on the day on which Gibraltar was ceded.'[42] Archibald Hunter, his no less bigoted successor, followed a similar tack by arguing that 'English is no better spoken here in general than by Kaffir rickshaw men in Durban, and nothing like so well as by a donkey boy at Suez or Cairo.'[43] A comparable line of reasoning was also propagated by the novelist Anthony Burgess, whose own Catholic and working-class background did not stop him from launching a scathing attack on the Rock's inhabitants.

---

[40] Anonymous, 'An Interesting Account of the present state of Gibraltar,' *Tradesman or Commercial magazine,* 7: 39, 1811, p. 208.

[41] Thomas Lister, 'Hunting at Gibraltar,' *Nineteenth Century: A Monthly Review,* 27: 158, 1890, p. 633.

[42] See William Jackson, *The Rock of the Gibraltarians* (1990), p. 238 footnote.

[43] Anonymous, 'Compares Gibraltar to Augean Stables,' *The New York Times,* 23 February, 1913.

Meditating upon the Gibraltarian fondness for historical events such as the 'Great Siege,' he complained that

> ...this is about the limit of their Britishness. They speak English, but only on a denotatory (sic) level which is wholly inadequate for commerce and local legislation. They know nothing of English literature and have not themselves produced either a poet or a novelist. Their primary language is Andalusian Spanish, but not even in this they have asserted a cultural identity. Their songs, dances and cuisine are Spanish.[44]

It is not surprising that the Spanish government saw fit to include Burgess's words in their *New Spanish Red book* of 1968, a revised edition of the book of the same name which had been first published some years earlier with the intention of vindicating Spain's claim to the Rock. By means of this jingoistic anti-Gibraltarian outburst, Burgess effectively validates the old Francoist claim that the civilian population of Gibraltar had no cultural identity of their own and could therefore be re-absorbed back into Spain at any given moment. Yet, even if Burgess is right and most post-war Gibraltarians spoke poor or heavily-accented English, he appears to forget that it was precisely the military establishment which forbade the Gibraltarians from developing either culturally, educationally, or politically. As David Lambert, writing about the same period in time, has pointedly declared: 'The lack of autonomy and dismissive imperial attitudes towards the resident population... [gave the]... Gibraltarian population... some of the characteristics of a colonial underclass.'[45]

---

[44] Anonymous, *New Spanish Red Book* (1968), p. 275.

[45] ' 'As solid as the Rock'? Place, belonging and the local appropriation of imperial discourse in Gibraltar,' p. 210.

(vi) 'This wretched little rock and its queer people':
gubernatorial attitudes to the Gibraltarians and the
preservation of a colonial underclass

If there is a historical moment which defines this lack of
Gibraltarian autonomy, it surely has to be the civilian evacuation
of 1940-1943, an event described as 'a defining moment in
the development of a distinct identity amongst the civilian
inhabitants of the Rock.'[46] In those days almost the entire
population of Gibraltar was relocated to London. Although
this measure was allegedly taken to protect the civilian
inhabitants, it did not escape the Gibraltarians' attention that
they were being deposited in London at the height of the
'Blitz,' at a time when 'real' British women and children were
being moved from the capital to the countryside. For many
Gibraltarians long-standing ideas about British overlordship
were shattered; for others the experience kindled a sense of
togetherness which had, perhaps, been missing in the interwar
years. What is certain is that, in each and every single case,
the evacuation caused prolonged hardship and suffering. Many
families were split up (with women and children being evacuated
first, and the men and adolescent boys following months and
even years later). The vast majority of these people were separated
from their homeland for 4-5 years, some of them not being
repatriated until as late as 1951. Along with this, there were
all those silent tales of individual suffering that history is
rarely able to record, several of which have been collated by
Tommy Finlayson in his admirable work *The Fortress Came*

---

[46] C. Grocott and G. Stockey, 'Uncontested Identity: Remembering and For-
getting the Past in the British Colony of Gibraltar,' p. 17 (www.lancs.ac.uk/
fass/eurolang/pg/phd/docs/gib_paper-07.pdf - 27-8-07).

First.[47] When I was growing up, for example, my grandmother used to recount tales of whizzing V-1s and sleepless nights in the underground shelters, her anti-British misgivings only palliated by the fact that, upon being finally repatriated in 1947, her family were allowed to travel back home in a luxury liner. On top of that, those evacuated were often derided as refugees by the native Londoners. My grandfather, who did not join my grandmother in London until ten months after her departure, once told me that he was regularly called a 'refugee' and a 'wop' by his workmates at the Rolls Royce Factory in Acton. The same thing happened when he was moved to an ammunitions depot in White City. ('They just kept on muttering things behind my back all the time,' I remember him rather sadly confiding, shaking his grey head at the memory. 'They were just constantly at it.') The irony, of course, was that the Gibraltarians had been removed from a relatively safe Gibraltar (it is computed that no more than a handful of bombs fell across the isthmus during the entire war) to be deposited in one of the most dangerous cities in the world. For me, this transforms the evacuation into a *wholesale crime against the native population* – even if the military authorities at the time were typically dismissive about the whole affair. When Miles Clifford, colonial secretary from 1942 to 1944, for example, heard that the Gibraltarians were against the idea of being forcibly evacuated, he casually wrote in his diary that he was 'getting more than a bit tired of this wretched little rock and its queer people.'[48] We can only surmise whether the pipe-smoking Mr. Clifford would have been so contemptuous of it

---

[47] Tommy Finlayson, *The Fortress Came First* (1991).

[48] Quoted in *The Rock of the Gibraltarians*, p. 123

all had he and his family been the ones evacuated to one of the most perilous places in Europe!

I believe that Clifford's remarks can be seen as a metonymy for British gubernatorial attitudes towards the local population. With the exception of one or two enlightened figures such as George Don or William Jackson (whose persistence pro-Gibraltarian politicking, it must not be forgotten, caused him to be chided on more than one occasion by Whitehall), the British military authorities have regarded the Gibraltarians as second-rate Britons and vestiges of this attitude still persist even to this day. In great part this has been due to the mechanics of imperial possession and the sense of superiority that comes from controlling an alien population. To quote the Marxist historian Ulf Hedetoft, '[s]uperiority is an integral part of the British character *per se,* owing to Britannia's centuries old colonial history and status as a world power during the whole of the 19c.'[49] Within a Gibraltarian context, I would argue, this translated into an almost visceral contempt for the local population:

> The officers of the garrison look upon the civilians, with a very few exceptions amongst the British, as immeasurably inferior to themselves [and] despise the natives of the Rock, many of whom are of great respectability and wealth, as mere 'scorpions'[50]

These words were printed in an American journal of 1839. Exactly one hundred years later, George Orwell was expressing

---

[49] Ulf Hedetoft, *British Colonialism and Modern Identity* (1985), p. 77.

[50] Anonymous, 'A Summer in Andalucia,' *The Museum of Foreign, Literature, Science and Art,* 8, 1839, p. 384.

amazement that 'even as near home as Gibraltar they [i.e. the British soldiery] walk the streets with a swaggering air which is directed at the Spanish *natives*.'[51] Although Hedetoft rightly highlights the ideological backdrop to such attitudes, it must not be forgotten that within Gibraltar itself they were encouraged, if not actively promoted, by a very deliberate series of local measures. Prominent among these were the divisive socio-spatial geographies prescribed by the ruling military establishment – most of which sought to segregate the British soldiers from the Gibraltarians and which also endowed the army with much better facilities than anything handed out to the colonials under them. Even during the late 70s and early 80s, I remember, the British military had an almost exclusive monopoly not just on the best housing, but also on the best sporting and leisure facilities, controlling the Rock's only swimming pool, its one bowling alley, eight out of its ten tennis courts and four out of its five football pitches. In addition, there was hardly any social interaction between the Gibraltarians and the British – with the bulk of the local population clustered around the old town and the majority of English personnel safely out of their way across the Rock's northern and southern extremities (around the areas known as North Front and Buena Vista/Windmill Hill). To my mind, these demographic divisions would have reinforced the sense of superiority which the military depended upon to control the civilian population. They would have also ensured that very few military personnel, other than men of the lowest rank, interbred with any of the local women. This was particularly true during the nineteenth and early twentieth centuries.

---

[51] See *Writing the Rock of Gibraltar,* pp. 262-263.

Although Joyce famously made the character of Molly Bloom the daughter of an Irish officer and a local Jewess by the name of Lunita Laredo, the fact is that such miscegenated alliances were highly unlikely.[52] Most British males would have preferred the company of prostitutes rather than the thought of courting locals, as evidenced by the cluster of brothels which sprung up around the area known as Serruya's Lane (nowadays New Passage) and which did not cease to operate until prostitution was effectively banned by Governor Smith-Dorrien in 1922. In fact, according to Herring, such Anglo-Gibraltarian unions would have been virtually impossible 'since [o]fficers would not have thought local girls their equals unless they were British.'[53]

How did the civilian community react to such a varied and extended array of inequalities and prejudices? Most of the time, it has to be said, they reacted just like any other colonial population would – accepting the status quo without any pronounced complaints. Post-colonial demagogues will tell you that this is one of the hallmarks of a colonised population: they accept the imposition of segregational policies *just because that's the way it is.* For example, during the years of my childhood and youth, no-one around me complained about the

---

[52] The unlikeliness of Molly's character is further highlighted by the lack of a Gibraltarian presence throughout the novel. 'Molly,' to quote Philip Herring, 'gives us a tourist-eye view, one nearly devoid of information about lives of her parents or other Gibraltarians.' 'Toward an Historical Molly Bloom,' p. 502. The same point is made by Sue Vice, who notes how '[s]muggling, prostitution, [and] the ghettoizing of different groups of people' are 'conspicuous by their absence' in the novel. See 'The Construction of Femininity in Ulysses and Under the Volcano: A Bakhtinian Analysis of the late draft version,' *Joyce/ Lowry: Critical Perspectives,* ed. Patrick A McCarthy (1997), p. 103.

[53] 'Toward an Historical Molly Bloom,' p. 515.

disparity between the MOD's leisure facilities and our own –
even though now, with the benefit of hindsight, everyone
recognises just how unfair the set-up really was. Yet it would
be a mistake to see the Gibraltarians as the passive or unwitting
accomplices of a subjugating imperialist order. Grievances did
occasionally give way to social unrest, as happened during the
1850s and later throughout the 1890s.[54] Likewise, when
tyrannous governors such as Sir Robert Gardiner or Sir
Archibald Hunter tried to oppress the population with their
whimsical rulings, concerted lobbying by the Gibraltarian
mercantile classes usually succeeded in either getting these
governors replaced or given a good rap on the knuckles by
Whitehall. Also – more importantly than any of all this -
great advances in political liberty and individual freedom were
made just after the second world war, a period during which
the Gibraltarian statesmen Sir Peter Isola and Sir Joshua
Hassan engaged and then successfully repelled the double threat
posed by a revitalised Francoist Spain and a war-weary Britain
intent on following a path of imperialistic self-destruction.[55]

(vii) Modern British attitudes to Gibraltar: imperialistic hangover or politically-orientated spindoctoring?

Since those days, of course, Gibraltarians have achieved a
considerable degree of internal autonomy and have largely
shaken off the colonial tag. Nowadays, Gibraltarian children

---

[54] Tito Benday, *The Gibraltar Police* (1980), pp. 17-20. See, also, Miles
Taylor's 'The 1848 Revolutions and the British Empire,' *Past and Present*,
166, 2000, p. 176.

[55] For Gibraltar's political and constitutional development in the twentieth
century, see Joseph J. Garcia's *Gibraltar: the Making of a People* (1994).

follow the UK national curriculum, conduct their lessons in English and attend higher education institutions in the UK. Yet – herein lies the rub – there are still a substantial number of British commentators who persist in questioning our right to a British Gibraltarian identity. In 2004, for example, the *Daily Mirror* journalist Anna Smith, whose knowledge of Gibraltar it appears was roughly equal to that of her colleague Brian Reade, wrote that Gibraltarians were 'as Spanish as a dish of paella.'[56] Even more offensive, perhaps, were the comments made by Peter Preston in *The Guardian,* a newspaper widely perceived as something of a rubber stamp to Blair's Europeanist ventures. In language that could have almost been lifted straight from a nineteenth-century handbook of gubernatorial practice, Mr. Preston wrote that that 'the people of Gibraltar must be told what's good for them' and that 'they couldn't raise two fingers to the wishes of the British majority.' He then questioned the Gibraltarians' right to British nationality, arguing that this was 'a slightly complex concept in a distant sub-colony largely populated by the descendants of Italians, Greek and Maltese.'[57] Many Gibraltarians, not surprisingly, resented being described as 'the descendants of Italians, Greek and Maltese.' They could not believe how in today's prevailing climate of political correctness, in which any form of discrimination against ethnic minorities is expressly frowned upon, they themselves could have been subject to such racist vilification. I myself wrote a letter to *The Guardian* newspaper at the time, in which I asked Mr. Preston if he

[56] Anna Smith, 'Rock off, Britain,' *Daily Mirror,* August 8, 2004.

[57] Peter Preston, 'The People of the Rock Must be told what's good for them,' *The Guardian,* 25 March, 2002.

would have dared to describe modern British Asians as no
more than 'the descendants of Bangladeshi, Pakistanis or
Nepalese' - but, predictably enough, the piece never got
published. The general feeling among politicians and academics
in Gibraltar was that, being white and Caucasian and actually
proud of their Britishness, they were seen as a more permissible
target than anybody else. One is reminded in this sense of the
current media backlash against Poles and other Eastern
Europeans. While no-one would dare question the rights of
Britain's Asian or African communities, the Eastern Europeans
are persistently vilified by the UK tabloid press.[58]

It could, of course, be argued that there are residual political
motives behind these sporadic anti-Gibraltarian outbursts, but
I think that this explanation only provides us with half the
picture. As I have tried to demonstrate during this course of
this article, racist discourses have long since underpropped
British attitudes to Gibraltar and I think that it would be
extremely naïve to read Preston's ethnological aspersions divorced
from this context. In fact, according to the cultural
anthropologist Gareth Stanton, 'racist attitudes survive to the
present day, with many Metropolitan British migrants and
military personnel viewing the 'Gibbos' as no more 'than English-
speaking spicks.' '[59] If this is the case, then it is very ironical
- given the way far-right political groups such as the National
Front or the Ulster Nationalist Party appropriate the discourse

---

[58] See, for example, 'The superloo where Polish Migrants are fighting to
spend the night,' *The Daily Mail*, 4 May, 2007; 'British Workers denied jobs
because they can't speak Polish,' *The Daily Mail*, 19 June, 2007.

[59] Gareth Stanton, 'Military Rock: a mis-anthroplogy,' *Cultural Studies*, 10,
1996, p. 280.

of 'British Gibraltar' to suit their own nationalistic ends. It is almost as if we are dealing with some kind of ideological schizophrenia, in which there is a pronounced bifurcation between the way Britons represent Gibraltar to other Britons and the way they view the Gibraltarians for themselves.[60]

But is Gareth Stanton right? Are Gibraltarians still looked down upon by a sizeable percentage of the migrant British population? Even if he is wrong and most British people do not share such attitudes, it is clear that there will always be one or two bigots who will classify Gibraltarians as 'spicks', 'dagoes' or 'wops' no matter what. To understand why this is happening, I feel, we need to take into account not only the *superior-rising* mechanics of imperialist discourse, but also other deeply-inculcated British prejudices. Prominent among these is a factor that most modern commentators on the topic of Gibraltarian identity, being British, have tended to ignore: the Protestant proclivity to marginalise and look down upon southern Catholic Europeans. Essentially, this attitude dates back to the time of the English Reformation, a period which saw Catholic Southern Europeans and Protestant Englishmen divided into two self-excluding, ideological poles.[61] Out of this dualism evolved a whole range discourses which sought to reaffirm the primacy of the North European Briton over the South European Catholic. Religion, exegesis, millenarianism: these and other key discursive areas were

---

[60] See, for example, 'The Big Issue: Don't let Spanish grab share of Gibraltar,' *The Sun*, 18 July, 2002; 'Rock On,' *The Sun*, Nov 8, 2002.

[61] See, for example, John Bale's *The Image of bothe churches* (Antwerp, 1548), part 2, sig. I1ᵛ. Bale's text is divided into three parts, each with separate title-page and signatures.

appropriated by different theoreticians and apologists of empire to underprop the inequalities of imperialist discourse as much as to smugly rationalise Britain's position of European hegemony. Well into the eighteenth century, for example, it was not uncommon for Englishmen to invoke a biblically-inspired supposition which maintained that Spaniards and Italians were descended from Japthet's son Tubal, one of the supposedly impurer genealogical lines stemming from Noah.[62] Samuel Taylor Coleridge, passing through Gibraltar on his way to Malta at the beginning of the nineteenth century, must have consciously or subconsciously imbibed some of these prejudices for him to describe the Rock's Spanish-speaking inhabitants as 'dirty dogs' and 'a degraded race that dishonor Christianity.'[63]

Coleridge entered those words into his journal in 1805, at a time when it was still possible to use exegesis and scriptural parallelisms to buttress one's understanding of the world. With the advent of Darwinism and its insistence on the primacy of the genetics,[64] however, there was a shift from pseudo-religion to pseudo-science as the preferred dialectical tool for the rationalisation of Empire. A case in point is William McDougall's *The Group Mind* (1920), a highly influential study which placed the 'homo mediterraneus' below the north European

---

[62] I have an engraving at home entitled *The Manner how the Whole Earth was Peopled By Noah and his Descendants after the Flood* (1749) which presents these very same ideas in diagrammatical format.

[63] See *Writing the Rock of Gibraltar*, pp. 227-229. That Coleridge, a Unitarian minister as well as an avowed Pantisocratist, should have held such pronounced racist opinions, I believe, only shows how strongly ideas of imperial overlordship and manifest destiny had been inculcated into the nineteenth-century Englishman's psyche.

[64] Charles Darwin, *The Descent of Man* (1871), vol. 1, p. 201.

Aryan (although, of course, above the 'homo africanus') on pseudo-scientific craniometrical grounds. Giving expression to what many of his Anglo-Saxon contemporaries thought, McDougall came to the conclusion that Mediterranean man 'differs from the northern or European type in having less independence and initiative, [and] a greater tendency to rely upon and seek guidance from authority.'[65] Echoes of this attitude, I believe, can be seen in a text written more or less around the same time, the autobiographical confessions of the notorious occultist and disciple of the black arts Aleister Crowley:

> We went on the next day to Gibraltar. It did not take us long to find out that we had left freedom behind us. It was hot; the Levanter was blowing and taking all the marrow out of one's bones. I was utterly tired: I sat down. I was perceived by a rock scorpion... as they call the natives of the fortress, a detestable and despicable breed, which reminds one quite unreasonably of the Eurasian...[66]

Do these attitudes survive today, we need to ask ourselves again. Are we still regarded as 'a detestable and despicable breed' behind our backs, as Gareth Stanton's research appears to indicate? It is a highly debatable point and one that I will only deal with briefly before ending this article. First and foremost, it has to be noted that Stanton was writing eleven years ago in 1996 and that, for a belatedly emancipated colonial territory such as Gibraltar, a lot can change within such a compressed time scale. Certainly, it is true that Gibraltarians

---

[65] William McDougall, *The Group Mind* (1920), p. 124.

[66] Aleister Crowley, *The Confessions of Aleister Crowley* (1929; reprinted 1969) p. 586.

were often racially abused by the British military in the 1970s and 1980s, and that racist attitudes still break out, rather like pus seeping from a badly-cured boil, from time to time in the English mainstream press. On the other hand, there is very little evidence that Gibraltarians are currently suffering from such pejorative attitudes in their own homeland. In no small way, I think, this has been due to the British government's decision to pull out the resident British battalion in 1991 and have them replaced by the Royal Gibraltar regiment. Although this was a purely political maneouvre that failed to take into account the subsequent impact upon the local Gibraltarian economy - the fortress, as usual, *did come first* – it has had a generally beneficial effect on Anglo-Gibraltarian relations by (a) depriving non-military English residents of pre-existing social networks and forcing them to interact more meaningfully with the locals and (b) breaking down those divisive geographies of space which kept the British soldiery and the local population apart. Also, in a bid to bring its numbers to an acceptable level, the Royal Gibraltar regiment was forced to recruit from English regiments, thereby throwing British and Gibraltarian soldiers side by side for the first time in many years. The results of this conflation, I believe, have been nothing short of remarkable. Just as a 'nigger' is only a 'nigger' until you actually get to know a black person; so, too, does a 'spick' stop being a 'spick' when you are living and working with a person of Mediterranean origin.

'The Great Depot for Smuggling'

(i) Introduction

An endless number of petty smugglers - chiefly women and children – manage[d] incessantly to go through with the forbidden merchandise secreted about their person. Large cartloads of tobacco... used to be driven up to the last limits of British territory.... [I]n the open air and in full day-light, those creatures, hundreds and hundreds at a time, divested themselves of their clothes and padded themselves all over with the contents of their carts, put their rags on again, and, thus laden, went their way into Spanish ground. The Spanish ... [have] remonstrated with the English authorities about these open-air toilets which [they] described as offensive to decency, and the police from the Rock have now orders to bid the women and children to 'move on'... 'The Smugglers Rock,' *The Times*, 3, September, 1877.

It was just before one in the morning when a Gibraltar family returning from Spain in their car could not believe their eyes.

There were scores and scores of Spanish women, known as 'matuteras' rushing up and down from the Gibraltar frontier gates to the Spanish side. 'I have never seen anything like it,' said the eyewitness. 'It was like a stampede!'

The Spanish women, in their hundreds, come to Gibraltar to buy cigarettes and take them back - hidden within their person - to others waiting on the other side. They do this once female customs searchers have left duty at the Spanish *aduana*. Then, they cannot be touched. Spanish customs men just watch the 'matuteras' go by....

Said an eyewitness: On the Spanish side there were at least 150 females of all ages, from young girls to elderly women. 'Many of those rushing up and down were wearing loose maternity-like dresses to hide the cigarettes,' we were told. The kiosk opposite the air terminal was crowded 'like a fair' and at *Cepsa* the women were in their hundreds, all queuing up to get their cigarettes....

It was about midnight, on the Spanish side. There was a large crowd of women, speaking excitedly, as if it was a crisis meeting. An old lady was saying at the top of her voice: 'Nothing is going to stop me from lifting up my dress and filling up with cigarettes.'.... 'Crackdown on Matuteras,' *Panorama*, 3, August, 1998.[1]

---

[1] This extract describes the period at the end of the 1990s, during which large groups of female tobacco smugglers would congregate across the Gibraltarian side of the border. Then, just like a hundred and thirty years earlier, passers-by were treated to something of a spectacle. Half-hidden behind parked cars or in some cases not bothering to hide at all, these women, mainly Spaniards from the deprived La Linea borough of La Atunara, but also from other towns further afield in the Campo area, could be seen undressing and stuffing packets of *Winston* into pockets, corsets, bras, underpants or anywhere else these could be concealed. Their operative methodology was simple yet effective. They would wait on the Gibraltarian side of the border until the only Spanish female customs officer retired for the day, then quickly cross over into Spain – knowing that no male customs officer was legally empowered to search them. Once on the other side, they would sell each packet of *Winston* bought in Gibraltar for about twice its original price, then return back to the colony to carry on crossing and recrossing the border. By means of this constant to-ing and fro-ing, 3000 or 4000 pesetas could be made in a few hours, a veritable fortune at time when the Campo was an economically-depressed region with seriously high levels of unemployment.

I have chosen to begin with these two extracts to emphasise the transhistorical dimension of the Gibraltarian smuggling phenomenon. Although it became something of a commonplace for people in the 1990s to complain that smugglers had never had it so easy, history clearly suggests otherwise. In the 1850s and 1860s, for example, the British authorities were extremely reluctant to clamp down on the practice of contraband, going as far as shooting at Spanish customs boats following the smugglers' brigantines back into Gibraltarian territorial waters. There was not even the need for smugglers to conceal the merchandise before loading it onto their boats — something that would have been unthinkable even during the height of the smuggling boom in the 1980s and 1990s. All this, not surprisingly, ensured that Gibraltar earned a reputation as the world's premier smuggling depot. One writer, for example, described Gibraltar as 'exceedingly convenient for... contraband traffic.'[2] 'Certain it is,' wrote another in 1839, 'that smuggling between [Algeciras] and Gibraltar is carried on more extensively and openly than I have seen elsewhere.'[3] Even a literary luminary of the stature of William Makepeace Thackeray could not help coming to a similar conclusion:

> Gibraltar is the great British depot for smuggling goods into the Peninsula. You see vessels lying in the harbour, and are told in so many words they are smugglers: all those smart Spaniards with cigar and mantles are smugglers, and run tobaccos and cotton into Catalonia;

[2] Anonymous, 'Barbarian Rambles,' *Blackwood's Edinburgh Magazine*, 67, 1850, p. 287.

[3] Gustavus Richard Brown Horner, *Medical and Topographical Observations Upon the Mediterranean* (1839), p. 72.

all the respected merchants of the place are smugglers...
[I]n this little corner of her dominions Britain proclaims
war to custom-houses, and protection to free trade.[4]

Within this short extract Thackeray rehearses the main points of
what could be termed the 'great Gibraltarian smuggling debate'
– the long and often acrimonious ideological struggle between
those who felt that Gibraltarian free trade had to be protected
at all costs and those who believed that unchecked protectionism
encouraged smuggling and was tantamount to criminal negligence
on the part of the British authorities. Although largely forgotten
by contemporary historians, this debate shaped the course of
nineteenth-century Anglo-Spanish relations and also attracted a
significant amount of political and literary attention. Searching
through back issues of *The Times* newspaper from 1875 to
1890, for example, I came across no less than fifty separate
references relating to the subject of Gibraltarian smuggling,
ranging from news reports to letters and full-scale articles such
as the one quoted at the beginning of this article.

This is all very ironical, given the modern historian's
reluctance to grapple with the topic of Gibraltarian smuggling.
Again and again we find that smugglers have been extirpated
from the annals of Gibraltarian history, removed, as it were,
from what we are supposed to know about our past. This crime
– for surely it is a crime to expunge what is objectionable from
our history – has been perpetuated by almost every major
British academic writing about Gibraltar's past. H. W. Howes's
*The Gibraltarian: the Origins and Development of the
Population of Gibraltar from 1704*, Maurice Harvey's *Gibraltar:*

---

[4] See M. G. Sanchez, *Writing the Rock of Gibraltar* (2006), p. 116.

A History, Philip Dennis's *Gibraltar and its People*: in all these texts smuggling is reduced to an anecdotal footnote, a matter of ancillary importance.[5] As a Gibraltarian interested in his own roots, I find this marginalisation somewhat demeaning, although not very surprising. As I have endeavoured to demonstrate in my previous writings, the history of Gibraltar has always been the history of the military men who transiently populated the place, never of the civilians who actually lived and died there. Battles, fortifications, the Great Siege of 1779-1783, the construction of the naval dockyard, the fluctuating state of Anglo-Spanish relations: these sort of topics have always been the domain of the historian writing on Gibraltar. Smuggling, by contrast, can be seen as a civilian enterprise *par excellence*, an activity that was literally as well as symbolically beyond the pale of military law. For this reason British historians have either ignored the historical reality of the smuggler, or, when they have deigned to write about smuggling, chosen to portray it as a metaphor for the social and moral degeneration of the native population. Witness the example of G. T. Garratt, the notoriously anti-Gibraltarian author of *Gibraltar and the Mediterranean* (1936), who chose to describe us as a motley crew of 'smugglers, gypsies, vagabonds, African rogues and Spanish rebels - a *sentina gentium*.'[6]

---

[5] William Jackson actually devotes a few pages to the question of Gibraltarian contraband – although, typically enough, he is more interested in the political subtext of smuggling than on how smuggling impacted on individual lives. See *The Rock of the Gibraltarians* (1990), pp. 235-239.

[6] Geoffrey Theodore Garratt, *Gibraltar and the Mediterranean* (1939), p. 124. Another anti-Gibraltarian writer who chose to focus on the smuggling trade from a pejorative angle, for that matter, was John David Stewart, author of the controversial *Gibraltar: the Keystone* (1967).

I believe that this situation needs to be redressed. If smuggling was as widespread as most nineteenth-century commentators would have us believe, then it is clear that it forms an integral part of our heritage that needs to be investigated and chronicled – just like any other aspect of our past. In fact, I will go one step further and contend that smuggling both emblematises and defines the experience of the nineteenth-century Gibraltarian - since it is one of the few forms of Gibraltarian activity that took place outside the sphere of British colonial influence. Countless, for example, are the modern Gibraltarian families who, were we to draw an extrapolatory genealogical line back in time, would be able to trace the origins of their present wealth to the schemings of some wily, moustachioed *contrabandista*. My aim in writing this short essay is not to uncover the names of these individuals (tempting as this prospect may be), but rather to recontextualise the practise of smuggling against a new historical framework, one in which smuggling can be seen as much as an accelerated ladder towards social and material advancement as a consequence of the politics and social conditions of the time. If in the course of doing so I can tempt some academic or journalist to embark on the full-scale history that a topic like this deserves, then the purpose of this short exploratory piece will have been amply served.

(ii) The Napoleonic Wars and the start of the Smuggling Trade

When did smuggling between Gibraltar and Spain actually begin? Although *contrabando* of one form or the other has existed almost from the day Gibraltar became politically and jurisdictionally autonomous from the rest of Spain,[7] it is generally recognised that large-scale contraband did not occur until the beginning of the nineteenth century. This, at least, is the view of conservative Spanish historians, nearly all of which stress that the smuggling trade was triggered by the Peninsular War and the stark imbalance of power which it left in its wake. More specifically, they point to the see-saw effect that the war had upon Britain and Spain, destabilising and impoverishing the latter at the same time that it strengthened and reinforced the presence of the former within the peninsular. For many subscribing to this view, Britain did not consciously set out to help the Spanish guerillas; she simply followed her own national interests:

> Por suerte que la Gran Bretaña con la insurreccion de España adquirió un campo ímmenso y seguro para combatir con su enemígo, con tan grande libertad y desahogo, como que no tenía que pagar las devastaciones que causaban sus maniobras; cayendo el peso de ellas sobre los españoles, que las toleraban resignados.

> (It was only thanks to the Spanish rebellion that Great Britain acquired a large and secure field of campaign against its traditional enemy. Nor did she have to worry about the destructive consequences of her military maneouvres, seeing that the brunt of destruction fell upon us Spaniards, who had no option but to tolerate them.)[8]

---

7 Tito Benady has recently looked at some aspects of this little-known eighteenth-century contraband trade – including the setting up of a snuff mill by the Dutch consul, Gerard Dierk, in the City Mill Lane area in 1711, and the execution of several peasants at San Roque in 1714 for smuggling tobacco into Spain from Gibraltar. See 'Smuggling and the Law,' *Gibraltar Heritage Journal*, 13, 2006, p. 90.

8 José Canga Argüelles, *Observaciones sobre la historia de la Guerra de España que escribieron los Señores Clarke, Southey, Londonderry y Napier* (1833), p. 222.

This view, I believe, has trickled into the popular Iberian consciousness and is reflected in the way that modern-day Spaniards – with the exception, of course, of one or two impartial historians[9] - continue to negate or willfully underplay British participation in what in Spain is known as 'la guerra de la independencia.' Go to Vitoria, for example, the site of the Iron Duke's decisive triumph of 1813, and you won't find a single statute commemorating the English participation in the battle.[10] Ask almost any Spaniard out in the street about Wellington and you'll probably get one or two shrugs of indifference, perhaps a

[9] See, for example, Jose Manuel Cuenca Toribio's *La Guerra de la Independencia: Un Conflicto Decisivo, 1808-1814* (2006):

La organización, el método, la disciplina y la constancia corrieron fundamentalmente a cargo de los ingleses, a los que, en buena lógica, cabe atribuir gran ...parte de la victoria sobre los franceses (p. 67).

(The discipline, methods, and constancy belonged essentially to the English, whose efforts, it naturally follows, were instrumental in the victory over the French.)

[10] There could be another reason for such mass indifference - Wellington's well-known contempt towards his Spanish charges. 'But I come now to another topic,' he famously wrote in one of his military dispatches, 'which is one of serious consideration, and has considerable weight in my judgment upon this whole subject, and that is the frequent, I ought to say, constant and shameful misbehaviour of the Spanish troops before the enemy..... In the battle of Talavera, in which the Spanish army, with very trifling exceptions, was not engaged, whole corps threw away their arms, and ran off in my presence, when they were neither attacked nor threatened with an attack, but frightened, I believe, by their own fire.... When these dastardly soldiers run away, they plunder every thing they meet; and in their flight from Talavera, they plundered the baggage of the British army, which was at that moment bravely engaged in their cause.... I have found, upon inquiry and from experience, the instances of the misbehaviour of the Spanish troops to be so numerous, and those of their good behaviour so few, that I must conclude that they are troops by no means to be depended upon.' *The Dispatches of Field Marshal the Duke of Wellington*, vol. 5 (1834), pp. 80-81.

quietly-whispered aside whether the chap in question plays for either Liverpool F. C. or Manchester United. This, again, is a most singular irony, considering not only that Wellington's tactical genius and authoritarian personality almost singlehandedly delivered the Spanish from their French oppressors, but that the Spaniards themselves, grateful for their liberation as only a liberated people can be, awarded Arthur Wellesley the dukedom of Ciudad-Rodrigo, the 'Toisón de Oro,' the gran cruz of San Fernando, and the cross of San Hermenegildo in the years between 1812 and 1815.

But the matter doesn't stop at willful negation or under-representation. Even more remarkably, perhaps, there has always been a tendency among Spaniards to resent the British military participation. Jose Maria Blanco Crespo, the Sevillian theologian who converted to Anglicanism and later changed his name to Joseph Blanco White, reveals an early instance of this attitude when complaining about certain Spaniards for whom 'los ingleses.... son mas odiosos... que los franceses mismos' ('the English are more hateful than the very French'). 'Si oyera usted,' continues the anglophilic Crespo with scarcely contained indignation, 'como yo he oído a los ecos de estos caballeros. Los ingleses nada han echo; ni los ejercitos que han mandado; ni los millones que han gastado en armas, municiones, y pertrechos de guerra: ni las batallas que han ganado... todo es nada.'[11] ('If only you would have heard some of the things I have heard these gentlemen say! To them the English have done nothing for us. Neither the armies they have sent, nor the millions they have spent on weapons, munitions and other equipment of war, not even the battles they have won... none

11 Joseph Blanco White, *El Español*, vol. 1 (1811), pp. 56-57.

of this means anything to them!'). Even now, almost two hundred years after the end of the Peninsular War, there are still some Spaniards who hold on to such attitudes. Consider the following lines, taken from a modern right-wing website:

Inglaterra nunca ayudó a España; se sirvió de España para ayudarse a sí misma. Así ocurrió cuando la guerra contra Napoleón. A los españoles que se replegaban a Gibraltar les abre sus puertas, pero nos obligan a destruir las fortificaciones por si acaso eran ocupadas por los franceses. Fuímos nosotros mismos - ingenuos españoles, siempre embaucados, engañados por el enemigo avieso de la sonrisa por fuera y el látigo por dentro - los que derruimos nuestras defensas, las que habíamos construido con nuestro dinero, con nuestro trabajo y con nuestro sudor.

(England never helped Spain; she exploited Spain to help herself. The same happened during the war against Napoleon. England may have opened Gibraltar to the Spaniards who travelled there, but she also forced us to destroy our land fortifications in case they fell to the enemy. It was us – naïve, foolhardy Spaniards, duped by an enemy who smiled on the outside but carried a dagger behind his back – who destroyed our own fortifications, the ones we had built with our own money, our own work, and our own sweat.)[12]

Subscribers to this view complain about the long-term consequences that British involvement had upon Spanish morale

---

[12] Anonymous, 'Historia de Gibraltar,' (http://www.ateneofalangista.es/forum/index.php?topic=1330.0;wap2 – 3-10-2007).

and national self-esteem. They argue – a little melodramatically perhaps, but not entirely unreasonably – that the British presence in Iberia had 'el aspecto humilante de una limosna, ó de un socorro prestado á un desvalido' ('the humiliating undertones of an act of charity towards a defenceless individual').[13] Among other things they point out that (a) Spain was suddenly forced to recognise her traditional enemy Britain as her foremost ally (b) that she had to suffer the indignity of seeing the Duke of Wellington take control of her homegrown troops and that (c) she was forced to feel eternally grateful for the troops and money which the British were ploughing into her territory. Thus, according to them, the Peninsular War cannot simply be seen as a war of liberation against a foreign invader; it also heralds the beginning of Spain's slide into what Santiago Ramón y Cajal later came to describe as a 'state of spiritual encystment.'[14]

It is against this backdrop of moral and economic bankruptcy that the origins of Gibraltarian smuggling have been repeatedly contextualised. Spain, for so long a dominant power on the world stage, suddenly finds herself emasculated, mortally wounded, her former power and prestige having haemorrhaged to nothing in the blood-soaked fields of Badajoz, Vitoria and Bailen. 'Desde el punto de vista económico,' accordingly writes the historian Emilio García Campra, 'la guerra de la Independencia supuso la destrucción continua y total de las pocas riquezas económicas con las que se contaba [en Espana].'[15]

---

[13] *Observaciones sobre la historia de la Guerra de España que escribieron los Señores Clarke, Southey, Londonderry y Napier*, p. 223.

[14] Quoted in John Armstrong Crow's *Spain: the Root and the Flower* (1963), p. 378.

[15] Emilio García Campra, 'Liberales y Contrabandistas en la Taha de Marchena' (http://ecoalhama.galeon.com/num008/liberal.html - 2-10-2007).

('From an economic perspective, the Peninsular War totally destroyed the few remaining economic riches [which Spain possessed]'). If that wasn't bad enough, Spain also had to endure the humiliation of finding herself yoked to her traditional Protestant enemy:

> De enemigo o de rival de Gran Bretaña, como lo había sido a lo largo del siglo XVIII, España pasó a ser su amiga y aliada. Una aliada menesterosa, sin medios y casi sin territorio, por estar en poder de los franceses la mayor parte de los núcleos urbanos de la Península. Una aliada cuyas autoridades dependían para sobrevivir del dinero que les suministraba el Gobierno británico y cuyos Ejércitos fueron puestos a las órdenes de un General inglés, Lord Wellington. Esta supeditación española fue la que permitió a Londres llevar adelante su política destinada a hacer más cómoda y barata su presencia militar en Gibraltar.... Despues de las guerras napoleonicas... Gibraltar... se convirtio en un centro de contrabando que cada vez fue adquiriendo mayor importancia...

(From being an enemy or rival of Great Britain, which is what she had been throughout most of the eighteenth century, Spain suddenly became her friend and ally. An enfeebled ally, it has to be said, without means and almost without territory, seeing that the French were in possession of almost all the major cities in the peninsula. An ally, what is more, whose leaders depended entirely on the money given to them by the British government and whose soldiers were placed under the command of an English general, the Duke of Wellington. Thanks to this state of Spanish subjection, London was able to pursue policies designed to make her military presence in Gibraltar easier and cheaper... After the Napoleonic wars... Gibraltar... became a centre of contraband which grew increasingly in importance...')[16]

The implication here is clear: the Peninsular War instilled a mentality of subservience ('supeditación') among the Spanish that enabled their British paymasters to play a game of political and economic brinkmanship within the colony of Gibraltar. If this is true, then smuggling begins at the point when Spain is at its lowest military and political ebb; it becomes a historical scar carrying the imprint of an unforgivable and unforgettable wound. 'Con todo eso podemos asegurar,' writes for example Professor Rafael Sanchez Mantero, 'que fue a partir de la finalizacion de la guerra de la Independencia cuando este trafico conocio su epoca dorad.'[17] ('For all that, we can safely say that it was not until the end of the Peninsular War that the Gibraltar contraband trade really flourished.') Perhaps this is why countless Spanish academicians and political commentators have taken such fierce and acrimonious exception to the Gibraltarian contraband trade: in their eyes it represents not just a clandestine assault against the Spanish economy, but a real-life metaphor of Spain's economic and military impotence.

What these and other Spanish commentators fail to realise is that smuggling, just like any other form of mercantile

---

[16] Fernando Olivie, Angel Liberal, Salustiano del Campo et al, *Estudios Sobre Gibraltar* (1996), pp. 80-86.

[17] Rafael Sanchez Mantero, *Estudios sobre Gibraltar: Politica, Diplomacia y Contrabando en el siglo XIX* (1989), p. 67.

activity, is regulated by the laws of supply and demand. This was never more the case than at the end of the Peninsular War, a period which saw Spain plunge to the depths of economic degradation chronicled in Goya's *Desastres de la Guerra*. Hungry, destitute, their traditional agricultural economy in ruin, the people of Spain were starving in their thousands and neither the provisional government in Cadiz nor the Spanish monarchists in exile could help redress this situation. Into this void stepped many of the garrison's 'Rock Scorpions,' hard-bitten Genoese and Maltese merchants who had been driven westwards by the Napoleonic wars and who now saw an opportunity to ply their considerable mercantile skills. Aided by the collapse of Spain's external borders – and helped, in no small measure, by Gibraltar's free port status - they began to sell tobacco, whisky, and other 'indispensable luxuries' to those Spaniards prepared to carry them into the hinterland. Sir William Francis Patrick Napier, one of the first British historians to have chronicled these heady events, explains what was happening in his *History of the War in the Peninsula* (1842):

> All the roads were infested with brigands, and in the hills large bands of people, whose families and properties had been destroyed, watched for straggling Frenchmen and small escorts, not to make war but to live on the booty; when this resource failed they plundered their own countrymen. While the land was thus harassed, [and] the sea swarmed with privateers of all nations ... the merchants of Gibraltar forced their smuggling trade at the ports.[18]

---

[18] Sir William Francis Patrick Napier, *History of the War in the Peninsula* (1842), p 236.

Nor was this influx of goods resented by the Spanish populace in general. Although Castilian historians have consistently complained about the negative effects of smuggling upon their native economy, all the evidence suggests that ordinary Spaniards in and around the Campo area[19] saw it as an acceptable form of living. In part this was because of dire necessity; in part it was also due to the pronounced stratification of nineteenth-century Spanish society and the accompanying fear of officialdom which this provoked among the disenfranchised classes:

> The certain fact is that between the Spanish people and their government there is at heart a traditional war, and that whatever is done to the government's injury is considered a meritorious action. It little matters whether Spain is a monarchy or a republic, an absolute or a representative state. The government is always a public enemy. The administration never changes, only from bad to worse. There has been of late a tremendous aggravation of public burdens, owing partly to the political convulsions of the past ten years, partly to the necessity of furthering long-neglected public works, but chiefly to the enormous number of state functionaries consequent on the very disorders of the revolutionary period, and to the incapacity, venality, and actual rapacity of many of them…. The delays and chicanes,[20] the capricious and uncertain rules and prescriptions, the circumlocution prevalent at Spanish Custom-houses have the effect of driving all trade from the frontier by main force, and many an honest man who

---

[19] 'The Campo de Gibraltar' is the area in Spain immediately adjacent to the Rock.

[20] 'Subterfuges' (Archaic).

would have no wish to cheat the revenue... is compelled
to put himself into the smuggler's hands solely to avoid
the trouble and inconvenience which await him at the
Custom-house. [21]

Our anonymous Victorian correspondent has captured here
something which most Spanish historians, in their readiness
to malign the British at all costs, have persistently forgotten:
the fact that most Andalusians simply did not give a damn
about their Madrid-based government or anything else to do
with those far-off plutocrats. This was as true in 1877, as it
would have been in 1810 or 1750: the character and aspirations
of the indigenous population were essentially regional and
inward-looking in orientation. Seen in this context, the argument
that the smuggling trade was precipitated by post-war Spanish
defeatism doesn't hold true — for the simple reason that there
wasn't much nationalist honour or moral backbone in Spain
there to begin with. This was particularly noticeable in the
area adjacent to the Rock, a region known for its dissoluteness
and primitiveness throughout the rest of Spain and across
most of Europe. Banditry, kidnappings, murders, rapes: it is
not for nothing that eighteenth, nineteenth and even twentieth-
century travellers venturing into Andalusia were warned about
the dangers facing them when going southwards beyond
Granada.[22] This is one of the more implacable ironies facing
those who link the rise of contrabandism to the so-called

---

[21] 'The Smugglers Rock,' *The Times*, 3, September, 1877.

[22] Even as late as 1926, the author Catherine Alison Phillips felt compelled to warn
her readers about the 'very dangerous' roads to be found in the deep south and the
presence in them of rateros — 'that is to say, peasants who, though not professional
brigands, will take a purse by the way.' *A Romantic in Spain* (1926), p. 304.

'supeditacion Española': they seem to forget just how rundown and morally bereft the Andalusian hinterland was *during* and *before* the war itself. Take the way the Andalusians conducted themselves during their 'Guerra de la Independencia.' Although it has become fashionable, thanks mainly to the re-imagining efforts of the Romantic movement, to portray the Andalusian 'insurrectos' as an indomitable force rising against their French overlords, the unpalatable truth is that, with a few notable exceptions, southern Spaniards were by and large passive and surprisingly acquiescent in the face of the French occupation. Consider the words of the historian Thomas M. Barker, writing in the year 2000:

> Apart from the bellicose populace of Estremadura, southern Spaniards failed to resist the invaders as northerners did. The south was arguably the section of the country with the highest ratio of collaborationists, fence-sitters, and profiteers... [I]f one may believe the captive Blayney and other observers, French officers were often personally consoled by Spanish women. Malaga harboured many Napoleonic sympathizers (*afrancesados*). Stooge King Joseph had received a tumultuous welcome both there and in Granada earlier in the year.[23]

If this is true (and we have no reason to doubt Professor Barker's historiographical objectivity, seeing that the extract in question is taken from an article highlighting *English* military incompetence during the Peninsular War), then it clearly makes a nonsense of the theory which blames the 'supeditacion Espanola'

---

[23] Thomas M. Barker, 'A Debacle of the Peninsular War: The British-Led Amphibious Assault against Fort Fuengirola 14-15 October 1810,' *The Journal of Military History*, 64:1, 2000, pp. 14-15.

for the subsequent rise in Gibraltarian smuggling activities. *That*, in my opinion, is no more than an ideological construct – designed to justify Spain's slide into international obscurity and the concomitant loss of its empire. Yes, Gibraltarian merchants did step in to plug a gaping economic hole and yes, many of them did profit immensely from the situation[24] - but it was market necessity, rather than premeditated political intent, that prompted their actions. This may be yet another of those subtle differences in opinion which have traditionally undermined Anglo-Spanish relations where Gibraltar is concerned, but in this case it does make a difference – since it unites Gibraltarian shopkeepers and Spanish smugglers in a web of transnational complicity first against the French invaders and then later against the Spanish government's treasury men in Madrid. What I am trying to say, in other words, is that smuggling was an expression of the popular will on both sides of the border, not the nationalised battle between a Castilian David and a British Goliath that Spanish historians in the nineteenth and twentieth centuries have made it out to be. As an anonymous author rather neatly put it in 1849:

---

[24] Just how much money was being made can be seen from an anecdote related in A. E. W. Mason's *The Four Feathers* (1902): 'Jose's father had left him... a couple of thousand pesetas. With this Jose Medina had gone to Gibraltar, where he bought a felucca, with a native of Gibraltar as its nominal owner; so that Jose Medina might fly the flag of Britain and sleep more surely for its protection. At Gibraltar, with what was left of his two thousand pesetas and the credit which his manner gained him, he secured a cargo of tobacco.... 'Gibraltar's a free port, you see,' said Hillyard. 'Jose ran the cargo along the coast to Benicassim, a little watering-place with a good beach about thirty kilometres east of Valencia. He ran the felucca ashore one dark night.' Suddenly he stopped and smiled to himself. 'I expect Jose Medina's in prison now.' 'On the contrary,' said Graham, 'he's a millionaire."

The Spaniards want our goods; their government will not
let them buy them in a regular way; and we, kind creatures,
let them have them without giving any trouble to the
custom house.[25]

(iii) The Contrabandist as hero: popular attitudes to smuggling in literature and the arts

If there is any doubt about the tacit approval with which most
working-class Spaniards viewed this illicit trade, one need
only look at the way that smugglers (or, as they were more
fashionably known, *contrabandistas*) were eulogised and even
feted in nineteenth-century writing. Again and again, we come
across representations of the *contrabandista* as a figure outside
the law yet firmly ensconced within the people's affections,
a sort of Hispanic Robin Hood or Dick Turpin. In some
ways, of course, this is due to the influence of the Romantic
movement. Beginning with texts like Byron's *Corsair* (1819),
there is a tendency among Romantic writers to eulogise
morally-indeterminate figures like highwaymen and smugglers
and to equate criminality and lawlessness with freedom of
mind and movement.[26] This nineteenth–century obsession with
criminality - in itself, one could argue, a sublimated reaction
against the widespread political and ideological repression of
the time - found its natural geographical complement in
Southern Spain, a region known for its wild, mountainous
topography and its gypsies and *bandidos*. Possibly one of the
earliest and most famous examples of this can be seen in the

---

[25] Anonymous, 'An incident in the Peninsular War,' *Chambers's Edinburgh Journal*, 11, 1849, p. 166.

[26] Martha Grace Duncan, *Romantic Outlaws, Beloved Prisons: The Unconscious Meanings of Crime* (1996) p. 82.

pages of Washington Irving's *The Alhambra*, a text that can almost be read as a manifesto on the potentialities of Romanticism within Spain. In his section entitled 'Local Traditions,' for example, Irving relates how in Andalusia

> ...they will gather round the doors of their cottages in summer evenings, or in the great cavernous chimney-corners of the ventas in the winter, and listen with insatiable delight to miraculous legends of saints, perilous adventures of travellers, and daring exploits of robbers and *contrabandistas*. The wild and solitary character of the country, the imperfect diffusion of knowledge, the scarceness of general topics of conversation, and the romantic adventurous life that every one leads in a land where travelling is yet in its primitive state, all contribute to cherish this love of oral narration, and to produce a strong infusion of the extravagant and incredible.[27]

It is no coincidence that the figure of the smuggler, possibly the most representative of all Andalusian outlaws, is offered a place of distinction by Washington Irving in his pantheon of 'otherness.' Wild, transgressive, unfettered by the dictates of law or morality, the smuggler is recast by the Romantics into a courageous, libertarian and anti-establishment icon who is admired by ordinary men and fantasised over by housewives who cannot help but 'have a natural love for *contrabandistas*.'[28] In fact, it is his very dangerousness that makes the smuggler so attractive in the first place:

---

[27] Washington Irving, *The Alhambra* (1832) (etext.library.adelaide.edu.au/i/irving/washington/i72a/part20.html - 2-10-07)

[28] Anonymous, 'Notes of Promiscuous Travels by Guy A. Scutis,' *The Knickerbocker: Or, New-York Monthly Magazine*, 51, 1858, p. 96.

> I had no doubt at all that I was in the company of a
> smuggler, and possibly a brigand. What cared I? . . . I
> was very glad to know what a brigand was really like.
> One doesn't come across such gentry every day. And there
> is a certain charm in finding oneself in close proximity to
> a dangerous being....[29]

The extract in question is related by the narrator of Prosper
Mérimée's *Carmen*, the original novel upon which Bizet's opera
was based. Coming across a smuggler near the town of Cordoba,
he feels irresistibly drawn to the man, almost overawed by his
presence. Many others, too, fell under a similar spell. Henry
Seton Merriman, a young Victorian gentleman on his way to
the Middle East, described Algeciras 'as the stronghold of
those *contrabandistas* whom song and legend have praised as
the boldest, the merriest and most romantic of law-breakers.'[30]
Likewise an article in the *London Saturday Journal* of 1842
recalls the experience of an English officer who encountered a
'handsome young man... [with] a short round jacket of brown
cloth' near Granada:

> I informed him [the handsome young man] we were
> Englishmen, from Gibraltar.
>
> 'From Gibraltar!' he exclaimed with admiration. 'That is
> indeed a fine place. What tobacco one finds there! What
> cotton goods!'
>
> These remarks at once informed me of the occupation of our
> new companion. 'You are a *contrabandista*, then?' said I.

---

[29] Prosper Mérimée, *Carmen* (1845) (www.gutenberg.org/etext/2465 - 2-10-07)

[30] Henry Seton Merriman, *In Kedar's Tents* (1897; reprinted 2004), p. 23.

He unhesitatingly assented.

'How I envy you such a wild life!' I continued. 'Your
excitement must be greater than can be imagined!'[31]

Mixed in with such unrestrained adulation there was a
tendency to present smugglers as glamorous and exotic figures
of 'otherness,' quite removed from the sartorial humdrumness
of everyday life. Thackeray, for example, described the smugglers
he saw in Gibraltar as 'smart Spaniards with cigar and mantles'
who wore 'tufted hats, with gay silk handkerchiefs round their
heads.'[32] Likewise Major Hort, author of *The Rock of Gibraltar*
(1839), commented that '[t]he streets [of Gibraltar] as usual
were crowded with *contrabandistas*, who, arrayed in their fanciful
yet picturesque costumes, were busily engaged in completing
purchases.'[33] Possibly the most exotic rendering of the Spanish
contrabandista, however, can be seen in Robert Sear's *Scenes and
Sketches in Continental Europe* (1867):

As the life of a *contrabandista* (which means, properly
speaking, a land smuggler) is to a certain extent roving
and romantic, so are his habits lively and energetic, and
his costume picturesque. The best accommodation the
inns can afford are his, whether on the road or in the
town, and frequently his gay and cheerful temper renders
him an agreeable visitant. As he has ample opportunities
of collecting information in his continuous perambulations,

---

[31] Anonymous, 'The Granada Smuggler,' *London Saturday Journal*, 3: 66,
1840, p. 222.

[32] *Writing the Rock of Gibraltar*, p. 116.

[33] Quoted in *The Rock of the Gibraltarians*, p. 235.

he is considered as a walking newspaper, and may be seen in his brown jacket with its gaudy embroidery and silver bell buttons, his red sash and shirt of lace, his short loose trouser and conical hat, standing at the hostel door, recounting the news to a group of eager listeners, or seated in the chimney-corner, with his wine-skin by his side, and cigar in his mouth, enlivening the company with his guitar.[34]

It is hard to imagine a less threatening figure than that portrayed by Sears here. With his 'red sash' and his 'silver bell buttons' and his 'gay and cheerful temper', this guitar-strumming smuggler reminds us more of a children's TV presenter than an outcast beyond the pale of the law. And yet, in a sense, Sears is taking the Romantic obsession with criminality to its most extreme – decriminalising the figure of the outlaw and turning him into a figure fit for middle-class consumption. This was yet another of those representational tropes which Romantic writers often employed: smugglers, like thieves and other brigands, were decriminalised and stripped of all sense of anti-social menace – just as policemen and *carabineros* and other representatives of the establishment were presented as corrupt and untrustworthy figures. Some authors even went as far as to invert reality altogether and turn smugglers into the very paragons of civility. Consider these two extracts on Spanish smugglers, written in 1839 and 1848 respectively:

The Spanish *contrabandistas* of the better class are a noble set of men, hardy and daring, generous, and strictly honourable. I have heard Englishmen who have travelled

---

[34] Robert Sears, *Scenes and Sketches in Continental Europe* (1867), p. 196.

and been entertained by them, speak in the highest terms of their courtesy and hospitality.[35]

To be a *contrabandista*, and a coward, is an utter contradiction. Courage is associated with his profession. He is a smuggler, because he is a hero,—a hero, because he is a smuggler. The ideas are convertible, not to say identical. The *contrabandista*, instead of being repudiated as the pest, is honored as the pet of society. Nobody classes him among the evil doers. He confers benefits. He breaks the statutes, but he serves the community. He incurs perils for the public good.[36]

But is this what nineteenth-century smugglers were really like? Could the lawless outcasts who roamed the Sierra Carbonera be no more than a bunch of universally-liked, highly-principled, dandified fops? Most attentive readers will have noticed that so far I have only quoted non-Spanish writers on the subject. This would seem to imply that the view of smugglers we have been getting here is one that stems from those who did not live in day-to-day proximity to the outlaws themselves. From this it would be easy to surmise that smugglers were neither as loved nor as well thought of as these foreigners made them out to be. Yet – surprisingly - this is not the case. Just as foreigners loved to romanticise the figure of the smuggler, so did Spaniards enjoy doing the same. Juan Carrete Parrondon, in fact, writes about *contrabandistas* and *bandoleros* occupying what he describes as 'una larga tradicion en la cultura popular' ('a long tradition in

---

[35] Anonymous, 'A Summer in Andalusia,' *The Museum of Foreign Literature, Science, and Art*, 8, 1839, p. 384.

[36] William Howitt and Mary Botham Howitt, *Howitt's Journal* (1848), p. 57.

popular culture').[37] This was particularly evident in the field of
the *cancion popular*, the Andalusian art form *par excellence*.
Time and again we come across lyrics in which *contrabandistas*
are portrayed in tragic, heroic or eulogistic terms, but never in
what could be described as a pejorative light. A typical example
of this can be seen in the work of the composer/lyricist Felipe
Pedrell, one of the *cancion's* foremost fin-de-siècle exponents. In
1889 he published two songbooks for voice and piano – *Aires
Andaluces* and *Aires de la tierra del cantaor Silverio*. The first
of these carried the subtitle 'coplas de contrabandistas para
piano' ('songs about smugglers for piano') and includes such
classics of the genre as 'Me metí a contrabandista' ('I became a
smuggler'), 'Todos los contrabandistas' ('All the smugglers'), and
'¡Arriba caballo moro!' ('Spring forwards, my Arab stallion').
Even more famous and widely-known, perhaps, was Manuel
Garcia's 'Polo de Contrabandista' ('Song of the *Contrabandista*'),
an early nineteenth-century *cancion* which, according to the
Spanish scholar Gerardo Fernández San Emeterio, served as the
basis for the 'Veil song' in Verdi's *Don Carlos* and also inspired
Schumann to write his little-known piano piece *Spanisches
Liederspiel*.[38] George Borrow admits to knowing the song in his
Bible in Spain (1841) – and actually starts humming it at one
point to defuse a tense encounter with a shifty Tagus boatman.[39]
Although Garcia's *cancion* is largely forgotten nowadays, its
strongly defiant tone suggests to what extent the average Spaniard

---

[37] Juan Carrete Parrondon, *El grabado en España* (1998), p. 691.

[38] Gerardo Fernández San Emeterio, 'Canciones líricas españolas del Siglo
de Oro y versiones musicales de Robert Schumann: El Spanisches Liederspiel
y las Spanische Liebeslieder,' *eHumanista*, 5, 2005, p. 87.

[39] George Henry Borrow, *The Bible in Spain* (1841; reprinted 1920), p. 19.

saw the *contrabandista* as a kind of renegade romantic hero:

Yo soy el contrabandista,

y campo por mi respeto.

A todos los desafío,

Pues a nadie tengo miedo.

¡Ay! ¡Jaleo muchacha!

¡Quién me compra

Algún hilo negro!

Mi caballo esta cansado.

¡Ay!

Y yo me marcho corriendo.

¡Ay! Que viene la ronda

Y se movió el tiroteo.

¡Ay! Caballito mío,

Caballo mío ligero.

¡Ay! ¡Jaleo que nos cogén!

¡Ay! ¡Sácame de este aprieto!

¡Ay! ¡Jaleo muchacha! ¡Ay!

¡Quién me compra

Algún hilo negro!⁴⁰

---

[40] 'I am the smuggler / And I do as I please / I challenge everyone / And fear no one. / Ay! Jaleo! My girl! / Who will buy from me/ Some black thread! / My horse is tired. / Ay! / And I run beside it. / Ay! The night patrol approaches / And they're starting to/Ay! My little horse, / My sprightly horse!Ay! Jaleo! They're catching / Ay! Get me out of this / Ay! Jaleo! My girl!Who will buy from me / Some black thread!'

(iv) Operation *Contrabandista*, part one (The Sea Run)

How was the contraband getting from Spain to Gibraltar and who was responsible for taking it there? The surest and most successful method, of course, was to load the goods into boats manned by eager *Campo de Gibraltareños* and then sail up the Spanish coastline with the intention of unloading them at a suitably hidden and sheltered location. Lord Castleragh, the British Foreign secretary between 1812 and 1822 and an enthusiastic proponent of the doctrine of free trade, has left us a short description of the smugglers' operational methods, as well as the simultaneous protectionism afforded to them by the military garrison:

> The goods themselves are forced in, by scores of large and small smuggling boats, who watch their time when the Spanish *guarda costas* are not on the alert, steal from under the Rock, run along the shore, and land their goods by previously planned stratagems. If chased, they retire under cover of Europa Point, and our guns do not hesitate to fire on any Spanish boat chasing within range of the fortress; our policy being to give encouragement and protection to the smugglers![41]

Castleragh presents us here with what could be termed an Anglo-Gibraltarian version of events. For a more balanced exposition of smuggling methods – one that also explains what happened to the goods *after* they were landed – we must turn to Rafael Sanchez Mantero's *Estudios sobre Gibraltar: Politica, Diplomacia y Contrabando en el siglo XIX* (1989), one of the

---

[41] Quoted in Severn Teackle Wallis's *Glimpses of Spain; Or, Notes of an Unfinished Tour* (1847), pp. 356-357.

few modern Spanish publications to have looked at Hispano-Gibraltarian contraband in an objective manner:

> El camino habitual que seguía el contrabando era el siguiente: las mercancias eran vendidas por los almacenistas, depositarios y comerciantes gibralteranos, hebreos en su mayoría, y que jugaban un papel muy importante en todo mecanismo. Posteriormente eran embarcadas en el puerto de Gibraltar en diferentes barcos que eran conducidos hasta el litoral español, eludiendo la vigilinancia que ejercien los generalmente escaos y mal pertrechados guardacostas del resguardo. Allí, los fardos eran recogidos por otros hombres, quienes a lomos de mula, a veces en reatas hasta de doscientas bestias, se introducían tierra adentro para distrubuirlos por aquellos lugares en los que tenían facil salida hacia los consumidores, siguiendo una ruta previamente concertada. En esa ruta, Ronda ocupaba un lugar de paso indispensible, ya que como cabecera de comarca, tenía una actividad comercial bastante considerable. Su proximidad a Cadiz y a Gibraltar y, al mismo tiempo, la difficultad del territorio que la separaba del mar, con intricadas sierras, muchos de cuyos pasos solos los conocían los contrabandistas, hacian de esta localidad un lugar ideal para la recepción de este tipo de mercancias y tambien para su distribución.

(The most common route followed by the contraband was as follows: the items were sold by the warehouse keepers, Gibraltarian merchants and tradesmen, largely Jewish in origin, who played a very important role in the whole distribution process. Subsequently they were loaded onto different boats at Gibraltar's harbour which would then be

Spain mainland. Consequently, it was not uncommon for their writers to employ metaphors of illness and contagion when describing the British-held dominion and its contraband-driven fiscality. Fernan Caballero, the famous nineteenth-century Spanish novelist, portrayed Gibraltar as 'esa úlcera de España - una porción de perdidos, desertores, presos fugados, contrabandistas y vagos.'[82] ('That ulcer of Spain – a haven for losers, deserters, escaped convicts, smugglers and good-for-nothings.') 'Gibraltar,' likewise echoed the historian Francisco María Tubino in 1863, 'ha sido una sanguijuela quo nos ha chupado muchas libras de sangre.'[83] ('Gibraltar has been a bloodsucker that has sucked many pounds of our blood.') Even General Franco's propagandists appear to have been caught up in this metaphorical conceit, describing Gibraltar as 'an economic cancer and a centre of moral corruption' in the early sixties.[84]

Why did the British and Spanish cling to these respective positions for so many years? From a Spanish perspective at least, the answer was very simple: Gibraltar was a thorn in their government's side and needed to be presented as negatively as possible. Smuggling, with its concomitant subtext of British lawlessness, fitted well within this scheme of things – fuelling the Spaniard's sense of self-righteousness as well as underpropping the 'moral argument' for the devolution of sovereignty. Yet, as I have already hinted at earlier in this

---

[82] Fernan Caballero, *Relaciones* (1862), p. 146

[83] Francisco María Tubino, *Gibraltar: Ante la historia, la diplomacia y la politica* (1863), p. 34.

[84] Anonymous, 'Spanish Outburst Over Gibraltar Contraband Traffic Denounced,' *The Times*, 13 April, 1964.

essay, there was a strong element of hypocrisy in all this. Even
if we disagree with the Victorian commentator who suggested
that the contraband trade was keeping some 400, 000 Spaniards
in employment,[85] it is clear that it was helping the financial
situation and purchasing power of a large percentage of *Campo
de Gibralteraños*, as well as other Spaniards further afield.
Rafael Sanchez Mantero, whose historiographical objectivity is
to be applauded, recognises as much when he admits that 'la
verdad era que tambien muchas familias españolas vivían del
contrabando'[86] ('the truth was that many Spanish families
lived from the contraband trade'). On top of that, we must not
forget that the *contrabandistas* were supplying the hinterland
with luxury goods that could not normally be found in Spain,
thereby bringing much pleasure to large sectors of the
population. All this, of course, may not have been recognised
by the Spanish government or its demagogues, but it was
certainly picked up by some of the more astute British observers.
'The anti-English party in Spain,' for instance wrote a
contributor for *Blackwood's Edinburgh magazine* in 1850,
'may occasional bluster about the hole in the national honour;
and so forth; but the great majority of the nation never bestow
a thought upon the matter, and the smuggling portion of the
community – no uninfluential class – find Gibraltar exceedingly
convenient for their contraband traffic.'[87]

Britain's reluctance to change the status quo was also fuelled
by ulterior motives of her own. Although Spanish propagandists

---

[85] William B. Dana, *Merchants Magazine and Commercial Review* (1846), p. 393.

[86] *Estudios sobre Gibraltar: Politica, Diplomacia y Contrabando en el siglo XIX*, p. 60.

[87] 'Barbarian Rambles,' p. 287.

liked to portray the Rock as a hive of decadence and luxury, the rather less varnished truth was that the garrison and everything that came with it was a major drain on the British economy. With over 10,000 troops, 15,000 civilians, and no agricultural or farming industries of its own, the fortress was a very expensive place to maintain and every trickle of financial help was to be welcome. That is why smuggling could never be entirely repudiated by the establishment. Not only did it plug these same economic deficiencies by circulating large sums of money through the garrison; it also, no less importantly, granted financial self-sufficiency to the locals and stopped them from becoming dependent on the military establishment.

(vii) Conclusion: the Gibraltarian attitude to the contraband trade

All this leads us to the final and most important variable within the equation: the Gibraltarians themselves. What did the 'Rock Scorpions' think of the smuggling trade? And how did they react to the interminable political wrangling between Britain and Spain over the same? Predictably enough, most Gibraltarian merchants were very keen to maintain the status quo and strongly opposed anything that would be prejudicial to their economic interests. John David Stewart, whose strongly anti-Gibraltarian disposition ensured that he devoted not just one but two separate chapters to the contraband trade in *Gibraltar: the Keystone*, gives us a glimpse into the dense web of economic interests at stake:

One Gibraltarian shopkeeper once told me that he was selling one-sixth of the total output of one of the world's most famous fountain pens. When I asked him how this could be, he replied: By supplying the whole Iberian Peninsula. I do not mean that he was a smuggler. He simply sold the pens, taking both wholesale and retail profits, to the ten thousand of Spanish commuters, who carried them into Spain at the rate of one per day per man. Another Gibraltarian, and a decent man he is, made himself independent for life, at this time, by selling saccharin alone. All he had to do was order it up by the barrel, break it down into tuppeny packets, and sell it to the Spanish workers...[88]

Under circumstances like these, it is not surprising that the Gibraltarian merchants reacted hostilely whenever individual governors took it upon themselves to redraft Gibraltar's mercantile laws or whenever Whitehall found itself bending under the weight of Spanish diplomatic pressure. An early example of the former occurred during the late 1840s, when Robert Gardiner was governor of Gibraltar. Irked by the political freedoms which had been granted to the native Gibraltarians over the preceding decades, Gardiner took a strong dislike to the Rock's population, particularly the members of the Exchange Committee, the forerunner of the modern Chamber of Commerce, which he rather memorably described as 'a tribunal for the propagation of smuggling.'[89] He also complained about the morale-sapping effects of smuggling upon the military garrison, arguing that it was not in the troops' interest 'to witness and become familiarised with all the crime and

---

[88] *Gibraltar: the Keystone*, p. 274.

[89] Quoted in *How to Capture and Govern Gibraltar: A Vindication of Civil Government*, p. 53.

profligacy of this deplorable traffic.'[90] Even more damaging from the Exchange Committee's point of view, perhaps, Gardiner saw fit to include these opinions in a pamphlet which he presented to the Secretary of State for the Colonies under the title of *A Report on the Military Defences, Government and Trade of Gibraltar, with considerations of the relative position of that fortress with Spain.*[91] This was the last straw for the disgruntled Gibraltarian merchants. Aided by their allies in the Chambers of Commerce of Manchester and Liverpool,[92] they began a long and systematic campaign against their high-minded oppressor which included the publication of the semi-libellous pamphlet *How to Capture and Govern Gibraltar* and did not abate until Gardiner, possibly the most unpopular governor in Gibraltar's long colonial history, was sensationally recalled from office in 1855.[93]

A similar scenario, though with slightly different permutations of its own, came to pass just over twenty years later in 1877. This time it was not the governor who wanted

---

[90] Quoted in *Gibraltar and the Mediterranean*, p. 131.

[91] Robert Gardiner, *A Report on the Military Defences, Government and Trade of Gibraltar, with considerations of the relative position of that fortress with Spain. Addressed to the Earl Grey, H.M. Secretary of State for the Colonies, by the Governor of Gibraltar, Major-General Sir Robert Gardiner* (1850).

[92] The support of the English traders can be explained by the fact that most of the cloths (cotton and linens in particular) smuggled into Spain were coming from the great Victorian textile factories in cities like Manchester and Liverpool.

[93] Although published anonymously almost a year after Gardiner's recall, *How to Capture and Govern Gibraltar* summarises all the arguments and tactics used in the smear campaign against the largely unwanted governor. Significantly, too, it carries a dedication to the Manchester Chamber of Commerce.

to clamp down on smuggling, but – even more dangerous from the Gibraltarian merchants' point of view - the Secretary of State for the Colonies. It all started a year earlier when a certain Mr. Reade, Her Majesty's consul at Cadiz and a typical FCO mandarin by all accounts, sent a letter to both Lord Napier of Magdala, the Governor of Gibraltar, and the Earl of Carnarvon, the Secretary of State for the Colonies, complaining about the vast amounts of goods being smuggled into Spain from Gibraltar. Magdala, a seasoned military man who had been awarded a peerage for his part in the second Afghan war, adopted what could be described as a diplomatic approach to this unexpected arrival from Cadiz: saying yes in principle to the letter's anti-contraband recommendations, but quietly deciding not to pursue the matter any further. Carnarvon, however, was neither as tactful nor as well-intentioned to the Gibraltar mercantile community. Displaying the crass disregard for colonial interests which would later see him clash with the Irish nationalist leader Charles Stewart Parnell, he immediately dispatched two English Custom officials on a fact-finding mission to Gibraltar, the aim of which was to uncover ways of curtailing the contraband trade. Shortly afterwards, the British government began talking about launching a customs scheme in Gibraltar similar to that employed in the Channel islands.[94] 'Against this ordinance,' wrote a reporter for *The Times* newspaper, 'a loud clamour arose on the part of many of the

---

[94] Specifically, the proposed regulations 'forbade the export or import of tobacco in packages of less than 80 lb,; they provided that the ships which export tobacco should be over 100 tons burden; and they required the exporter of tobacco to furnish a bond showing that it had been landed at the port for which it had been cleared to the satisfaction of the Governor - unless, of course, stress of weather interfered.' See Appendix A of this book, p. 163.

most respectable citizens of Gibraltar.'[95] Among the various expressions of discontent was a memorial (or letter of protest) sent directly to Carnavaron by the Exchange Committee of Gibraltar. Drafted by Judah Levy, Richard Abrines, J. A. Crooks, J. H. Recaño, and the committee's own chairman, Francis Francina, this unique document argued that 'if the measures in the proposed scheme are carried out, it will cause most material injury to all classes of this community, destroy Gibraltar as a commercial centre and free port, and bring untold misery on a large proportion of its poorer inhabitants.'[96] Even the Bishop of Gibraltar himself, the Right Reverend Dr. John Baptist Scandella, could not help getting embroiled in the controversy, writing to Lord Carnarvon in early 1877 to let him know that the banning of smuggling would

> cause deep irritation throughout the great neighbouring towns…. whose inhabitants depend, in a very great measure, on their trade with Gibraltar… It is unquestionable that The Lines, Campamento, San Roque, Algeciras, Marbella and Estepona will be almost ruined.[97]

According to the anti-Gibraltarian Stewart, Scandella's sudden interest in the welfare of Marbella and Estepona opens him to the charge of self-serving hypocrisy. Yet, in all fairness to the outspoken prelate, it must not be forgotten that similar arguments were being made across the border, most notably by the liberal politician and political commentator Francisco Maria Montero, who thought that the proposed legislation

---

[95] 'Smugglers Rock.'

[96] Quoted in *Gibraltar: the Keystone*, p. 131.

[97] Ibid., pp. 134-135.

would leave many Spanish children on the throes of starvation.[98]

In the end, however, letter-writing proved something of a political blank cartridge and the Gibraltarians had no option but to once again rely on their powerful friends within the English mercantile classes. Thus, with the help of the Chambers of Commerce of Liverpool, Glasgow and Manchester, a meeting was arranged on 26 July, 1877 between Carnavaron (whose anti-smuggling efforts, it should be noted, had by now earned him the unflattering soubriquet of 'el Earl Cabron' within Gibraltarian bourgeois circles[99]) and Francis Francina, the Exchange Committee's formidable chairman. Flanked by Mr. Hardcastle and Mr. Mundella, two members of parliament, and by Mr. Ashworth, the president of the Manchester Chamber of Commerce, Francina proceeded to set out the Gibraltarian case before the Secretary of State. In clear and surprisingly articulate language for a nineteenth-century 'Rock Scorpion,' he pointed out that he had not come to defend the practice of smuggling, but to uphold the right of the native mercantile classes to engage in free trade. 'We are convinced,' Francina ended up declaiming, 'that the fiscal system of Spain and the administration of the Spanish revenue service are such that no measures taken by the British government can diminish smuggling in that country.'[100] Although Carnavaron initially looked unimpressed – he is said to have shaken his head several times

---

[98] 'Smuggling and the Law,' p. 97.

[99] This anecdote was related to me by my maternal grandfather, who in turn had heard it from his own grandfather.

[100] Quoted in *Gibraltar: the Keystone*, pp. 137-138.

while Francina was speaking - he soon relented and promised to consult parliament before proceeding any further, something which, in the highly codified language of political diplomacy, was tantamount to an admission of defeat. Remarkably, the interests of the Gibraltarian mercantile classes had once again been preserved.

That there was a strong vein of self-interest behind the actions of the Exchange Committee in both 1850 and 1877, of course, cannot be denied.[101] Yet it would be wrong to dismiss Francina and company's protestations as the inevitable rejoinder of a self-seeking oligarchy. Just as the contraband trade kept the Gibraltarian business classes economically self-sufficient, so too, as Edward G. Archer has argued, '[during] times of difficulty, smuggling became the mainstay of the economy.'[102] Simply put, whenever the Gibraltarian economy floundered or went through a period of uncertainty, there was a corresponding rise in smuggling practises. One such time, Archer maintains, was the period stretching between the 1830s and 1840s. Still reeling from the cholera epidemic of 1834 and the moratorium on trade that accompanied it, the British garrison found itself in a position of grave economic insecurity, quite unlike anything seen within its 130 year long history. So precarious was the Rock's plight during this time, in fact, that even the Spaniards began to turn the screws. Witness, if not, George Newenham Wright's words of 1838:

> Various circumstances have occurred to diminish the trade
> of Gibraltar; among the most prominent are the creation

---

[101] Francina, the Exchange Committee's chairman, was actually the largest importer of tobacco into Gibraltar! See 'Smuggling and the Law,' p. 97.

[102] *Gibraltar, Identity And Empire*, p. 54.

of a free port at Cadiz, the establishment of manufactories in the eastern parts of Spain, and the various royal orders of the Spanish government, which place Gibraltar almost in a state of commercial non-intercourse with Spain, under the plea of preventing smuggling into the provinces adjacent to the fortress.[103]

Of course, rather than stemming the tide of Gibraltarian contraband, the new anti-mercantile prohibitions made it even worse. It is surely no coincidence, after all, that the origins of the first cigar-making factories, as well as those of *Saccone and Speed*, Gibraltar's oldest wine and tobacco merchants, can be traced back to this time. In fact, so much tobacco was passing through the Rock during the 1840s that one early Victorian writer could not help joking about the 'frightful deal that they must smoke in Gibraltar!'[104]

A similar pattern emerges during the next one hundred and fifty years. In periods of social or financial hardship, such after the second world war or when the resident British battalion pulled out of Gibraltar in the early 1990s, there has always been a corresponding rise in contraband activities. This is because smuggling not only consolidated the financial independence of the Gibraltarian merchants; it also, as has

---

[103] George Newenham Wright, *A New and Comprehensive Gazetteer* (1838), p. 158. The new Spanish measures included the formation of three border-protecting agencies - the *cuerpo de resguardo* (1822), the *cuerpo de carabineros de costas y fronteras* (1829) and the *guardia civil* (1829), the last of which is still engaged in customs operations. See *Estudios sobre Gibraltar: Política, Diplomacia y Contrabando en el siglo XIX*, p. 73.

[104] Anonymous, 'A Glance at the Peninsula,' *Blackwood's Edinburgh Magazine*, 67, 1845, p. 603.

already been stated, acted as the lifejacket which kept the garrison afloat during times of economic uncertainty. Indeed, it is no coincidence that the most unpopular governors of Gibraltar were the ones who spoke out against smuggling. One could even argue that to be anti-contraband was to be anti-Gibraltarian – since smuggling was the one area of mercantile activity which the Gibraltarians, dispossessed, as most colonial peoples are, of the right to social and economic advancement, could claim as their own. That is why, in the final analysis, Whitehall not only tolerated smuggling, but sometimes chastised those within its own ranks who thought otherwise (such as those two implacable foes of the *contrabandista*, Sir Archibald Hunter and Sir Robert Gardiner). It is also the reason why, despite the growing number of anti-contraband measures designed to placate the increasingly remonstrative Spaniards - such as the ordinance which forbade the movement of sea vessels after dark in 1890, or that in 1896 which made it compulsory to store tobacco in bonded warehouses – the British military junta persisted in leaving loopholes for the exploitation of the *contrabandista*. Yes, there were times when *it appeared* that the British government was finally clamping down on smuggling – that cannot de disputed; but, as a recent analysis of import trends between 1900 and 1920 has demonstrated, the amount of tobacco sold in Gibraltar remained fairly constant in spite of all those supposedly restrictive measures.[105] Whitehall, for all its anti-Gibraltarian prejudices, knew better than to sever the one economic lifeline that stopped the civilians becoming utterly dependent on the garrison.

---

[105] See 'Smuggling and the Law,' p. 97.

'That Dreadful Scourge of Humanity'

'The great distress which the garrison experienced during the fever no-one can describe.' [1]

(i) The Tragic Tale of the Reverend McMullen

In 1804 Thomas Coke, the fifty-six year old secretary for the British Methodist Conference, decided to establish a permanent Methodist mission in Gibraltar. For the task at hand he chose the Reverend James MacMullen, a young and energetic preacher known for his 'amiable and compassionate disposition.'[2] After a short period of instruction, MacMullen set off towards the colony at the beginning of September, 1804, accompanied by his wife and young child. What happened next is best related in the words of Thomas Coke's own nineteenth-century biographer:

> It was in the autumn of 1804, that Mr. MacMullen, with his wife and an infant daughter, went thither as a missionary. Their voyage was long and dangerous; but storms and contrary winds were to his family only the beginning of sorrows. After having been driven on the Barbary coast, they reached Gibraltar about the end of September, but found, on their arrival, that the yellow fever was raging among all ranks with unexampled violence. Everything was in confusion. Consternation everywhere prevailed. The report of death was heard in

[1] J. Gill, 'The yellow fever at Gibraltar,' *Methodist Magazine*, 37, 1814, p. 385.

[2] Joshua Marsden, *The Narrative of a Mission to Nova Scotia* (1816), p. 265.

almost every dwelling; and every face was covered with horror.... The child was taken ill almost immediately on their arrival, but survived the disease. On the first of October Mr. MacMullen wrote a letter to England, describing the calamities of their condition. With the same fatal disease he was seized on the tenth, and on the eighteenth he was a lifeless corpse. At the time of his decease his wife felt symptoms of the same disorder; and after lingering a little longer than her husband, followed him to the world of the spirits and the house appointed for all living, leaving their surviving orphan in the hands of strangers, in the midst of pestilence, in a foreign land.[3]

Reverend McMullen and his wife had the extreme misfortune of landing at Gibraltar halfway through the first and most serious outbreak of yellow fever that the fortress has ever witnessed. Over the next few decades Gibraltar suffered several episodic recurrences of the fever, most notably in 1813, 1814 and again in 1828. So strongly did the disease become associated with the fortress that it started to be known as 'Gibraltar fever,' a term that remained synonymous with yellow fever until recently and shows how much the events gripped the consciousness of the English nation. Nelson, writing home to a worried Lady Hamilton, felt obliged to assure his paramour that 'we are entirely free from [yellow fever], and in the most perfect health, not one man being ill in the fleet.'[4] Robert Southey, the poet laureate who happened to be in the Iberian

[3] Samuel Drew, *The Life of the Rev. Thomas Coke* (1837), pp. 309-310.

[4] Quoted in Thomas Joseph Pettigrew, *Memoirs of the life of Vice-admiral Lord Viscount Nelson* (1849), p. 427.

peninsula during an outbreak of the disease, likewise penned a quick note to his mother in which he stated how '[t]he plague, or the yellow fever, or the black vomit, has not yet reached us, nor do we yet know what the disease is, though it is not three hundred miles from us, and kills five hundred a day at Seville!'[5] Back within the British mainland, meanwhile, the wheels of speculation kept on spinning, with almost everyone venturing an opinion on how to treat the disease. S. H. Jackson, a noted nineteenth-century doctor, launched a stinging attack in 1807 against some of these armchair theorists, complaining how 'sitting in [their] closet... without the slightest opportunity... of becoming acquainted with the nature of this fever....[they] devise a theory of the disease; the application of [which] is to work wonders on the Gibraltar fever.'[6] In the meantime the virus continued unabated, striking down rich and poor, soldiers and civilians alike. In the outbreaks of 1813 and 1814, some 1245 people died, out of which 505 were soldiers and 740 civilians. In 1828 the overall figure rose to 1677, this time divided between 507 soldiers and 1170 civilians. In this essay I will look at the first epidemic of 1804 and how it came to affect the local population, focusing, among other things, on contemporary medical treatments, mortality rates, popular misconceptions about the illness, and the varied and in many cases desperate strategies used to cope with the onset of the disease. In doing so I am conscious that I am not the first to write about the Gibraltarian yellow fever epidemics. Much

---

[5] See Charles Cuthbert Southey, *The Life and Correspondence of Robert Southey* (1850), p. 125.

[6] S. H. Jackson, 'Observations on the Epidemic Disease which lately prevailed at Gibraltar, *The Critical Review, Or, Annals of Literature,* 9, 1807, p. 446.

sterling work, for example, has already been undertaken by
Dr. Sam Benady and Professor Larry Sawchuk.[7] Should this
article of mine prove interesting, I urge the reader to consider
looking at their more detailed *oeuvre*.

(ii) The Black Vomit: A Layman's Introduction

Yellow fever, otherwise known as yellow jack, black vomit,
vomito negro, or Gibraltar fever, is an extremely dangerous
vector-borne virus.[8] It is typically found in tropical or sub-
tropical areas and is primarily transmitted by the *Aedes egyptii*
and the *Aedes africanus* mosquitoes. Although the virus is not
transmissible through human contact, a non-infected mosquito
can pick it up from an infected human and in this way spread
it to other humans. The disease first attacks the lymphatic
system and then spreads to most internal organs, including the
heart, kidneys, adrenal glands and liver. While every single
case of yellow fever has its own distinct symptomatology, as a
rule there appears to be two distinct phases. The first normally
lasts twenty-four hours and is often characterised by nothing
more than fever, headache and muscle spasms. Provided they
receive adequate medical attention, most patients entering
this first phase are able to make a full recovery. If the victim
has not recovered within the first twenty-four hours, however,
he or she enters a second 'toxic shock' phase. This is much

---

[7] See, for example, Lawrence A. Sawchuk and Stacie D. A. Burke's
groundbreaking essay 'Gibraltar's 1804 Yellow Fever Scourge: The Search for'
Scapegoats,' *Journal of the History of Medicine*, 53, 1998, pp. 3-42; and
Sam Benady's and Larry Sawchuk's *Diary of an epidemic: Yellow Fever in
Gibraltar, 1828* (2003).

[8] I have, it should perhaps be noted, a special interest in vector-borne
viruses, having spent eight days in an Indian hospital with Dengue fever in
October, 2006.

more dangerous than the first and carries with it an attendant
risk of death. Even contemporary doctors, mystified as most
of them were by the disease's aetiology, were able to grasp that
much:

> The late Gibraltar epidemic was a fever of one paroxysm—
> cold, hot, sweating. If slight, nothing more. If severe,
> yellowness about the third day, black vomit, hiccup,
> total suppression of urine, copious haemorrhage of black
> blood from the nose, gums, anus, vagina, and death from
> the 4th to 6th or 7th day, always without a fever.[9]

Despite the coldly scientific tone employed here, it is easy to
imagine the distress which this second phase of the disease
must have brought upon the patients in question. Thomas
Bennion, a British surgeon present at Gibraltar in 1804, talks
about the 'incessant sighing, the greatest dejection of spirits,
with apprehensions of the most distressing nature,' adding,
almost as a postscript, that 'the fear of death is very great'
among the sufferers and that 'friendship for the nearest kin is
extinguished.'[10] An even more chilling account of the patient's
sufferings, if anything, has been left to us by Thomas Ross,
another British doctor resident in Gibraltar during 1804:

> It commences with the usual symptoms of fever; sometimes
> vomiting with the cold fit, but not always; when the hot
> fit comes on there is a violent pain in the head, chiefly

---

[9] Hugh Fraser, 'Review of the fact and arguments brought forward by
Dr. Barry... relative to the late epidemic fever in the fortress of Gibraltar,'
The Medico-chirurgical Review, 13, 1830, p. 338.

[10] Thomas Bennion, 'Bennion, on the Gibraltar Fever,' *The Philadelphia
Medical Museum*, 3, 1807, p. clxii

across the forehead, throbbings of the temporal and carotid
arteries... These were the symptoms of the first stage of
the disease, which, if not relieved by nature, (which was
very seldom the case) or by medicine, in twenty-four
hours, the eyes became more suffused and dull, the heat
of the skin continued, and all the other symptoms increased
till about the end of the second day, when a dull heavy
pain was felt at the pit of the stomach, which was soon
followed by an effort to vomit... The patient now becomes
very restless and delirious; the skin puts on a slight
yellow tinge, beginning about the neck, and which in a
few hours changes to a dull yellow livid colour; the
irritability of the stomach continues, and every thing is
rejected; the vomiting becomes constant; what is brought
up is a dirty brownish coloured liquor like the washings
of Port wine bottles; it gets darker and thicker, and has
now the appearance of coffee-grounds; the desire for cold
water now comes on, the restlessness increases, and frequent
attempts are made to get out of bed; the delirium is
generally expressed in mutterings, but sometimes the
convulsions are violent and the ravings frantick... Petechiae
now appear about the breast and arm-pits, and then
spread over the whole body; the vomiting continues,
attended with hiccup, and a cold, greasy, clammy moisture
on the skin, of a peculiar and cadaverous smell; the
yellow colour of the countenance acquires a darker hue,
and it is strongly marked by the expression of horror;
sometimes there are tremors and convulsive motions of
the eyes and muscles of the face or limbs; constant
muttering; partial intervals of recollection, during which

the patient seems sensible of his state, and approaching dissolution, although unable to express himself in words; the extremities are cold; the pulse sinks; and on the third, fifth or seventh day he dies; in some instances the whole train of symptoms were run through and terminated by death in thirty-six hours from the first attack.[11]

(iii) The background to the 1804 outbreak

In 1800 and 1803 yellow fever attacked the south of Spain. Cadiz first in 1800, and then Malaga in 1803 succumbed to the ravages of the disease, bringing mass panic to an already impoverished populace. Across the neutral lines, meanwhile, the British authorities decided to take no chances. On the orders of the Duke of Kent, strict quarantine measures were enforced to keep the disease from crossing over into the fortress - including the indefinite suspension of Anglo-Spanish trade and the prohibition of all crossborder traffic. While they were in place, too, these worked perfectly well: not a single case of yellow fever was reported within the garrison. Then, in August 1804, came the news of another outbreak in Cadiz. This led to the enactment of a government proclamation which ordered that 'commencing with tomorrow and until further orders all communications with Spain both by Land and Sea shall be cut off.'[12] Unfortunately, as usually happens in cases like these, there was something of a time lag between the passing of the

---

[11] Thomas Ross, 'Symptoms of the fever which prevailed at Gibraltar in September, October, November and December, 1804,' *The Philadelphia Medical Museum*, 3, 1807, pp. clxvi-clxviii

[12] Larry Sawchuk and Stacie D. A. Burke, 'Gibraltar's 1804 Yellow Fever Scourge: The Search for Scapegoats,' *Journal of the History of Medicine*, 53, 1998, p. 6.

proclamation and its implementation. It was during this window of opportunity, as it were, that a resident of Gibraltar coming back from Cadiz 'was taken ill the first day after his arrival in the garrison, and communicated the fever to the whole of the inhabitants in Boyd's Buildings.'[13] The name of this man was Santos and he was a shopkeeper who travelled frequently between Spain and Gibraltar. He arrived at Gibraltar on the 27th of August, just days after the outbreak in Cadiz. The first victim of the newly-imported disease, it appears, was 'a bombardier... residing next door to the house of the person Santos' in Boyd's buildings.[14] From that moment onwards the disease appears to have taken a demonic momentum all of its own:

> Mrs. Fenton [the Bombardier's wife] was the second person attacked; she was taken ill on the 3rd of September, her husband and a child of the name of Roland, were taken ill on the 8th, and died on the 12th. Mrs. Boyd, who had visited Mrs. Fenton, was taken ill on the 13th, and died on the 19th; her husband was taken ill on the 14th, and died on the 16th.[15]

These early transmission rates were helped by the condition of Boyd's buildings, 'that notorious fever-nest of the town' as one commentator later came to describe the dwellings.[16] Situated

---

[13] William Pym, 'Observations in Proof of the Contagious Nature of the Bulam Fever, and on the Mis-statements of Dr. Burnett regarding that Disease,' *The London Medical Repository and Review*, 6, 1816, p. 190.

[14] James Copland, *A Dictionary of practical medicine*, vol. 4 (1858), p. 159.

[15] William Pym, *Observations upon Bulam, Vomito-Negroor Yellow Fever* (1838), p. 21.

[16] *The British and Foreign Medico-chirurgical Review*, 34, 1864, p. 179.

at the junction between modern-day Governor's Street and Library ramp, these were 'small, dirty, and ill-ventilated tenements, into which individuals of the lower class were generally crowded.'[17] Victorian commentators talk about their cisterns being 'full of stagnant water' and their saw-pits 'filled with putrid animal and vegetable matter.'[18] Hugh Fraser, a medical inspector who came to Gibraltar in 1816 and published his findings in 1820 under the title of *A Letter to the Earl of Chatham, Governor of Gibraltar, relative to the Feverish Distempers of that garrison*, could not believe what he saw inside some of the tenements during the course of a routine sanitary inspection:

> In the middle area of Boyd's buildings, confined and choked up by lumber, 18 persons were crowded together, some of them sleeping and cooking, in places called rooms, not larger than two ordinary sentry-boxes. Some of the areas are crowded with water butts, old mats, oil jars, and lumber of all description, affording a nest for filth, and a fruitful source of putrescent exhalations, independent of their seriously diminishing the cubic mass of air, the circulation of which is still further obstructed by lines and poles crossing the areas for the purpose of drying linen. In many tenements there are no necessaries; in many others, one small hole serves to receive the ordure of twenty families. In the centre of the area, there

---

[17] René La Roche, *Yellow Fever, Considered in Its Historical, Pathological, Etiological, and Therapeutical Relations* (1855), p. 385.

[18] 'Observations in Proof of the Contagious Nature of the Bulam Fever, and on the Mis-statements of Dr. Burnett regarding that Disease,' p. 190.

is, in the best class of houses, a grating, which communicates with a drain; in several, this grating and drain are altogether wanting.[19]

The condition of Boyd's building can in some ways be seen as a metonymy for the lack of hygiene prevalent throughout the whole of Gibraltar. Contemporary travellers describe the Rock as a filthy and depressing place, its decrepit, little buildings heaving under the kind of filth and rubbish that is nowadays only associated with third-world countries. 'Although it has the appearance of great cleanliness without,' for example wrote one commentator in 1854, '... yet within, the houses are admitted to be, and are notorious for their filth, crowdedness, and want of ventilation...'[20] This was not helped by the Gibraltarian habit of keeping working animals within reach of living quarters. Mules, horses, goats: the only way livestock could be protected was by keeping it in close proximity at all times.[21] Larry Sawchuck, in his pioneering essay 'Gibraltar's 1804 Yellow Fever Scourge: The Search for Scapegoats,' has already documented how these and other aspects of 'patio living' contributed to the high mortality rates of 1804. In particular, he singles out the Gibraltarian tendency to collect rainwater and wash clothes in shady, unventilated courtyards as factors which would have facilitated the breeding of *aedes egyptii*.[22]

---

[19] Quoted in John Hennen, 'Sketches of the Medical Topography of the Mediterranean,' *The London Medical and Physical Journal*, 9, 1831, p. 546.

[20] Anonymous, *Report of the Sanitary Commission of New Orleans on the Epidemic Yellow* (1854), p. 369.

[21] Ann Herring, Alan C. Swedlund, *Human Biologists in the Archives: Demography, Health, Nutrition and Genetics* (2003), p. 195.

[22] 'Gibraltar's 1804 Yellow Fever Scourge: The Search for' Scapegoats,' pp. 8-9.

This lack of hygiene in the domestic space was also reflected in the state of Gibraltar's public areas. Due, in great part, to a lack of co-operation between the military and civilian authorities, there were no effective arrangements for waste disposal. Household rubbish, for example, was left lying about in courtyards, accumulating in gigantic vermin-infested piles that did not stop attracting mosquitoes until the advent of the late autumn rains. A similar story applied to the way people disposed of their own ordure. 'In many houses,' explains the disgusted historian Frederick Sayer, 'cesspools or accumulations of night soil exist, which, through the apathy of the inhabitants and the disregard for stench and filth, remain untouched for years.... When they are emptied, a course usually resorted to in summer, when the fetid effluvium overcomes the callous tenant, their contents are carried in open barrels along the streets, spreading their deadly exhalations through the crowded dwellings.'[23] This situation, moreover, did not improve with the passing of the years. Even after Governor Don built a rudimentary sewer in 1815, there were constant blockages and overflows, enveloping the adjacent town with a variety of unhealthy vapours and pestilential stenches. The area known as the Camber, now the site of the prestigious Waterfront development, was particularly notorious due to its proximity to one of the main sewage outlets. 'Besides this drain,' wrote one sickened commentator, 'there is a stagnant piece of water, called the Camber, in which boats are hauled up to repair; this, it is said, has three or four feet of mud in it, and receives a great part of the filth of the shores at the south, and emits

---

[23] Frederick Sayer, *The History of Gibraltar and of Its Political Relation to Events in Europe* (1862), p. 475

a very offensive effluvium.'[24] Sawchuk recalls the case of one
Major-General Pilkington who, arriving to Gibraltar in 1819,
was greeted by a stench so 'intolerable... and so diffuse that it
was experienced in his own quarters, in the very centre of the
town, at a distance of several hundred yards from its probable
source.'[25] Many, of course, deplored such lack of hygiene and
saw it as a possible contribuent to the spread of disease – yet
the majority of Gibraltarians appear to have been strangely
reluctant to accept this last possibility. The historian Robert
Montgomery Martin, author of the seminal volume *History of
the British Colonies*, even complained that '[t]he old inhabitants
of Gibraltar can never be got to admit that collections of filth
have any effect whatever in favouring the breaking out of the
yellow fever.'[26]

(iv) Quarantine or Escape?: Reactions to the advancing epidemic

There were some who... congregated and shut themselves
up in houses where no one had been sick.... Others... said
there was no better medicine against the plague than to
escape from it. Moved by this argument and caring for
nothing except themselves, a large number of men and
women abandoned their city, houses, families and
possessions in order to go elsewhere.[27]

---

[24] *Yellow Fever, Considered in Its Historical, Pathological, Etiological, and
Therapeutical* Relations, p. 222.

[25] 'Gibraltar's 1804 Yellow Fever Scourge: The Search for' Scapegoats,' p. 22.

[26] Robert Montgomery Martin, *History of the British Colonies* (1835), p. 77.

[27] See http://www.history.vt.edu/Burr/Boccaccio.html - 17-10-2007.

So wrote Giovanni Boccaccio in 1348. Since time immemorial, it appears, individuals caught up in areas of plague have agonised over the choice between barricading themselves in their own homes or moving away from the locus of infection. The matter has always had a stark simplicity to it: stay and protect your property and belongings, or run away and risk losing everything to marauding looters. A similar idea, though with certain peculiarities of its own, can be seen in early nineteenth-century Gibraltar. Because of the garrison's all-enclosing structure – and because the Spanish authorities, in any case, would have been most reluctant to allow anyone into Spain coming from a known centre of contagion – the Gibraltarians had to relive this human drama almost exclusively within the two and a half square miles of their rocky peninsula. That is to say, they had to decide between barricading themselves in their own homes or decamping to the upper rock caves and other unpopulated areas away from the city.

It is difficult to imagine the pressure these families must have faced. By the end of September, just a few weeks after Santos had arrived in the garrison, around 15,000 people were infected, the area of contagion having extended all the way down from Boyd's buildings to Main Street and Line Wall. Civilians were now dying at a rate of close to one hundred a day. Undertakers complained that they could not keep up with the demand for more coffins.[28] Around this time, too, the seriously overstretched military authorities began to force civilians to help bury the dead. Men were thus obliged to carry the corpses of their neighbours. Mothers were compelled to

---

[28] 'Gibraltar's 1804 Yellow Fever Scourge: The Search for' Scapegoats,' p. 13.

drag their own children to the grave. The Reverend James McMullen, who by this stage was already infected with the disease and days away from dying himself, sadly noted in his journal how 'half-infected soldiers were seen reluctantly patrolling the panicstruck natives to carry out the corpses of the poor, whether relatives or strangers, and drop them promiscuously into trenches, opened day by day to receive the multitudes of dead.'[29] Entering the month of October, if anything, things got even worse. Unattended corpses now lay at every corner. Survivors were seen throwing their relatives out of windows.[30] More and more cases of looting were reported. From the safety of a well-provisioned hulk anchored in the middle of the bay, Sir Thomas Trigge, the acting governor of Gibraltar, wrote anxiously to London asking for financial help to assist with the burials, arguing that if the bodies kept on accumulating across the street it would occasion 'a Pestilence more fatal than the disease we have experienced.'[31]

It is against this dantesque backdrop that many Gibraltarian families agonised over the most important decision of their lives: choosing between barricading themselves at home, or fleeing beyond the limits of town. In some cases, this decision had already been taken for them, *The Gibraltar Chronicle* of 22 September noting how a number of sickly-looking individuals had being forcibly evicted from their own homes by frightened neighbours and landlords.[32] Ironically, too, this would have

---

[29] Ibid., p. 13.

[30] William Jackson, *The Rock of the Gibraltarians* (1990), pp. 196-97.

[31] 'Gibraltar's 1804 Yellow Fever Scourge: The Search for' Scapegoats,' p.13.

[32] *The Gibraltar Chronicle*, 22 September, 1804.

been something of a blessing in disguise. For one thing, those who stayed at home were being forced to carry the rotting corpses of their neighbours - hardly the most salubrious of occupations. Secondly, the wooden shutters with which most working-class dwellings were fitted – there were no glass windows for Gibraltarians at the time – offered little if any protection against the flight paths of the *aedes egyptii.* To stay at home, under the circumstances, would have been tantamount to signing your own death warrant.

The simple truth was that self-quarantining did not work. Sir James Fellowes, the military surgeon who was knighted in 1809 for his efforts at Gibraltar five years earlier, relates the example of a certain Mr. George Cooper, a military man who 'confined himself and family to his house in a garden at Rosia… [b]ut .. far… from being preserved by this precaution, eight out of the nine persons connected with the family had the disease and five died.'[33] A similar demographic pattern of mortality can be seen in the epidemics of 1813, 1814 and 1828. René La Roche, one of the members of the Anglo-French commission who came to Gibraltar to investigate the causes of the 1828 outbreak, tells the story of three Irish Town merchants by the names of Mr. Kerling, Mr. Lindblad and Mr. Morrison. 'On the first alarm of the fever,' La Roche tersely remarks, 'they placed themselves in strict quarantine; yet, nevertheless, they were all attacked with the disease.' La Roche, not surprisingly, concludes from this that 'those who shut themselves up, and who may be considered to have

---

[33] Quoted in David M. Reese's 'Observations on the epidemic of 1819, as it prevailed in a part of the city of Baltimore,' *The North American Review and Miscellaneous Journal,* 10, 1821, p. 393.

placed themselves in quarantine, perfectly insulated, were attacked as readily as those who mixed indiscriminately with the people.'[34]

Those who fled town would have ventured slightly better. By leaving the mosquito-infested streets behind, these individuals would have reduced the chance of coming into contact with *aedes egyptii* and therefore stood a much greater likelihood of survival. A particularly salubrious locality, in this respect, appears to have been the flatlands of the neutral ground. In 1804, 1813 and again in 1828, the British authorities moved most of the garrisoned troops to this area - convinced that they stood a better chance of survival there. They were largely right too. 'In all these instances,' wrote one anonymous commentator, 'as soon as the troops were removed to encampments on the *Neutral Ground*, they became in a measure exempt, notwithstanding it continued to rage in the town.'[35] Why the troops and not the civilians were moved to the Neutral ground is, of course, another matter. As always throughout Gibraltar's long colonial history, the military authorities appear to have put the interests of the soldiers above those of the civilians, thereby consigning hundreds of Gibraltarian men, women and children to almost certain death. Just how much of a crime this was against the local population can be gleaned from a simple comparison between the rates of civilian and military deaths in the different outbreaks:

---

[34] *Yellow Fever, Considered in Its Historical, Pathological, Etiological, and Therapeutical Relations*, p. 534.

[35] Anonymous, 'Statistical Reports on the Sickness, Mortality and Invaliding among the troops in the United Kingdom, the Mediterranean, and British America,' *The American Journal of the Medical Sciences*, 1, 1841, p. 448.

Year of Epidemic	Number of Military Deaths	Number of Civilian Deaths
1804	860	4867
1813	391	508
1828	507	1170

[36]

Incidentally, there was a category of Gibraltarian that never had to face the ordinary town dwellers' dilemma: those who were able to pay their way out of the garrison. These were mainly merchants and their dependants - that is to say, members of the Rock's colonial aristocracy. Like the wealthy Gibraltarian evacuees who managed to pay their way to Madeira during the 1940s (while their less affluent compatriots were deposited in war-torn London), they relied on money to escape a potentially fatal predicament. In doing so they were only following the example of the British military high command, most of which had retired to a large hulk anchored in the middle of the bay while the rest of the garrison's population suffered. Unlike the governor and his cronies, however, these rich Gibraltarians were not guaranteed an easy way out. Some managed to bribe their way into Spain and settle in San Roque.[37] Others, particularly those of Jewish descent, were able to take shelter among the Sephardic settlements lining the Tangiers coastline. Others, still, were not so fortunate. La Roche relates the example of Mr. Cardozo,[38] 'the highly respected chief of the Jews at Gibraltar, who embarked with his wife and twelve other persons

---

[36] Source: *History of the British Possessions in the Mediterranean*, p. 177.

[37] Anonymous, 'Fever in Gibraltar,' *The Annual Register, Or, A View of the History, Politics, and Literature for the year 1828* (1829), p. 128.

[38] This, of course, was the famous Gibraltarian patriarch and merchant Aaron Cardoso. See Tito Benady's *Aaron Cardoso: Life and Letters* (2004), p. ix.

in a small vessel which sailed for the coast of Barbary.' 'Having a foul bill of health,' La Roche continues, 'they were not permitted to land at Tetuan' and were forced to spend the next few days wandering through the straits, seven of them dying in the process.[39] Money, although a considerable help in times of plague, appears not to have been much use on this particular occasion.

(v) Medical treatments during the 1804 epidemic: a case of trial and error?

'The Gibraltar Fever, about which the doctors disagreed so much,' writes Ford in his famous travelogue, had nothing remarkable about it save that 'the patients [were] dying in the mean while, *como chinches*.'[40] This was one of the most tragic aspects about the 1804 epidemic and those that followed it in 1813, 1814 and 1828: the medical establishment had little, if any idea how to deal with what was happening. Although most doctors instinctively grasped that lack of hygiene was a major contribuent to the spread of the sickness - La Roche, for example, was convinced 'beyond a doubt that whenever the yellow fever has made its appearance in Gibraltar, [it] has always commenced in the filthiest and most crowded spots'[41] - the disease's origins appear to have 'baffled the researches of the most learned physicians of all countries.'[42] Some blamed the Levanter winds – that 'tyrant

---

[39] *Yellow Fever, Considered in Its Historical, Pathological, Etiological, and Therapeutical* Relations, p. 534.

[40] Richard Ford, *A Handbook for Travellers in Spain* (1855), p. 274.

[41] *Yellow Fever, Considered in Its Historical, Pathological, Etiological, and Therapeutical Relations*, p. 385.

[42] T. Smith, 'Brief Sketch of the Fever which prevailed at Gibraltar in the Autumn of 1828,' *Edinburgh Medical and Surgical Journal*, 35, 1831, p. 26

of Gibraltar' and the bringer of dangerous miasmata.[43] An
article in the September 22 issue of *The Gibraltar Chronicle*,
for example, equated the high mortality rate 'with the
continuance of the Easterly wind' and expressed the hope
that 'the first favourable change in the weather will put an
end to the sickness.'[44] Others blamed the heavy rains.[45]
Others, still, were convinced that excessively high temperatures
lay behind the illness.[46] To make matters even more
complicated, medical men were divided between those who
believed that the disease could be transmitted from person to
person (the contagionists) and those who refuted the idea
(the noncontagionists.) The two groups frequently argued
between them, publishing virulent, libellous pamphlets in
which they denounced each other and their ideas and
sometimes, as in 1804, totally revising their former opinions
about the fever:

> We are informed by Sir W. Pym, that at the commencement
> of the epidemic of Gibraltar, in 1804, the medical officers
> were nearly unanimous with respect to the non-
> contagiousness of the disease; but that, before long, they
> became unanimous, with one exception, on the other side
> of the question.[47]

---

[43] *A Handbook for Travellers in Spain*, p. 271.

[44] *The Gibraltar Chronicle*, 22 September 1804.

[45] *History of the British Possessions in the Mediterranean*, p. 77.

[46] Daniel Blair and John Davy, *Some Account of the Last Yellow Fever
Epidemic of British Guiana* (1850), p. 58.

[47] *Yellow Fever, Considered in Its Historical, Pathological, Etiological, and
Therapeutical Relations*, p. 207.

The actual dispensation of medical treatments was no less uncertain. Mercury, bloodletting, opium, quinine, enemas, poultices, emetics, hydrotherapy: every doctor seemed to have a different opinion on how to go about treating the disease. The situation is best described by La Roche in his monumental *Yellow fever, considered in its historical, pathological, etiological, and therapeutical Relations*, possibly the sanest and most commonsensical of all the publications on 'yellow fever' issued at the time:

> [O]ne [doctor] advocates active depletion by the lancet, and measures the blood abstracted not by ounces, but by pounds... Another dreams of nothing but mercury, and would salivate all cases. A different writer preaches the necessity of free and profuse purging, and attributes the large mortality of the disease to a neglect of that indispensable means. Another, again, holds that neither bleeding, purging, nor mercury has ever done, or can do, any good, and strongly insists on the propriety, in all cases and under all circumstances, of administering the Peruvian bark in large doses. Some insist on the necessity and possibility of cutting short the fever by means of sulphate of quinia, and accuse those who call for proof of the success of the abortive method with being behind the times. Some discard every method heretofore suggested, and aver that the true plan of treating the yellow fever is to oxygenate the blood by means of neutral salts.[48]

La Roche highlights in this extract the use of blood-letting and mercury-laced preparations, two of the commonest (and most

---

[48] Ibid., p. 629.

dangerous) treatments used during the epidemic. Mercury – in the form of calomel, or mercurous chloride – was often administered to patients to promote salivation. Although a potent neurotoxin that can cause brain damage, it was believed to act as a purgative that helped cleanse disease out of an infected body. Dr. Robert Amiel, one of the British physicians present at Gibraltar during the epidemic of 1813, said that calomel was 'the only remedy to be relied on, and in a manner our sheet-anchor, in the disease.'[49] 'Calomel, given at first in a full dose,' likewise wrote his colleague George Gregory, 'so as to operate freely as a purgative... was the most approved practice among the English practitioners at Gibraltar in 1813.'[50] Others, by contrast, were not so sure of mercury's restorative qualities. La Roche vehemently and consistently decried the use of mercury, arguing that it produced 'sloughing of the gums, accompanied with a perpetual oozing of a considerable quantity of blood.'[51] Dr. P. Louis, one of La Roches's colleagues in the Anglo-French commission, similarly held that 'there was no reason to think that the mercurial practice was of any utility in the yellow fever' - although, unlike La Roche, he did believe in the value of 'moderate blood-letting.'[52]

Whether undertaken moderately or not, of course, bloodletting had absolutely no therapeutic value. The removal of blood from

---

[49] Hugh Fraser, 'Reply to Dr. Barry's Remarks on the Gibraltar Epidemic of 1828,' *The London Medical and Physical Journal*, 56, 1831, p. 412.

[50] George Gregory, *Elements of the theory and practice of physic* (1835), p. 94.

[51] *Yellow Fever, Considered in Its Historical, Pathological, Etiological, and Therapeutical Relations*, p. 663.

[52] Anonymous, 'Medical Pathology and Therapeutics,' *The American Journal of the Medical Sciences*, 14, 1847, p. 465.]

an infected patient would have only decreased the body's supply
of red blood cells, thereby obstructing the delivery of oxygen
from the lungs to the organs. This would have led to extreme
fatigue and periods of dizziness, not exactly the most appropriate
side-effects for individuals already labouring under the strain
of an extremely debilitating virus. Sir William Pym, a lifelong
opponent of the use of venesection, tells us how in Gibraltar
'bleeding was held in the greatest dread, and... was imagined to
induce such debility as to produce death.' Uncompromising as
ever, Pym blamed this phobia on 'the fatal effects resulting
from blood-letting in 1804,' and gave as proof the example of
one Mr. Martindale, a resident surgeon who 'laid aside the use of
the lancet... in consequence of its bad success.'[53] A similar
opinion was shared by Surgeon Thomas Bennion, another medical
man caught up in the great 1804-1805 epidemic, who 'considered
blood-letting as a great cause of mortality.... in the fever of
Gibraltar in 1804.'[54] Despite this, the practice continued to be
popular with practitioners not just in 1804, but in the outbreaks
of 1813 and 1828 as well. Particularly infamous in this regard
was a certain Dr. MacMullen, a military surgeon who arrived in
Gibraltar from the West Indies halfway during the yellow fever
outbreak of 1813. Claiming to have had 'ample opportunities of
observing this disease and its treatment' in the West Indies, he
employed bloodletting as a standard practice, much to the dismay
of William Pym and other members of the anti-venesection
brigade.[55]

---

[53] 'Observations in Proof of the Contagious Nature of the Bulam Fever, and
on the Mis-statements of Dr. Burnett regarding that Disease,' p. 193.

[54] Ibid., p. 192.

[55] Ibid.

Alongside the more traditional purgative treatments, there were, of course, all manner of alternative therapies. Surgeon Thomas Bennion, whose opposition to bloodletting has already been noted, believed in administering regular doses of calomel in conjunction with warm baths and emetics (i.e. vomit-inducing solutions) of antimony and Glauber salts. 'This [treatment],' Bennion wrote with a certain element of self-satisfaction, 'generally operated pretty smartly both on the stomach and the bowels.'[56] His colleague, Dr. Thomas, by contrast, claimed to 'have never lost a patient...[by]... directing him to drink a few cups of strong infusions of camomile flowers,' to which was later added 'a quantity of wine, proportionable to the age of the patient.'[57] By far the strangest form of treatment, however, was that advocated by a certain Dr. Barry, who arrived in Gibraltar towards the final stages of the 1828 epidemic. This eccentric individual was given charge of 'a small detachment hospital on the glacis, on the north front.' A few weeks later, we are told, '[i]t was... discovered that his success was not greater than that of his neighbours, with all his boasting. For... even by the aid of his own energetic treatment of a cataplasm of port wine and bread to the pit of the stomach and five leeches to the ankles, he lost every fever-patient under his care.'[58]

---

[56] Thomas Bennion, 'Bennion, on the Gibraltar Fever,' *The Philadelphia Medical Museum*, 3, 1807, p. clxv.

[57] Dr. Thomas, 'Thomas, on the Gibraltar Fever,' *The Philadelphia Medical Museum*, 3, 1807, pp. clxx- clxxi.

[58] 'Review of the fact and arguments brought forward by Dr. Barry... relative to the late epidemic fever in the fortress of Gibraltar,' p. 349.

(vi) Conclusion: the Yellow Fever legacy

The last reported case of yellow fever associated with the 1804-1805 epidemic came on 2, January 1805, just over four months after the beginning of the outbreak. By then some 5727 people had died, leaving Gibraltar with a serious shortage of manpower and a sense of collective bereavement that would take many decades to erase. Despite this, very little was done to improve the garrison's notorious lack of hygiene. A few vermin-infested shacks were torn down in the uppertown area and one or two landlords were ordered to clean up their properties – measures that seem almost laughably inadequate in retrospect. Given such levels of governmental apathy, it is not altogether surprising to hear that only eight years later, in 1813, a second outbreak of yellow fever was declared. What *is* highly surprising, however, is that the epicentre of the disease was once again Boyd's buildings, that 'notorious fever-nest of town.' The following year, too, there was another outbreak, this time beginning in Cavallero's buildings, in what is now known as Palace Gully.

The twin outbreaks of 1813 and 1814 finally stirred the authorities out of their period of dormancy. Governor Don, who had spent the 1814 outbreak sequestered aboard a ship anchored in the bay, gave orders in 1815 for the building of Gibraltar's first sewers – a system of primitive subterranean pipes which, though having a tendency to clog and choke, at least promoted a sense of civic pride among the inhabitants. He also subdivided the colony into twenty-eight administrative districts, each under the command of local inspectors, who were empowered to deal with issues such as hygiene, social problems, and law and order. Not content with this, Don also went on to establish Gibraltar's first Sanitary Commission, a body specifically set up to deal with issues of health and hygiene, although the efficacy of this organisation has been recently called into question.[59]

Even with these measures in place, yellow fever struck again in 1828. Thanks to the improvement of administrative records witnessed under Don, we are able to follow the initial geographic spread of the disease as it passed through Hargreaves Parade (27 August), Victualling Office Lane (31 September) and George's Lane (2 October). By the time the last case was reported on 25 December, some 1675 deaths had been recorded, inspiring the well-known English poetess Letitia Elizabeth Landon to write the moving 'Scene during the Plague at Gibraltar':

> And Terror by the hearth stood cold,
> And rent all natural ties,
> And men, upon the bed of death
> Met only stranger eyes...
> Heavily rung the old church bells,
> But no one came to prayer:
> The weeds were growing in the street,
> Silence and Fate were there. [60]

---

[59] 'Gibraltar's 1804 Yellow Fever Scourge: The Search for Scapegoats,' p. 38.

[60] In my 2006 book *Writing the Rock of Gibraltar*, I mistakenly stated that Landon had penned this poem in response to the cholera outbreak of 1834. In fact, Landon herself mentions that the poem was partly inspired by a conversation she had with 'a clergyman, Mr. Howe, whose duty enforced residence during the ravages of the fellow fever.' See *The Poetical Works of Miss Landon* (1839), p. 331.

Nearer to home, meanwhile, Governor Don reacted to the crisis with a raft of extemporary measures – including the establishment of an Anglo-French commission whose aim was to investigate the causes of the outbreak. Even so, very little appears to have been achieved in practical terms. 'Matters are now perhaps better,' accordingly wrote one commentator in the early 1830s, 'but still there is a fair proportion of poor people who live entirely by charity; and the houses of this class are extremely dirty and ill-ventilated.... [F]ilth, wretchedness and poverty are apparent at every step.'[61] In fact, it was not until after the notorious cholera outbreak of 1865 – which killed over four hundred people in a period of two months – that concrete steps were taken to improve Gibraltar's hygiene, the most important among these being the reconstruction of the sewers and the establishment of an improved and much-reformed sanitary commission. By then, over ten thousand lives had been lost to the ravages of yellow fever, a figure that gains in poignancy when we consider that the nineteenth-century garrison rarely held more than thirty-thousand individuals at any one given moment. It is still possible to see the graves of some of the English victims at Trafalgar cemetery, quietly ensconced among the vaults and mildewed sepulchres of those who died through the Napoleonic campaigns. The Gibraltarian dead, by contrast, were almost all buried in mass graves that have long-since been destroyed.

St. Pancras, London - Walkeshwar, Bombay,

August-October, 2007

---

[61] 'Brief Sketch of the Fever which prevailed at Gibraltar in the Autumn of 1828,' p. 51.

Appendix A: The Smugglers Rock
A newspaper article from 1877

It is not without considerable sensation that a man revisits a well-known spot after a 43 years' absence. What interest one feels in seeing the marks of human progress perceptible in the look of familiar objects! How strange it seems to find the world proceeding at a so much more rapid rate than one's own life! And in what other half-century in the history of the past, or probably of the future, can it be said that so portentous a change has been or may be effected as in these last four or five decades; or what other nation can boast of having given it a more momentous impulse than the one which, more than a century and a half ago, planted its standard on the Moor's castle from which Gibraltar was named?

One cannot help inquiring what would be the condition of the Rock if it had been left in the Spaniard's possession these last 175 years, or to what extent the place would have grown had it been merely a Russian or Prussian garrison town. What had its former rulers ever done with it? Or what evidence had they given of their consciousness of the importance of its position? The 'Pillar' in antiquity had barely a name. In his description of Ulysses' venturous voyage, Dante, who mentions Ceuta and Seville, ignores the appellation of Abyla and Calpe, the two mountain masses on which Hercules was said to have written his *Ne plus ultra*. What part has Gibraltar ever played in the great achievements of Transatlantic discovery or of African circumnavigation? Or when did the world-wide Empire of Charles V, or Phillip II, claim this spot as the key of the Mediterranean, or use its Bay as a naval station, or assume the actual command of the Straits of which both coasts acknowledge the Spanish away? The English alone may be said to have found out Gibraltar and to have turned it to some purpose, first as the Gate of the Inland Sea, and now as the inlet to the remotest Eastern oceans.

The movement of the Straits as it was in the early part of this century was about the hundredth part of what it has become since the opening of the Suez Canal. Gibraltar levies no toll; it sets no hindrance to this immense traffic; hardly profits by it, for it buys but little and has nothing to sell. It has not grown much, nor has it been greatly enriched; but how wonderfully improved it is! How beneficially has the advances of English civilization been at work upon it! What rows of neat houses, what sweet tropical gardens, what smooth, solid, well-watered streets and paths, what cleanliness; how much comfort and luxury; what hotels, what libraries, what amount of wellbeing one finds in the narrow ledge of rock which the exigencies of military defence have been able to spare to its motley population; what immense relief it is to come to this oasis of English thrift out of the wilderness of Spanish dinginess and sloth! There is only one drawback to it all - Gibraltar lives by smuggling. The people themselves have no hand in the unlawful business; they are honest traders and keep open shops. They no more inquire what becomes of the goods they dispose of than did the shopkeepers of Leghorn when that city was the free port of Tuscany. Within their walls and as far as the 'line' there is absolute free trade. It is for their neighbours to see to the protection of their frontier. Gibraltar looks not into the faces of its customers; they may or may not be contrabandists. But what concern is it or the

Rock? The Rock simply pockets its money and asks no questions.

Spain is surely not the only State which thinks itself aggrieved by the contraband that its own people or its neighbours carry on its frontier. Italy has just as much to endure on the side of Switzerland. Enterprising men have established themselves at Chiasso, at Locarno, and other places south of the Alps, who take upon themselves the conveyance of any goods free of the duties which insure their safe deliverance upon a moderate consideration. 'Your merchandise would be taxed 25, 30, or 40 per cent for the benefit of the Government,' says the smuggler; 'you shall have it at your door upon a charge of only 10 per cent.' How the smuggler can manage it we shall see by and by. Meanwhile it is very clear that the smuggler's trade would not so easily thrive if the duties were only 10 per cent and that he would be utterly bankrupt if there were no duties at all. Whether the Spaniards in general and especially the people on the borders are smugglers, as they are gamblers, by natural instinct, it would be un-profitable to inquire. The certain fact is that between the Spanish people and their Government there is at heart a traditional war, and that whatever is done to the Government's injury is considered a meritorious action. It little matters whether Spain is a Monarchy or a Republic, an absolute or a representative State. The Government is always a public enemy. The administration never changes, or only from bad to worse. There has been of late a tremendous aggravation of public burdens, and particularly of indirect taxes, owing partly to the necessity of furthering long-neglected public works, but chiefly to the enormous number of State functionaries consequent on the very disorders of the revolutionary period, and to the incapacity, venality, and actual rapacity of many of them. The system here seems intended to create new offices and officials; to exact from them the smallest amount of work, pay them the lowest wages, and allow them to 'help themselves'. I have spoken to many of the peasants on my way from Malaga and Ronda, and I found among them one universal cry that the labouring poor are robbed to enrich a set of idle high officials. And the heaviness of the taxes, oppressive as it is, is further aggravated by the vexatious, unequal, and senseless manner in which they are raised. The delays and chicanes, the capricious and uncertain rules and prescriptions, the circumlocution prevalent at Spanish Custom-houses have the effect of driving all trade from the frontier by main force, and many an honest man who would have no wish to cheat the revenue, and might even submit to unjust extortions, is compelled to put himself into the smuggler's hands solely to avoid the trouble and inconvenience which await him at the Custom-house, and to deal with one thief for the mere chance of escaping a host of worse thieves.

I found at Gibraltar, somewhat to my surprise, the Spanish and English authorities living on terms of perfect understanding and mutual amity, the Spaniards acknowledging that the English meet their wishes in everything that lies in their power to oppose the contraband trade, and the English quite charmed with the politeness and even indulgence with which the Spaniard allow them a free intercourse across the 'lines', and the still freer use of the territory about St. Roque as the field for those hunting, shooting, and horse-racing sports, without which the pent-up garrison and the best part of the population would find the Rock a much less endurable prison than military rule unavoidably makes it.

Smuggling goes on from Gibraltar by land and sea, and the chief articles in which it is carried on are tobacco which in Spain is a Government monopoly, tea, coffee, sugar, and other colonial goods, upon which heavy duties are demanded at the Spanish Custom-houses. The smuggling of cotton tissues and other English manufactured goods has of late greatly decreased, and almost ceased the Spanish authorities told me, because 'protection has given so great a development to Catalan industry that home competition has driven foreign produce from the Spanish market'. Tobacco is the chief offender; and these same Spanish authorities contend that the tobacco with which their Government supply the consumer is infinitely better than the stuff which is smuggled in, and that contraband only affects their monopoly by the lowness of the prices at which the smuggled goods are sold. With respect to this latter statement I must observe that public opinion in Spain somewhat disputes its correctness, for there is no end to the complaints of the 'infamous cigars' and cigarettes of the *Regia* on the part of the amateurs who have nothing else to smoke. Suffice it, however, to assert that there must be something in the unlawful importation of tobacco to make it a profitable business, and that it constitutes the chief grievance of the Spanish revenue officers against their neighbours. The so-called 'lines' which separate the British from the Spanish territory across the narrow neck or isthmus which makes the Rock a peninsula are only a few hundred yards distant from the gates of Gibraltar. The Spaniards have on their own side so barred the way across the

sandy flat, and allowed so narrow a way through, that persons
walking, riding, or driving past their lines, must as they go
past brush past their Custom-house officials and *Carabineros,*
or Custom-house guards. Here, nevertheless, an endless number
of petty smugglers go through with the forbidden merchandise
secreted about their person. Large cartloads of tobacco used
till lately to be driven up to the last limits of British territory,
where, in the open air and in full day-light, those creatures,
hundreds and hundreds at a time, divested themselves of
their clothes and padded themselves all over with the contents
of the carts, put their rags on again, and, thus laden, went
their way into Spanish ground. This practice is now
discontinued. The Spanish Consul, Don Francisco Yehra de
Sanjuan, with the zeal of a newly appointed functionary,
remonstrated with the English authorities about these open-
air toilets which he described as offensive to common decency,
and the police from the Rock have now orders to bid the
women and children to 'move on' and the carts to 'move off'.
In spite of this restrictive measure, however, there is little
doubt that this same contraband trade by land is still carried
on very nearly to the same extent, and one might ask why the
Spanish *Carabineros* do not submit suspected persona, laden
mules, and vehicles to so strict a search as to put a stop to
the lawless traffic; but the movement of people across the
line, only allowed from sunrise to sunset, is very brisk, and
cannot be easily interfered with; and it is extremely probable
that the speculators, of whom all that rabble of women and
children are the mere agents, have the means of inducing the
Carabineros to wink at the tricks those monstrously-stout
boys and girls and those big women in an 'interesting state'

play upon them. Independently of their alleged venality it is also possible that these wretchedly-paid officials, being themselves Spaniards, are not without some sneaking sympathy with the instincts of their offending countrymen, and are loath to look too closely under the clothes of pedestrians, or into the packs of laden mules, or boxes and boots of the spring vans used here as hackney carriages. For these officials are aware, and everybody is aware, of the sore distress prevailing at this moment all over Spain, and especially in these Southern Provinces, and they, perhaps, consider that any efficient check put on that contraband trade which is the only resource of vast numbers of the population would at once bring them to the verge of actual starvation. For such is the result of unwise laws, especially with regard to oppressive taxation, that the very officials who are charged with their execution, listening rather to humane feelings than to a proper sense of their duty, are too often disposed to connive at, and thus indiscreetly to encourage, their infraction. And, after all, even the higher Spanish authorities seem to think that such smuggling as is here still going on by land and across the lines is almost beneath their notice; and that as far as any extensive trade is concerned, Gibraltar, unapproachable as it is by carriage road from any part of Spain, may be looked upon as an island and its main intercourse must be by sea.

As an isolated spot, Gibraltar is not much more favourable to the Spanish smuggling trade than Tangiers, Tetuan, and the Spanish dependencies, Ceuta, Melilla, or any other port across the straits would be, and indeed there is already a loud complaint against the French authorities at Oran - a place where large cargoes of tobacco from Gibraltar are landed, and whence they are afterwards stealthily conveyed to various points on the coast of Spain; for so lucrative, as it seems, is this clandestine and criminal tobacco trade that it can easily bear the expenses of two or more voyages. Gibraltar, however, in the Spaniard's opinion, offers to the smuggler the especial advantage of immediate proximity. Algeciras, at only five miles' distance across the Bay, is visited almost hourly by small ferry steamers and boats, with shoals of smugglers as their only passengers. And small craft of every description carry on the same intercourse with Estepona, Marbella, and all the coast as far as Cadiz on the other. Steamers of larger size, of Spanish and other lines, take passengers on board with little attention to what they take with them as luggage, and as they proceed along the coast, they are in the dark, or even by daylight, approached by fishing boats, into which bales of tobacco and other forbidden merchandise are dropped, probably without the knowledge, possibly with the connivance, of the captains. For so universal, so all-pervading, is this smuggling business, if you believe the Spanish authorities, that many of the richest merchants, shipowners, and shipmasters, as well as all the well-to-do mountain population of these districts, are more or less actively engaged in it; and enrich themselves by it.

Against this wholesale trade, to prevent which the Spanish revenue officers by land and sea seem so utterly helpless, how can the English authorities at Gibraltar lend efficient aid? The Spanish Consul would wish that no steamers or sailing vessels should leave the harbour without giving a strict account of the cargo they had on board and of its destination, and, indeed, all particulars to that effect are not only supplied to him, but also published in the bulletins of the local Press. But the difficulty lies in the verification of the correctness of the statement given, which would involve a search and vigilance extremely troublesome and vexatious, and which would not, after all, be satisfactory, unless at least in the case of vessels sailing under Spanish colours, the Consul himself or his agents were allowed to exercise the right of personal inspection. To prevent a vessel hiding a few bales of tobacco under a cargo of fruit or any other free merchandise, or even landing off Malaga or Cadiz a *bona fide* cargo of tobacco nominally intended for and booked for Oran or Mogador, would be no easy matter, and the Consul insists that Spanish vessels, at least, should give him a declaration of the cargo they embark here, and a similar statement of that which they land either at the appointed port or at any other to the Spanish Consular agents at every stage of their voyage.

Were he, the Spanish Consul, to receive correct information of any cargo of forbidden merchandise leaving Gibraltar, no matter for what foreign port, he thinks he could telegraph a timely warning all along the Spanish coast, so as to put the revenue officers at all points on their guard against any deviation of the vessel from her appointed course. He contends that a similar mutual understanding was and is established between his own Government and that of Portugal, and that it was by this strict surveillance of the vessels of both nations from port to port, and from the account they were made to give of their cargo at every stage of their voyage, that the contraband of English cotton goods with which the Peninsula was till lately inundated to the detriment of home industry has now been brought to an end.

Perhaps this worthy functionary does not make due allowance for the difference between the views entertained in different countries as to commercial freedom. But even if England were to go hand-in-hand with Spain in any measure tending to exercise so vexatious a check on the trade of Spanish vessels, it is very evident that the unlawful business could easily be carried on in foreign boats, upon which the English authorities might not be entitled to exercise the same control; so that Spain would not be to any great extent rid of her great plague of contraband, and she would lose much of that coasting trade to which she attaches the utmost importance.

But it is very evident that even with the most earnest goodwill, and with no matter how gross a violation of her principles as to the freedom of commerce and navigation, England could do next to nothing towards checking the contraband which is so grievously damaging the interests of the Spanish revenue. In the port of Gibraltar, as at the gates of the town, in obedience to indispensable military rule, ingress and egress are forbidden between sunset and sunrise, and no vessels are allowed to leave harbour at night without special permission. But vessels which have left harbour before sunset cannot easily be prevented from tarrying in the Bay at their own pleasure, and taking in such contraband merchandise as small boats may manage to convey to them by stealth under favour of darkness. Owing to want of space in the cramped-up wharves and docks of the town, large stores of coal are kept in hulks anchored outside the port. These coal-depots, the Consul asserts, take in large loads of tobacco bales, and these are easily transferred from the hulks to the smuggling vessels while these are waiting outside the harbour either for daylight or a fair wind. It is obvious, in short, that vessels with contraband on board cannot be hindered from leaving Gibraltar, and the question is, to what extent the Spanish revenue officers by land or sea can intercept their further progress. The rule of the sea allows every State full jurisdiction over three maritime miles round its coasts. But between Gibraltar and Algeciras the Bay, as I have said, is only five miles across, and the claims of England and Spain to their respective three miles of water cannot be easily reconciled. A Spanish revenue cruiser has no right to search or otherwise interfere with suspected vessels within English water, and as at night or in foggy weather a nice calculation of distances and discrimination between English and Spanish waters are not easy, a vessel hugging the eastern side of the Bay down to Europa Point at the extremity of the Rock and three miles beyond has a fair chance of gaining the open sea and baffling the vigilance or out-speeding the chase of the Spanish revenue boats. Should the latter stop or seize the vessel anywhere within the limits of English waters the seizure could be lawfully resisted, and any contest arising from it would become matter for lengthy and not always temperate international discussions. The present Governor of Gibraltar, Lord Napier of Magdala, an amiable as well as gallant soldier, has done all in his power to hinder the illegal traffic both by land and sea, and by his order patrolling boats now row all night outside the harbour to oppose the egress of boats at unlawful hours. But the Spanish authorities show an ungenerous mistrust of British vigilance, and there have been recent instances of Spanish revenue cruisers chasing smuggling boats across the Bay and attempting to seize them within a few yards of the Gibraltar mole, to which the smugglers in the night had ventured to fly for shelter. His Excellency then issued an order that all boats should forcibly be prevented from coming in the night time within 400 paces of any point of the Rock; and, as this measure made no exception in favour of the Spanish revenue cruisers, it has been most unreasonably resented by the Spanish authorities as an insult to their national flag.

It is clear, therefore, that this smuggling evil has roots not easily to be reached by any well-meant exertions on the part of the British Government, and, to give some idea of the difficulties the Gibraltar authorities have to contend with, it will be sufficient to state that the Spanish revenue cruisers, whenever in the discharge of their duties they are allowed to visit Gibraltar, seldom go back without some bales of tobacco on board - a substantial evidence that, with all their parade of real in the service, they are not themselves above dabbling in the unlawful trade they are appointed to put down.

Her Majesty's Government, at all times, and especially after the restoration of the Bourbon Dynasty in 1875, yielding to the diplomatic solicitations of the Ministers of King Alfonso XII., have taken this painful subject into serious consideration, and a variety of schemes have been proposed and discussed with a view to lend Spain all the assistance in the protection of her revenue which a friendly State could reasonably expect from a just neighbour. A 'Draft of an ordinance relating to trade and Customs at Gibraltar', with the 'Correspondence relating to it,' was laid before both Houses of the Imperial Parliament in June and August, 1877. It was proposed, in the first instance, that a duty on tobacco should be levied upon

Gibraltar itself, and subsequently that the trade of this place should be subjected to the same rules that are observed in the Channel Islands, and which, it seems, were adopted upon the solicitation of France and in the interest of her revenue. These rules, as embodied in the ordinance and summed up by Lord Carnarvon, then Colonial Secretary, amounted to this: - They 'forbade the export or import of tobacco in packages of less than 80 lb,; they provided that the ships which export tobacco should be over 100 tons burden; and they required the exporter of tobacco to furnish a bond showing that it had been landed at the port for which it had been cleared to the satisfaction of the Governor - unless, of course, stress of weather interfered'.

Against this ordinance a loud clamour arose on the part of many of the most respectable citizens of Gibraltar, backed by some influential members of the House of Commons, and by the Chambers of Commerce of Liverpool, Manchester, Glasgow, and other British trading communities, whose interests are closely connected with the business of the Rock, whose written addresses and whose arguments, delivered by a numerous deputation appearing before Lord Carnarvon on the 27th of July, 1877, had the effect of thwarting the intended measure for the time, upon the understanding that the subject should at no distant period be referred to the deliberation of the Imperial Parliament.

And it seems, indeed, as necessary that something should be done in this matter as it is difficult to come to any conclusion as to what should be done. It is very certain that no Englishman and perhaps, also, no British subject, at Gibraltar has a direct hand in the smuggling trade of which Spain complains; but it is equally evident that all Gibraltar and the English merchants connected with the Gibraltar trade profit by it. The sale of tobacco, which is in Spain a Government monopoly, yields to that country an annual income of GBP 3,200,000, one-half of which, however, is absorbed by the purchase, freight, and manufacture of the leaf, while the Custom-house officers, guards, &c., entail a further expense of GBP 600,000 – a charge especially arising from a vain endeavour to oppose the tobacco contraband. With all this the Government supply of tobacco (7,426,937lb) only meets one-half of the demand; the other half is introduced by the smuggling trade. Gibraltar is undoubtedly the chief depot of this illicit trade, the quantity finding its way from the Rock into Spain averaging between 80,000 cwt and 100,000 cwt yearly. The persons engaged in and living by this trade in Gibraltar, as manufacturers or dealers, number between 1,600 and 2,000, constituting with their families a population of 4,000 to 6,000.

To doom these people to starve or to look for other employment, and to suffer Gibraltar and her trade, the imports of which from England amount to three millions sterling a year, to perish; to do away with the commercial importance of this Rock, past which British property to the amount of GBP 100,000,000 goes every year – and all that only to do justice to Spain, and lend her a hand in the protection of her revenue – might well strike every sensible man as a desperate measure; and it might naturally be expected that it would paralyze the deliberations of a Parliament, as it evidently two years ago shook the resolutions of a Cabinet. Yet even from such extreme expedients it would not be unreasonable to shrink, if the application of the most stringent rules could lead to any practical results. Lord Carnarvon justly observed to the deputation which waited upon him as objectors to the ordinance that 'it is certainly not obligatory on one nation to protect the revenue of another, but it would be a mistake to suppose that friendly assistance and co-operation in relation to the fiscal system of two neighbouring countries is unknown in the history of civilized nations.' What has been done in the Channel Islands to prevent smuggling into France, what might be done in Canada for the benefit of the revenue of the United States, might equally be attempted at Gibraltar in behalf of Spain, if any good could be expected to come of it. Lord Carnarvon, while admitting that 'the Spanish revenue authorities deserve no special consideration at England's hands, that the Spanish system is a bad one, as bad perhaps as any that exists in Europe' – while acknowledging that 'the Spanish revenue officers are very corrupt (a matter', he added, 'which will be accepted on all hands') still insists that 'the circumstances of Gibraltar are peculiarly exceptional and,' he thought, 'gave a friendly nation the right to appeal to Great Britain as far as possible for the exercise of that comity and fair co-operation which one nation, when in good relations with another, ought to give'.

In the position in which the noble lords left the question when he withdrew from the Cabinet it is still at the present day. Lord Napier of Magdala told the Spanish authorities that he would undertake to do away with all smuggling from Gibraltar if they would only place their Custom-house officers and guards on their own side of the frontier under the orders and management of one of his own officials whom his Excellency has particular reasons to trust. The remedy of the evil and of all evils in Spain would then be the same as is being applied to Egypt, and will probably soon have to be extended to Turkey. It consists in taking the direction of the Customs, of the Finance, and in general of every branch of the Government, from the hands of a hopelessly rotten native administration and making it over to the trustworthy.

Appendix B: 'Scene during the plague at Gibraltar' (1839)

A Poem by Letitia Elizabeth Landon on the 1828 epidemic of Yellow Fever

At first, I only buried one,
And she was borne along
By kindred mourners to her grave,
With sacred rite and song.
At first they sent for me to pray
Beside the bed of death:
They blessed their household, and they breathed
Prayer in their latest breath.
But then men died more rapidly -
They had not time to pray;

And from the pillow love had smoothed
Fear fled in haste away.
And then there came the fastened door -
Then came the guarded street -
Friends in the distance watched for friends;
Watched - that they might not meet.
And Terror by the hearth stood cold,
And rent all natural ties,
And men, upon the bed of death
Met only stranger eyes:
The nurse - and guard, stern, harsh, and wan,
Remained, unpitying, by;
They had known so much wretchedness,

They did not fear to die.
Heavily rung the old church bells,
But no one came to prayer:
The weeds were growing in the street,
Silence and Fate were there.

O'er the first grave by which I stood,
Tears fell, and flowers were thrown,
The last grave held six hundred lives,
And there I stood alone.